Sojourners in the Capital of the World

SOJOURNERS IN THE CAPITAL OF THE WORLD

Garifuna Immigrants

Maximo G. Martinez

EMPIRE STATE EDITIONS

AN IMPRINT OF FORDHAM UNIVERSITY PRESS
NEW YORK 2023

Copyright © 2024 Fordham University Press

Map credit: Map of the Caribbean Sea and its islands, by Kmuser, licensed under CC BY-SA 2.0.

All rights reserved. No part of this publication may be reproduced, stored in a retrieval system, or transmitted in any form or by any means—electronic, mechanical, photocopy, recording, or any other—except for brief quotations in printed reviews, without the prior permission of the publisher.

Fordham University Press has no responsibility for the persistence or accuracy of URLs for external or third-party Internet websites referred to in this publication and does not guarantee that any content on such websites is, or will remain, accurate or appropriate.

Fordham University Press also publishes its books in a variety of electronic formats. Some content that appears in print may not be available in electronic books.

Visit us online at www.fordhampress.com.

Library of Congress Cataloging-in-Publication Data available online at https://catalog.loc.gov.

Printed in the United States of America

26 25 24   5 4 3 2 1

First edition

CONTENTS

Preface   vii

Introduction   1

1. Origins, Surviving, Ensuring Subsistence, and Culture   27
2. Livelihood on the Caribbean Coast   41
3. Early U.S. Garifuna Communities   51
4. Identity and Cultural Growth: *Garifunadao*   74
5. Music, Dance, and Sports from the 1990s to the Present   101
6. Social Issues in New York City from the 1990s to the Present   118
7. Central America and St. Vincent from the 1990s to the Present   155

Conclusion   179

Appendix A: U.S. Garifuna Merchant Marine Seamen Crew Ship List, 1920s–50s   193

Appendix B: Honduran Garifuna Organizations Participating at the Garifuna Nation Pocono Retreat, 2005   211

Appendix C: U.S. Immigration Data from Belize, Guatemala, Honduras, 1930–2017 213

Appendix D: Bronx Community Board Appointees, 2019–20 215

Appendix E: Founding Members of the Garifuna Coalition USA 217

Acknowledgments 219

Notes 221

References 237

Index 259

PREFACE

Coming up in the Bronx during the late 1970s and 1980s, I was surrounded by abandoned buildings and zombie-like individuals addicted to crack and heroin. My summer pastimes included jumping on discarded mattresses lying outside derelict buildings and trapping bees in an empty bottle. My parents were strict, limiting the amount of time my siblings and I were allowed to play outside. Our baseball games in the park would be cut short to meet our five o'clock curfew. We attended Garifuna religious events at Roman Catholic churches and homes. There were Garifuna folk dance presentations at local community centers and schools or at outdoor gatherings in the summer. Traditional Garifuna food, call-and-response chants during the singing and drumming, and patterned rhythmic dancing were common. As a family, we frequently watched the soccer matches (*fútbol* in Spanish) at Van Cortlandt Park. There were Garifuna soccer tournaments, and sometimes mixed Garifuna, Central American Latino, Caribbean, and West African teams would play. Visitors to our home told stories of their life in the United States and Central America, in both Spanish and the Garifuna language, and I listened attentively. A tall, fair-skinned man often visited our apartment, and sometimes we went to his home. Later I learned that he was the founder of the first Garifuna organization in New York City. Such was my early education about the Garifuna. All these social events motivated me to document the community's development in New York City, forming the basis of this work.

As a Garifuna born in the United States, I appreciate the opportunity to view the world through different perspectives. Being raised in a low-income community of the South Bronx, I was fortunate to acquire Caribbean, Black, and Latino friends and acquaintances, and my interactions with them became the foundation of my worldview. My unique position allowed me to live in the world as a Black American through my complexion and to identify as a Caribbean through my cultural background and as a Latino through my Spanish surname, language, and culture. My father, who was a merchant marine seaman, arrived in the United States in the 1940s from Honduras and eventually established himself in New York City. Both my paternal and maternal grandfathers had immigrated to the United States much earlier. My grandfathers and my father experienced life as African Americans and embraced the African American culture of their time: conking their hair, dating African American women, and enjoying rhythm and blues music. Sam Cooke, Fats Domino, Marvin Gaye, Smokey Robinson, the Temptations, James Brown, the Neville Brothers, and Mahalia Jackson were some of the artists in their diverse music collections. Interestingly, my father's musical tastes also extended to Latino and Afro-Latino artists such as Celia Cruz, Orlando Contreras, Beny Moré, and Rolando Laserie. Caribbean artists such as Toots and the Maytals, Jimmy Cliff, and Bob Marley were also popular in my household. My spiritually inclined grandfather served as an usher in a Southern Baptist church in North Carolina. He also described visiting Daddy Grace's church in New York City.

As a youth growing up in the Bronx, I struggled to define my identity. Because of my first name, I was treated differently. The Black Latino presence was not as large or as well recognized as it is now. Black Americans and Puerto Ricans were the dominant minority groups in the Bronx during the 1980s. They were our neighbors, and my family developed bonds with them. In school, I was chided and mocked because of my uncommon first name. When classmates heard my parents speaking our Garifuna language, they thought we were Jamaicans.

There were pockets in the neighborhood where drug addicts loitered. My strict parents would tell my siblings and me that we were different, that we should not be like "those people"—meaning the many youths who had succumbed to society's ills. Later, I realized that I was part of that general community and was fortunate to have chosen the correct path in life. In addition, the discrimination I experienced both outside and inside my community—for instance, police officers stopping and frisking me—consolidated my sense of belonging.

In college, I embraced my multiple cultural identities, with African American and my Black phenotype being the most significant. As a Black studies major, I learned about African American culture and history, which expanded my outlook. I validated my identity as an African American when I sang in the gospel choir at college and later joined the Church of God in Christ. The Latino food I had once rejected at home I now enjoyed during Latino night at the college cafeteria. I associated with Latinos and enrolled in Spanish courses to acquire proficiency in the language to complement my Spanish surname. I bonded with my roommates, some of whom were international, and we identified various cultural similarities. Eventually, I also participated in the Caribbean Club, the Black Students Union, and the Latin American Association. After completing advanced studies in international affairs and political science, I noticed similarities between the Garifuna and other U.S. ethnic groups I had studied and researched. This discovery contributed to my interest in the Garifuna in New York City.

My father and grandfather collected music, pictures, videos, and movies of the Garifuna from the time of their initial presence in New York City and throughout the twentieth century. As a social science researcher, I was motivated to document the information they left behind to complement this study. This study has also been enriched by my participation in Garifuna community events, interviews with relevant individuals, and my personal witnessing of the community's growth. Several of these events were recorded in blogs, email, and local newspapers, which are referenced in this book.

INTRODUCTION

SINCE THE 1930s and 1940s, Black immigrants from Cuba, Panama, Puerto Rico, and elsewhere in the Caribbean, including the Garifuna[1]—an ethnic group from Honduras, Belize (formerly British Honduras), Guatemala, and Nicaragua—settled in established New York City African American neighborhoods. They were subjected to de facto segregation. These groups engaged with one another and enjoyed the social dance culture of the period that included the mambo, cha-cha, and boogie-woogie. In studies of Latinos—the dominant and fastest-growing U.S. minority group—the Afro-Latino segment of the population is seldom discussed.[2] This is especially relevant for New York City, which has the fastest-growing population of Black immigrants, including non-Latinos ("The State of Black Immigrants" 2014). Black immigrants are contributing to both the African American and the Latino populations in the United States, and the Garifuna ethnic group is a significant factor. Recently, Latinos—primarily Central American migrants—crossing the southern U.S. border have dominated the national media, as the legitimacy of their detention and of U.S. immigration policy in general is debated by partisan politicians and pundits. Among these migrants seeking economic opportunities and fleeing violence from gangs and drug traffickers are many Garifuna from Honduras. New York City newspapers, particularly the Spanish-language *El Diario*, feature articles about the experiences of Garifuna from Honduras, many of whom were held in the city's detention centers (Cortes de Solano 2015). Local TV news reports highlight Garifuna organizations in the city that are seeking to preserve their culture, as well as Garifuna struggles over land rights in Central America. New York City has the largest population concentration of Garifuna, as this ethnic group coalesces in the region.

This study highlights the different ways the Garifuna have organized their community life in New York since their settlement in the 1940s. Their concentration in the city has facilitated collective engagement among themselves and with the general community. Although the men migrated first, the women who arrived in greater numbers later were important in preserving the culture, taking several leadership roles. As the population increased with various waves of immigrants, the Garifuna continued to integrate into society, maintain their identity, and organize their growth. The title of this book reflects the Garifuna's status as immigrants settling in New York City. Although some return to their home countries when they retire, many remain in the United States. The title derives from scholar Nancie Gonzalez's early study, "Garifuna Settlement in New York: A New Frontier." She is also the author of the book *Sojourners of the Caribbean: Ethnogenesis and Ethnohistory of the Garifuna* (1988), a pioneering study of the ethnic group that presents their historical origins in the Caribbean, migrations, culture, social relations, and settlement in Central America. Since her study, many scholars have described Garifuna migration to the United States from the 1940s to the present. These studies also show that Garifuna have a long history of organizing in the United States, ranging from cultural clubs, to hometown associations, to political and civic engagement.

Garifuna history begins on the island of St. Vincent, where Africans who either made their way to the Americas prior to the arrival of Columbus or were brought as slaves in the 1600s mixed with the native Carib/Arawak population, forming a new ethnic group referred to by the European colonizers as the Black Carib (England 2006; J. Palacio 2005). After repeated eighteenth-century wars with the British to defend their early settlement on the island of St. Vincent, in 1797 the remaining Garifuna were rounded up and expelled from the territory by the British and embarked on an arduous journey, during which many died. Those who survived eventually settled throughout coastal Belize, Guatemala, Nicaragua, and Honduras, where their population increased. In Honduras, there are approximately forty-eight Garifuna townships along the Caribbean coast, accounting for the largest concentration of this ethnic group. There are two primarily Garifuna communities in Guatemala, six Garifuna communities in Belize, and five in Nicaragua. Although Garifuna are concentrated in these locations, they also have communities in the peripheries and in each country's main city. The Garifuna language is spoken in their communities and reflects their Amerindian heritage, which is part of their culture. Their African heritage is also notable in their Black phenotype. Most Garifuna speak Spanish, the language of their countries. However, Garifuna in Belize speak English, the national language, as do those in Nicaragua, where English is spoken along the coast. Beginning in the 1930s, many Garifuna relocated in increasing numbers to U.S. cities, particularly New York. These early immigrants were primarily merchant marine seamen. The Garifuna are now dispersed throughout the United States, with population concentrations in Los Angeles, New Orleans, Houston, Seattle, Boston, Chicago, and Miami. However, New York City still has the largest concentration of Garifuna in the United States (J. Palacio 2005; Mark Anderson 2012).

Garifuna have overcome many challenges in the past and have contributed to U.S. society as military officers and enlistees, staff members of high-profile public officials, educators, scientists, athletes, and musicians. Some well-known individuals with Garifuna roots are DJ Evil E and Hen-Gee, O.T. Genasis, King Tiger, and Mahogany Beatz in the rap and hip-hop music industry; Brian Flores, coach of the NFL's Miami Dolphins (2019–21); and African American Simone Biles, the Olympic gold medal–winning gymnast who was raised by a Garifuna woman. The ethnic group's unique blend of African and Amerindian culture, music, language, and spirituality facilitated recognition of the Garifuna as an Intangible World Heritage Culture in 2001 by UNESCO.

In New York City, Black and Latino public officials have established ties with Garifuna organizations. Beginning in 1991, the Garifuna gained recognition at various levels of state and local government. Mayoral administrations since 1990 have held town hall meetings with the Garifuna community (Garcia 2013). These contacts with local officials reflect the Garifuna's importance as an electorate in local districts.

As Black ethnic groups contribute to the Black population in the United States, the Garifuna provide an important case study to determine whether and how Black ethnics assimilate with African Americans. This study of the Garifuna also presents perspectives for determining their classification in the American Descendant of Slaves (ADOS) reparation debate. Although the ancestors of many Black ethnics did not experience U.S. slavery, those living in the United States today are subjected to its legacy of systemic structures of discrimination in American society. Like African Americans, the Garifuna experience the effects of unfair educational, housing, and criminal justice policies in their communities.

As a Black immigrant population, the Garifuna have established cultural, social, and other groups that facilitate their subsistence, retention of their unique culture, and participation in New York City, as well as the ability to address issues in their homeland. In this book I show that Garifuna have a history of organizing collectively, beginning in St. Vincent by resisting slavery and colonialism. Their resistance continued as they settled in Central America, opposing racial discrimination, land grabbing, and political repression. Because of their past experience in organizing, Garifuna immigrants in the United States were able to establish groups to retain their language and customs upholding their identity. The evolution of Garifuna organizations (cultural, religious, social service, sports) reflects their identity even as they engage with other ethnic groups. The Garifuna early immigrant population socialized mainly with African Americans and West Indians, but later they also associated with Latinos, and presently Garifuna establish alliances with all minority groups in their communities. Garifuna became civically engaged, allying with different minority groups in their communities to address their shared concerns, such as citizenship status, housing, and education, among others. Although many generations of Garifuna integrate into the U.S. population, their organizations and hometown associations engage in community development and address political concerns in their Central American homelands. This sustains their organizing as both local and transnational, in common with other Black immigrant populations.

Black Immigrants in New York City

The presence of several Black ethnic or immigrant groups in New York City, each with its own common culture, language, and religion, results in a beautiful mosaic throughout the boroughs, which includes the Garifuna. The West Indians are one Black ethnic immigrant group in New York City that has been studied extensively. Like Garifuna, West Indians of different nationalities and cultures are unified as a group in the city. Kasinitz (1992) focuses on the evolution of the English Caribbean community in the city and the development of a common identity. That study also shows that English Caribbeans were pioneers among Black public officials in New York City, including J. Raymond Jones, the first Black Democratic county leader; Bertram Baker, the first Black elected to the New York State Assembly from Brooklyn; Fred Samuels, a councilmember from Harlem; Basil Patterson, a former state senator; and New York judge Bruce Wright (Kasinitz 1992; News Americas 2017). Garifuna, however, have been unsuccessful to date in several attempts to promote their candidates for local office in the city (see Chapter 6).

Studies of Black ethnics in New York City have also analyzed their political engagement and relations with African Americans. For example, Greer (2013) explains the theory of "elevated minority" imposed by society on Black ethnic immigrants, favoring them as different from and better than Black Americans. This erroneous perception is reinforced by constant negative representations of African Americans in movies, news, and various social media. Unfortunately, some recently arriving Garifuna immigrants adopt these views.

Haitians are another Black ethnic group with a history of political activism in New York City. One of their early organizations was the Haitian American Citizen Society, which was established in 1968 but later dissolved (Laguerre 1984; Pierre-Louis 2006). For the most part, Haitian Americans' political engagement became centered around political issues in their home country, which has resulted in political support in the United States. Haitian American organizations in New York City endorse their own candidates and others for local office. Wright Austin (2018) shows that Haitian organizations have allied with African Americans to support political candidates in New York. In 2013, Michaelle Solages was the first Haitian elected to the New York State Assembly. Another woman of Haitian descent, Rodneyse Bichotte Hermelyn, was elected to the Assembly in 2015. Haitian candidates were prevalent in the attempt to replace Una Clarke on the New York City Council, but internal divisions and competition among several Haitian candidates resulted in failure (Wright Austin 2018). The first Haitian elected to the New York City Council was Mathieu Eugene, through a special election in 2007. He represented District 40, which includes parts of Crown Heights and Flatbush in Brooklyn. The Haitian community's ability to overcome divisions and come together to support a candidate of their own for local office indicates that the Garifuna can take similar action. Among the many similarities between Garifuna and Haitians is their long history of sustaining transnational associations. Like the Garifuna, these association developed in various sections of the city, contributing to their communities and reinforcing their strong identity (Pierre-Louis 2006; Zéphir 1996, 2004; Laguerre 1984).

Sub-Saharan Africans are a growing Black ethnic group with a strong identity, and many of them are neighbors of the Garifuna in the Bronx. Immigrants from sub-Saharan Africa are the major Black ethnic population in several counties. They sustain high social and economic gains and high educational attainment. According to Hamilton (2019), failure to account for diversity in the Black population may lead to incorrect estimates of African American progress. Black ethnics are often included as part of the data collected on African Americans. Cooper and Ibrahim (2020) share similar views in their study of Black immigrants in the United States. This study and others highlight the importance of analyzing Black ethnic or immigrant groups separately as an aid to understanding diversity in the U.S. Black population (Hamilton 2019).

Identity, Territorial Challenges, and Migration

Although the Garifuna are a relatively small Black immigrant population, many scholars find them an interesting subject, with most studies focusing on Honduran Garifuna, the majority population.[3] The group's mixed heritage and multiple ethnic and racial classifications tend to attract researchers' attention. In addition to indigenous and African identities, they have English, Spanish, French, and Caribbean cultural influences. Native Belizean Garifuna Joseph O. Palacio edited *The Garifuna: A Nation across Borders* (2005), which presents the common themes of identity, gender relations, music, spirituality, and historical resistance. These themes are addressed in separate essays by Garifuna and non-Garifuna scholars, such as ethnomusicologist Oliver Green (2018), who studies Garifuna music's ties with spiritual and cultural celebrations, and Alfonso Arrivillaga Cortés (2009, 2017), who has researched Garifuna historical migrations and their settlement in Guatemala.

Four waves define the periods of large-scale Garifuna migration to the United States, with the majority of immigrants coming from Honduras. The first wave occurred in the 1940s, as a result of World War II. Garifuna seamen predominated in this wave. Years after the war ended, the growing need for workers in the U.S. service sector motivated Garifuna to leave their countries and seek economic opportunities abroad. They were part of the Latin American and Caribbean population encouraged to immigrate to the United States due to the elimination of race-based prohibitions with passage of the 1965 Hart-Celler Act. During this second wave, women, children, and other family members of previous Garifuna immigrants predominated.

During the Cold War period of the 1970s and 1980s, the ruling military and the elites in power in Central America feared subversion by communist guerrilla groups. At the same time, peasants were losing their lands to large plantation owners seeking to expand productivity. Economic and social conditions were declining as human rights abuses were committed by government security forces. Thus, peasants, independent laborers, students, and Catholic-based church groups began to mobilize. The military and the police sought to counteract these mobilization efforts by repressing citizens. Repression in Honduras was less severe than in the neighboring states of Guatemala, Nicaragua, and El Salvador (Reklitis 2003, 21; Johnson 2007). For the most part, countries in the region suffered from gross income inequality, extensive corruption, widespread poverty, weak democratic institutions, and large foreign debt (Booth and Walker 1999). In addition, natural disasters and civil wars motivated migration northward, with the United States being the most popular destination.

Although Honduras experienced no civil wars during the turbulent 1970s and 1980s, the country endured economic and social deprivation that contributed to migration. Thus, many Garifuna families left in the 1980s and 1990s, constituting the third wave of migration (Johnson 2007). Established networks facilitated the settlement of Honduran and Guatemalan Garifuna individuals and families in New York. At the same time, many Belizean Garifuna settled in Los Angeles, California. U.S. economic growth in the 1980s and 1990s, particularly in the service sector, allowed many Garifuna to obtain employment. Some were hired as building superintendents, maintenance workers, home-care providers, and factory workers.[4]

The most recent large-scale Garifuna migration, considered the fourth wave, took place between 2013 and 2014 (Castillo 2019a). Economic insecurity caused by gang violence and narcotics trafficking spurred this migration wave, primarily from Honduras. Both Honduran and Garifuna migration has increased since this period, with some risking their lives on the perilous journey to reach the United States. Others have migrated to Spain and Italy. Most of the migrants are young; entire Garifuna families, mothers (some pregnant) with their children, and single fathers with children have left their homes and headed for the United States (Iborra Mallent 2021). In many Central American communities, the Garifuna population has decreased, as evidenced by the number of students who have left school.⁵ Seeking better economic opportunities was the primary motive of fourth-wave Garifuna migrants. Another motivating factor was the misinformation provided by "coyotes" that the Obama administration was granting entry to those accompanied by children (Castillo 2019a). Garifuna migrants also included college graduates unable to find employment and professionals seeking better opportunities due to various challenges, including discrimination based on skin color. Also included in the fourth wave were community activists seeking political asylum to avoid assault and death threats because of their activism. Due to the sizable numbers of undocumented Garifuna, accurate data are unavailable. However, estimates can be made by looking at 1930–2017 immigration data from Belize, Guatemala, and Honduras in appendix C.

The challenges Garifuna experience in their Central American communities motivate them to seek better economic opportunities elsewhere. Like their Honduran counterparts, Belizean Garifuna migrate primarily to raise their standard of living and to escape the lack of employment opportunities in their country. Belizean Garifuna researcher Myrtle Palacio (2001) found that migration increased from the 1950s to the 1980s, and many migrants remained in the United States permanently. Similarly, Guatemalan Garifuna migration to the United States is differentiated by decade, such as those who migrated legally in the 1960s versus those who arrived undocumented after the 1980s to seek employment opportunities (Collado 2007). Castillo Lewis (2005) studied the various reasons Guatemalan Garifuna cited for their migration. Key issues for Garifuna in Livingston—where their population is most concentrated—included restricted employment opportunities, discriminatory hiring practices, and the lack of academic preparation and training.⁶ In the town of Livingston, foreigners control tourism, and Ladinos dominate the main source of revenue, which is the fishing industry. They have modern vessels for large-scale industrial fishing, surpassing the Garifuna fishing business and depleting the fishing stock.

In Belize, formal institutions and established procedures specifically targeting Garifuna are nonexistent. In the state's view, a diverse multiculturalism exists in Belize. The needs of ethnic minorities are addressed on a regional basis rather than as individual groups. In Belize, there is no large-scale policy framework to address the issues of its minority populations (J. Palacio 2005). Belizean government ministries are assigned to attend to social, health, and educational needs on a regional basis. For the most part, Garifuna reside in the southern districts (Toledo, Stann Creek), which have the lowest indices of health, economic status, and education, with the exception of Garifuna residing in Belize City (located in Belize district).

Recently, the Garifuna's land rights activism in Central America has garnered attention. Since arriving in Central America, the ethnic group has encountered constant territorial challenges. Early studies by Thorne (2004) emphasized prominent Garifuna organizations' attempts to convince the Honduran government to recognize their land rights, linking this to their identity in the late twentieth and early twenty-first centuries. In the past, many indigenous groups' cultures and territorial sovereignty were acknowledged in their countries, and the Garifuna pursued the same recognition, based on their Amerindian heritage. Brondo (2017) studied associations between Honduran Garifuna identity politics and the neoliberal policy of development, which challenged the ethnic group's land rights and subsistence in several regions. Garifuna women activists led the resistance against coastal development initiatives as Garifuna organizations allied with Black hemispheric groups and Honduran indigenous organizations to pursue their rights. The Honduran group Consejo Cívico de Organizaciones Populares e Indígenas de Honduras (Council of Popular and Indigenous Organizations of Honduras, COPINH) collaborated with the Garifuna organization Organización Fraternal Negra de Honduras (Black Fraternal Organization of Honduras, OFRANEH) on many occasions (Lakhani 2020). COPINH leader Berta Cáceres was assassinated in 2016 while defending the indigenous community's lands against large dam projects supported by the government and private businesses. This reflected the increased violence faced by the indigenous and Garifuna populations after the 2009 coup that ousted Honduran president Manuel Zelaya. Since then, Garifuna in Honduras have experienced violence, repression, and adverse legislation seeking to nullify their land rights. Loperena (2010), who conducted extensive research on the roles of the Honduran government and multilateral agencies in usurping Garifuna lands, was among the scholars analyzing the coup's impact on ethnic groups' activism. Although Zelaya's progressive government did not intervene in municipalities' initiatives to usurp Garifuna territories, he supported projects promoting African and indigenous art, culture, and education, which ceased after the coup. After the coup in Honduras, Garifuna joined the resistance movement to carry on their activities in pursuit of racial justice and territorial rights. The new politically conservative government adopted a different multicultural policy to serve African descendants and indigenous people, as violence, disappearances, and deaths increased, along with development initiatives (Euraque 2010; Mark Anderson 2012; Gordon and Webber 2016; Loperena 2016, 2021).

In this book, I highlight Garifuna organizations in New York City responding to the crisis in Honduras as it impacted their friends and families. Increased government corruption, drug trafficking, and gang violence contributed to the economic decay after the coup. This caused many Hondurans, including Garifuna, to migrate from their communities, leading to large "migrant caravans" heading to the United States. Studies of Garifuna migrants indicate that they prefer safer and more discreet ways of migrating (Reyes and Gallo 2021; Castillo 2019a). Iborra Mallent (2021) analyzed Honduran Garifuna migrants to the United States, including one organization seeking political asylum for women recently arrived in New York as part of the large 2013 migration wave. The forced removal of Garifuna from their lands in certain communities was cited as justification for their applications for political asylum. Different views of Honduran Garifuna migration related to territorial challenges are discussed in Chapter 7. For the most part, better economic opportunity is the primary motivating factor for migration from Honduras. As a minority population, the Garifuna also experience discrimination as a barrier to opportunity (Castillo 2019a, 2019b).

The current Garifuna migration wave from Honduras motivated New York City Garifuna organizing addressing personal needs and advocating on their behalf. Compared to the past this migration wave is undocumented and many consider themselves refugees. This Garifuna population is among the unaccompanied minors and women in Mexican shelters waiting to cross the borders who appear in the news. Many who have made it to the United States apply for asylum and are monitored with ankle bracelets. Unlike others of their population who migrated legally in the past and are able to obtain employment, participate in elections, and become citizens, the new Garifuna migrants, many of whom are undocumented, are marginalized, unable to become employed, participate in elections, and become citizens. Many factors motivate Garifuna organizers who address concerns back home, seen as motivating migration, as well as immigration and other social concerns in New York. This is further discussed in Chapter 7. One factor is that ongoing migration has facilitated transnational connections with their Central American communities. As a result, cultural, political, and economic exchanges decrease the distance between their U.S. and Central American communities. Scholars provide evidence of Honduran Garifuna's different forms of transnational ties with their communities (Johnson 2007; N. Gonzalez 1979, 1969; López Oro 2016a, 2016b; England 2006).

Residence in U.S. Cities

Studies of Los Angeles, Houston, New Orleans, and New York Garifuna communities became more common in the latter part of the twentieth century. An early study by Nancie Gonzalez (1979) described Garifuna establishments in New York City since the 1950s. She focused on the migration patterns of primarily Honduran Garifuna and saw New York as an extension of their Central American communities. Other details included the Garifuna's adjustment to life in the city and maintenance of their culture during the 1970s. Years after Gonzalez's study of Garifuna in New York City, their population increased in other cities, leading to additional research.

Matthei and Smith (1998) focused on a Belizean Garifuna community in Los Angeles and how transnationalism and a changing identity influenced communities back home. Similarly, the role of Garifuna women migrants altered family and parenting styles back in Belize. Also in Los Angeles, Joseph O. Palacio (1992) examined several formal institutions and voluntary associations supporting primarily Belizean Garifuna cultural and social advancement, highlighting how immigration facilitated the Garifuna's improvement of their community in Los Angeles.

In the Deep South, Honduran Garifuna dispersed, living in predominantly Latino or African American communities in the New Orleans metropolitan area. According to Chaney (2012), most Garifuna live in the Latino area, and their common Spanish language supports their employment, social services, and other needs. Thanks to their connections with Latinos, the Garifuna obtained permission to use their facilities to hold Garifuna activities as their community grew. West of New Orleans, the Garifuna population has also increased in Texas, following the national trend. Garifuna have traditionally settled in Houston, but they are scattered throughout different parts of the city (Rodríguez 1987). For the most part, Honduran Garifuna are the majority in metropolitan Houston, with some of their Belizean counterparts present as well (Hutchinson et al. 1996).

These past studies show the Garifuna tendency to cluster and keep to themselves, forming their own organizations and activities such as soccer clubs and festive celebrations. Although this is also common in New York Garifuna communities, I uncovered some differences. A recent study of Garifuna in New York City highlights some generational variance in terms of associating with Blacks and Latinos in their communities. Paul Joseph López Oro (2016b, 2021), himself a Garifuna, explores Garifuna identity (Honduran, Latino, Black) in both Honduras and New York City, analyzing census campaigns in both locations. He relates the experience of an early Honduran Garifuna migrant who was rejected by Black Americans, which, he concludes, was common among her generation of migrants in the late 1960s. López Oro interviews Aida Lambert, featured in a chapter of *The Afro-Latin Reader*, about her community organizing and difficulties assimilating with Black Americans. In my studies, I found this to be true in some cases but not all (see Chapter 3). Doris Garcia (2013), another Garifuna scholar, writes about Garifuna organizational activities in New York City and Honduras, including how the group was influenced by U.S. Black activism in the 1960s. Garcia explores the historical origins of Garifuna organization and their transnational engagements in New York City. She argues that by developing transnational organizations Garifuna were able to challenge the Honduran government and neoliberal economic reforms threatening their territorial rights. Recent Garifuna groups in New York City are highlighted as being focused on redefining their identity and less concerned with land rights activism. Mark Anderson (2009) also presents a segment on Black Americans' influence on Honduran Garifuna; however, he focuses on the impact of the hip-hop culture. He explores the evolution and identity of Honduran Garifuna in relation to the survival and maintenance of their culture and the political and territorial challenges in their country. Other research also mentions Garifuna challenges sustaining their culture with their younger generation in New York City. Cosgrove et al.'s (2021) recent study presents Garifuna youth as less connected with their culture, with greater challenges and distractions compared to past generations. The authors focus specifically on Garifuna in Nicaragua, briefly analyzing Honduran Garifuna in New York upholding their culture. Their central theme is that Garifuna and their culture continue to persevere as in the past, adjusting to the forces of changes faced since colonialism and up to the present social media age. My study shows that each generation of Garifuna has been influenced by African American culture. In addition, I found evidence of friendship and marital relations between early Garifuna migrants and Black Americans.

Sarah England's *Afro–Central Americans in New York: Garifuna Tales of Transnational Movements in Racialized Space* (2006) and Paul Christopher Johnson's *Diaspora Conversions: Black Carib Religion and the Recovery of Africa* (2007) are the only books specifically on the Garifuna in New York. Johnson compares Garifuna religious traditions and practices in the city with rituals in Honduran villages. He explores the alterations in religious practices due to so many Garifuna relocating to New York and shows how Garifuna in the city adopted elements of Caribbean religions. England examines the transnational social activism of Garifuna organizations in Honduras as they defend their rights against agro-export businesses and tourism. Race, class, ethnicity, gender, and nationhood are explored within the Garifuna community as it deals with these challenges. Also highlighted are Garifuna volunteer organizations in New York supporting the Garifuna community in Honduras. My research complements England's and other studies addressing the Garifuna Black identity in the city, showing that past and present generations of the ethnic group have identified and associated with Black Americans. In addition, I present Garifuna organizations in the community prior to the 1990s; these groups were not village oriented but were open to all, including those outside the ethnic group.

Furthermore, I highlight Garifuna political engagement beginning early in this century in New York City. This topic is briefly covered by Garcia (2013) and is also part of a chapter in *Latinos in New York: Communities in Transition* (Baver et al. 2017) analyzing Central American immigrants in the city. There, the authors illustrate the diversity of recent Latino populations in New York City, exploring race, culture, and ties to home countries. *Latinos in New York* also shows how the Garifuna increased their contact with local public officials and city agencies after the 1990s Happy Land Social Club fire in the Bronx, where many died. This led to the formation of an umbrella organization, FEDHONY (Federation of Honduran Organizations in New York), which became central to their political participation in the city (England 2006; Garcia 2013; Jones-Correa 1998). In

Jones-Correa's *Between Two Nations: The Political Predicament of Latinos in New York City* (1998), FEDHONY and an earlier organization are briefly described, although the Garifuna are not listed as participants. Nor is Honduran population diversity explored in this analysis. This is important because although Garifuna are a minority in Honduras, they are the most visible Honduran population in New York City and are estimated to be the majority (England 1999). Concentrating on first-generation Latino immigrants in New York, Jones-Correa finds that they are unable to cut ties with their home country, which deters them from becoming citizens or engaging civically. Instead, he claims, the Garifuna's New York organizations prefer to address concerns in their home countries, such as the 1969 soccer war in Central America, which resulted in aid and goods being sent back home. Here, however, we learn that the Garifuna community evolved and became politically engaged while simultaneously addressing issues back home (see Chapter 7).

The Garifuna as an Organized Entity

Although assimilation and integration can occur through various means, for the Garifuna in New York City, organizations have been the primary method of community integration. Garifuna maintain many kinds of organizations: informal, formal, religious, recreational, cultural, civic, and township associations, among others (Endo et al. 2010). Because Garifuna come from different countries, nationalism and regionalism are common, and this is evident in their organizations. As the largest Garifuna population, Honduran Garifuna have the greatest number of organizations in the city (Brondo 2017; Endo et al. 2010). Garifuna from Belize and Guatemala have different groups to represent their hometown communities and interests; thus far, Nicaraguan Garifuna do not have an organized group, likely due to their small population in the city. However, Garifuna Carib descendants from St. Vincent and the Grenadines recently established an organization, strengthening their connections and embracing their ethnic heritage. Because of their different nationalities, many New York City Garifuna associate with non-Garifuna groups from their respective countries. Their consulates in New York maintain a network of functions in which many Garifuna participate. For example, each year a mass is held at St. Patrick's Cathedral honoring the Honduran Garifuna's patron saint, the Virgin of Suyapa. Honduran Garifuna leaders also represent Honduras in the annual New York City Hispanic parade (*Catholic NY* 2022; *Queens*

Latino 2021). Several Belizean Garifuna organizations hold annual celebrations of Belize Independence Day and sponsor town hall forums. In addition, Belizean Garifuna leaders are part of the Belize Ex-Servicemen's League, a U.S. satellite of the Belize veterans' organization (Belize Ex-Servicemen's 2021).

It is important to note that although there have been four generations of Garifuna in the United States, for the most part their organizations have been founded and led by individuals born in Central America. These organizations' culture and structure and their members' heritage are sustained as new Garifuna migrants join the community upon their arrival, strengthening its cultural identity. As Garifuna organizations integrate into the community, culture is promoted, and identity remains important. That cultural identity includes traditional culinary dishes, artisanal work, attire, musical styles and instruments, dances, folktales, language, traditional medicines, and religious ceremonial practices.

Central Theme and Theoretical Foundation

To gain a thorough understanding of Garifuna community growth, this study utilizes key components of the social capital literature to examine the relationship between this group and its community. Social capital also supports this study's explanation of how Garifuna organizations evolved, becoming civically engaged. Putnam defines social capital as the "connections among individuals—social networks, and the norms of reciprocity and trustworthiness that arise from them" (Putnam 2000, 19).[7] Effective social networks and connections allow groups to achieve their goals and objectives. This theoretical concept has been used to study different Garifuna communities, such as those on the island of St. Vincent. Social capital strategies were used to analyze Garifuna communities in remote areas of St. Vincent that were negotiating to ensure their fishing and farming livelihoods, which were threatened by economic neglect, droughts, and tropical storms (Barker and Smith 2013; Smith 2016). This theoretical concept was also applied to analyze issues in the ethnic group's Central American communities. For example, Garifuna fishing families living along the northern coast of Honduras built social networks that gave them access to marine resources and allowed them to organize against state regulations (Lansing 2009). Curran (2002, 12), in her studies of migration, social capital, and the environment, highlights the commercialization of fisheries in Livingston, Guatemala, where, compared with Ladinos in the area, the Garifuna had few social and economic networks and institutions, preventing them from obtaining fisheries resources at lower commercial prices and supplementing their diets.

Social capital concepts, group connections, and networks are applicable to various subject areas. This includes Black immigrants and African Americans encountering challenges such as discrimination and inequalities in their communities, a central theme in this study. Social capital theory is used by Rodriguez, Hawkins, and Wilkes (2019) to analyze past African American experiences of inequality during the civil rights era and how organization networking and forming coalitions contributed to successful legislation. In contemporary times, the authors recommend, Blacks need to form selective economic and political partnerships to bring social change and close the gap of existing inequalities.

Scholars also highlight churches as historically key to African Americans in dealing with discrimination and racism. They show that in the late 1700s Blacks were able to congregate in church and that over time their involvement in church evolved to facilitate their organizing and civic engagement for securing their collective rights (Shaw-Taylor and Tuch 2007; Averett 2021). Churches continue to be key meeting places for Black immigrants, as listed in Averett (2021) and other literature. In the case of the Garifuna, in addition to serving as meeting places, their churches played a role in their initial phase of civic engagement in New York, highlighted in Chapters 4 and 6. Similarly, social capital theory is also applied to analyzing Black immigrant groups in New York overcoming discrimination and living in racially segregated communities. Grasmuck and Grosfoguel (1997) explore social capital among Puerto Rican, Dominican, Cuban, Jamaican, and Haitian immigrants in New York City. An analysis of women's function in their families provides the basis for a comparison of the socioeconomic conditions of each immigrant group. In a more recent study using social capital theory, Shaw-Taylor and Tuch (2007) compare English Caribbean and African immigrants to African Americans in terms of their success in obtaining economic resources. The social capital concept has been applied to challenge views that African Americans' cultural traditions contribute to their lower earnings compared to Caribbean immigrants'. Concentrating on another Black ethnic population, Opoku Donyina (2020) highlights that African immigrants in New York City from different countries sustain their livelihoods through social networks. He expresses their success in spite of facing many challenges, including living in racially segregated Black and Latino communities with limited opportunities to advance in education and employment. For Dominicans, another immigrant group in New

York City some consider to be Black, economic and local political gains are attributed to social capital and the group's organizational growth and networks (Reynoso 2003). Their success is credited not merely to their increasing population but to their entrepreneurial drive and acquisition of political power in the city. Reynoso (2003) also finds that racial discrimination is among the obstacles confronting this immigrant population living in the city.[8] These studies are among many others that use social capital to study the circumstances of Black immigrants.

Black Immigrants and African Americans: Similar Experiences yet Different Organizing

The concept of Black immigrants and African Americans establishing social networks also complements a central theme in this study: that Black immigrants' and African Americans' cultural differences do not pose significant barriers to their uniting to address racial inequities in their communities and to support policies that improve their social mobility. Yet their organizing differs based on continued ties to their homelands. Earlier in this introduction, research on Black immigrants (African and Caribbean) was mentioned. Wright Austin's study (2018) was based on surveys and interviews in Boston, Chicago, Miami, and New York showing African Americans' and Black immigrants' racial group consciousness, supporting political coalition alliances between them. She states that Black immigrants living in minority communities and experiencing discrimination also vote in support of Black candidates. In addition, the author highlights that the increase in the population of Black immigrants over past generations, their gains in education, and residence in Black neighborhoods foster greater racial solidarity. This outcome is also evident with generations of Garifuna living in New York assimilating and integrating in society. Kasinitz (1992) analyzes different generations of a Black immigrant group's relations with African Americans. In his study, focusing specifically on New York City, he shows how during three waves of West Indian immigration, community formation differed, as well as West Indians' relations with African Americans and whites dominating society. At first, West Indian immigrants resided with Blacks in Harlem, before many migrated to Brooklyn because of changes in housing policies. Garifuna experience parallels that of West Indians sustaining different waves of migration, as Garifuna also first settled in Harlem before moving and establishing their population concentration in the Bronx. Kasinitz shows that West Indians' advanced British model of education contributed to their early involvement in city politics. Periods when some of their associations allied with white public officials as well as Blacks are highlighted. Though many maintain cultural and political ties to the Caribbean, in New York politics they identify as Black. The author further argues that a change in the post-1965 period (of progressive immigration and civil rights legislation) resulted in West Indians' increased promotion of their ethnicity with their annual parades and in new neighborhood population concentrations. Relations with African Americans also fluctuated during this period as West Indians supported policies and political candidates. Nevertheless, Kasinitz illustrates how West Indians embraced being Black as they also experienced discrimination, structural racism, and police brutality in the city.

Greer (2013) also focuses on this book's central theme. Her study is also based in New York City but concentrates on the post–civil rights era. She acknowledges the cultural differences between African immigrants, Afro-Caribbean (West Indian) immigrants, and African Americans. In her argument based on the elevated minority concept and "linked fate of Black ethnics," she analyzes how all Blacks come together in supporting shared political issues. She concludes that although culturally different, Black ethnics share some features of the "linked fate" of African Americans in that racial discrimination and inequality limit their socioeconomic advancement. Greer states that although their similarities could be expected to result in coalition building between the groups, that expectation is challenged because of Black ethnics' "elevated minority" views. She finds both Afro-Caribbean and Afro-American pessimism regarding equal opportunity in the United States. Nevertheless, Greer observes that labor union membership brings the groups closer together in becoming politically knowledgeable. Through the labor union they ally with the Democratic Party supporting liberal views, including on government spending for issues concerning their Black communities such as education, health care, and the environment. Similarly, many Garifuna also belong to unions, opening opportunities for their civic engagement highlighted in the book. Interviews with union members, national survey data, and data from New York City's Social Services led to her findings. Greer concentrates on extensive national demographic data analysis to arrive at her conclusions.

In contrast to studies that feature multiple Black immigrant groups, Pierre-Louis (2006) focuses on a single immigrant population, Haitians in New York City, observing their strategies for accommodating to life in the United States to protect themselves from the discrimination they experience as a minority. They organized, becoming civically engaged in New York City, and formed hometown associations that continue their ties to their homeland. Conflicts occurred between Haitian immigrants seeking to sustain ties to their home country and those wanting to focus instead on participating in local politics and integrating into society. The author presents Haitian immigrants as accepting their common African heritage with Black Americans. Nonetheless, Haitians have also asserted their cultural differences to enhance their economic and social positions compared to other Blacks. The author presents this as "segmented assimilation."[9] In part, this entailed Haitians participating in African Americans' and other groups' activities yet retaining their unique ethnic identity as they assimilated. This condition is also evident in the way some Garifuna, especially their more recently arrived immigrants and long-standing leaders of their organizations, have promoted their culture while associating with different community groups. Pierre-Louis presents the advancement of Haitians in local city politics and the tensions that occurred with English Caribbean descendants and African Americans. However, he shows these Black groups forming alliances that support policy issues affecting their minority communities. Another similarity to studies on Black immigrants presented by Pierre-Louis is that second and subsequent generations of Haitians identify as African Americans.

Haitians, West Indians, Africans, and Caribbean Black immigrants described by the authors come together in spite of their differences. The studies focus on a specific Black immigrant group or on multiple groups in their analysis. The authors observe differences in culture, language, political issues, and educational background of the immigrant groups compared to African Americans. For example, Haitians and West Indians in New York City have transnational ties to their home country, highlighting a difference in their organizing compared to African Americans. In addition, "elevated minority" was listed as a coping strategy of Black immigrants dealing with racism in the United States, separating themselves from African Americans. In contrast, Haitian immigrants' "segmented assimilation" promoted their unique culture as they sought to assimilate with other groups (Greer 2013; Pierre-Louis 2006). The authors show that Black immigrants, like African Americans, acknowledge that their social, political, and economic opportunities are limited in the United States because of racial discrimination. Migration waves of Haitians and West Indians to the United States, before and after the civil rights era, highlight the longevity of these immigrant populations in New York City, as they established separate neighborhoods after residing in segregated communities with African Americans. These two immigrant populations were shown at times to be selective in their political alliances with African Americans and other groups. Nevertheless, each Black immigrant group through subsequent generations in the United States identifies as African Americans.

These authors' topics and shared conclusions support the thematic analysis of this study that Black immigrants experience many circumstances similar to those of African Americans in terms of discrimination and structural racism. In addition, these immigrants also have cultural and linguistic differences from African Americans that have caused tensions. Nevertheless, although Black immigrants' organizing differs, they tend to form alliances with African American for a common good. Subsequent generations of these immigrant groups begin identifying as Black Americans. Similar to other Black immigrants, Garifuna also organize to address issues in their homelands. The Garifuna in this research exhibit these attributes, as well as social capital trends. The theoretical framework of social capital shows that African Americans and Black immigrants who organize themselves and network with other groups are able to advance by overcoming barriers of discrimination and racism. Sander (2015), in his study of U.S. civic engagement, defines the social concept as "the collective value of all social networks" when people collaborate with one another. Voluntary and social organizations are the prerequisites for civic exchanges. When Garifuna organizations engage in these networks, just as with Latinos, African Americans, and Black immigrants, this engagement becomes an effective means of increasing their political participation (Coleman 1988; Segura et al. 1999, 2003; Bedolla 2005). Garifuna organizations began as social networks, and over time many of them became civically engaged, accounting for their community growth and development.[10] Social capital applied in this context shows that networking and forming alliances contributed to many Garifuna organizations becoming civically engaged to address their needs, and also to challenge inequalities residing in New York's racially segregated communities. This study explains Garifuna's present political participation in New York City through this theoretical framework. The central theme and framework complement the argument that establishing different groups facilitates Garifuna's maintenance of their subsistence, culture, and participation, in addition to engaging in their homeland issues.

Methodology

The New York City boroughs of the Bronx, Brooklyn, and Manhattan were selected for this study due to the sizable Garifuna populations there.[11] It is common to hear the Garifuna language on buses, in subways, in local parks, and in shopping districts in the region. I was born in New York

City, and have often returned to the city to visit family and friends. During one visit I told them about my research project, and they were happy to refer me to individuals in the community who were leaders of or associated with Garifuna organizations. I scheduled meetings in 2006 and began interviewing several Garifuna leaders and attending events in the city. Interviews were conducted in either Spanish or English, based on the interviewee's language proficiency. Sometimes phrases or words in the Garifuna language were used to express strong sentiments or situations. I developed a network that led to multiple other contacts and friendships with many leaders. In addition, I reviewed all the literature I could find focusing on or relevant to the Garifuna, visiting research libraries in the city and at universities.

My move back to the Bronx in 2012 facilitated my attendance at more activities in the city and extended my Garifuna networks. I attended Garifuna cultural masses, evangelical church events, and folkloric dance presentations, where I met the individuals involved in these groups. In addition, I visited Garifuna political forums, meetings associated with the 2020 census, and gatherings to address the political challenges in Belizean and Honduran Garifuna communities. I also attended planning meetings among local officials for Garifuna Heritage Month celebrations in the city. At these gatherings, Garifuna of various social classes were present, allowing me to socialize with them and hear their different views. In addition, I was invited to meetings of Garifuna professional associations, where I interviewed leaders of the various organizations and learned about their history and experiences. Elder members of the community provided photos and documents from past Garifuna organizations.

During the early phases of my study, one of the Garifuna leaders recommended that I visit Garifuna communities in Central America to gain a comprehensive understanding of the ethnic group. Many Garifuna from the United States move back home when they retire, and their families visit during summers and holidays and to attend traditional ceremonies. Beginning in 2010 I spent summers at Garifuna communities in Honduras and Belize, where I interviewed elders and community leaders to learn about past and present challenges. I also visited Garifuna communities in Guatemala. Since that time, I have made annual visits to Central America, particularly Honduras, where I travel to different communities, including those in remote areas. I also keep in touch with friends who inform me of present conditions. In 2019 the Garifuna experienced an unprecedented number of deaths due to criminal acts. Many of these murders were associated with the usual cycle of violence in Honduras, but some deaths and threats were associated with Garifuna activists' organizing and resisting the seizure of their lands by outsiders. Occasionally, Ladinos approach a Garifuna community seeking to seize its territories. In other cases, drug traffickers come looking for members of the community involved with them. Garifuna leaders are sometimes threatened. Although this happens more often than it did in the past, fortunately it is not a daily occurrence and occurs only in certain communities. Overall, Garifuna communities remain relatively peaceful and safe, as they are located over a range of 600 kilometers along the Atlantic coast. Many villages are tourist attractions, as both non-Garifuna and Garifuna come for weekends and holidays to enjoy the natural scenery and beaches. Foreigners visit the tourist resorts along the coast.[12] Unfortunately, although those resorts are in Garifuna communities, for the most part they are owned by outsiders.

Organization of this Book

This book is structured chronologically, tracing the organizational development of the Garifuna community through the decades. Their historical and cultural background is presented first, beginning on the island of St. Vincent, followed by their early experiences in Central America in the 1940s through 1970s and the wave of Garifuna migration in the 1980s and 1990s as they sought better economic conditions and opportunities (Johnson 2007). In the twenty-first century, gang violence and the drug trade have had a negative effect on economic security in Central America, spurring Honduran Garifuna to migrate to the United States as well as to Europe (Spain and France), where they have also started to organize. These migrants maintain both social and financial ties to their Central American communities, benefiting those countries' economies (Guzman 2018; Endo et al. 2010).[13]

Chapter 1, "Origins, Surviving, Ensuring Subsistence, and Culture," presents Garifuna origins and culture, beginning on the island of St. Vincent in the Caribbean. Their Black Carib descendants struggled for autonomy during the colonial period before being forcibly removed from the island and sent to Central America, where they settled along the coast. In their pursuit of autonomy, they formed alliances with political factions, reminiscent of what they had done on St. Vincent. Garifuna political partnerships during and after Central America's independence period are also highlighted. Such partnerships became common, as Garifuna continued establishing ties with other groups to ensure their subsistence in locations they settled. Included also in the chapter is a section about Garifuna culture, which is helpful in understanding their differences and similarities with other groups in their communities.

Chapter 2, "Livelihood on the Caribbean Coast," provides background on the Garifuna's Central American experiences that later influenced them as immigrants in New York. I describe the influence of a foreign agro-export company, Garifuna interactions with English-speaking Black laborers, and Marcus Garvey's United Negro Improvement Association (UNIA), all of which had an early impact on Garifuna men, some of whom eventually migrated to New York City (López Oro 2016b). The Garifuna in British Honduras (now Belize) established organizations to promote their culture, and these groups played a role in the formation of the Garifuna seamen's association in New York (covered in Chapter 3). In Belize, Garifuna joining the UNIA assisted in managing discrimination and inequalities experienced in the country. Later they established their own group helping to preserve their culture and address their community social needs in Central America. Eventually, economic decline and World War II caused many Garifuna men to leave their Central American communities. Many became seamen and ended up in New York.

Chapter 3, "Early U.S. Garifuna Communities," covers the immigrant group that initially settled in Harlem in the 1940s and started the first Garifuna organization. I describe the early period of racial tension in Harlem, where West Indian Black Hondurans formed an organization and the Garifuna started a separate organization. This chapter includes a discussion of the Garifuna's associations with African Americans, Garifuna seamen's experiences during World War II, and the postwar period and Garifuna settlement in the Bronx and New Orleans. As the immigrant population grew, Garifuna organizations increased their membership and activities, and they associated more often with Latinos in the Bronx. Programs and advertisements for Garifuna activities in the 1960s, written in English and Spanish, demonstrate that they welcomed a diverse population to their events. Like other Black immigrants, Garifuna first settled in Harlem before later moving to other boroughs. Groups established during this period assisted in sustaining their culture. Early established groups were the foundation for an evolution to civic engagement. Garifuna connected with African Americans, West Indians, and Latinos, also marginalized and discriminated against in this period.

Chapter 4, "Identity and Cultural Growth: *Garifunadao*," offers an account of the Garifuna in New York City in the 1970s and 1980s, including the increased recognition of their heritage and their ongoing activities and organizational growth. During this period Garifuna integrated more into their NYC communities. Their networks expanded with other ethnic groups but sustained their unique Garifuna culture. They also continued to identify and sustain outreach efforts with their Central American communities. The chapter is divided into two periods. In the first period, the 1970s, Garifuna cultural awareness and population growth included the addition of musicians to their social scene and the initiation of new groups, including Belizean Garifuna organizations. Another important community development was the creation of Garifuna hometown, sports, and Catholic associations. With the new wave of immigrants in the 1980s, there was a change in musical performances, with greater use of the Garifuna language and traditional instruments. Through their organization activities they interacted with other minorities whose communities also experienced socioeconomic challenges. In addition to upholding their culture, Garifuna groups during this period provided for their social development needs.

Each of the following three chapters covers the same year range, from the 1990s to the present, from different angles. Remarkably, in this period Garifuna population and organizations substantially increased. Chapter 5, "Music, Dance, and Sports from the 1990s to the Present," shows these activities upholding Garifuna culture and identity. The chapter presents Garifuna amateur soccer clubs (for which organizers volunteer their time and hold fundraisers to cover expenses), folkloric dance groups, and social organizations' cultural events significance, leading Garifuna functions in the city in these decades. Some groups were short-lived while others became established in the community, evolving from previous years. Introduced in the first segment of the chapter are amateur soccer clubs, folkloric dance groups, and organizations' cultural events, contributing to sustaining their identity. Their activities bring Garifuna together engaging in their language and culinary traditions, part of their identity. This is followed by Garifuna organizations uniting to celebrate their culture in their annual parade. The last segment of the chapter includes discussions led by their organizations about their ethnic classification and origins. The chapter shows how these Garifuna group activities allow them to network with non-Garifuna. These groups lead Garifuna in integrating into their local communities as a separate ethnic group promoting and conserving their identity.

Chapter 6, "Social Issues in New York City from the 1990s to the Present," explains how Garifuna organizations managed social issues in their communities during this period, becoming civically engaged. Some issues they encountered were police brutality, gun violence, and lack of adequate health care and housing, among many other needs. At first Garifuna capitalized on both private and public support received after many died in one of New York City's worst fires. Key contacts they acquired after the incident contributed to a surge in new Garifuna organizations, including a health care–related agency, a group offering trade education, and umbrella organizations seeking to address issues collaboratively. Once they became politically active, they succeeded in acquiring discretionary and private funding support and legislation recognizing their cultural contributions. Garifuna organizations' various alliances with African American and Latino candidates facilitated some of their gains.

The next chapter demonstrates how Garifuna, like other Black immigrant groups, continued ties to their homelands. Chapter 7, "Central America and St. Vincent from the 1990s to the Present," explores Garifuna organizations' connections to their countries and the outcomes of these contacts during this period. The first chapter segment describes Garifuna groups holding transnational forums beginning in the late 1990s to plan how to support their communities abroad. In the new century, Garifuna New York City organizations have responded to their human rights and territorial challenges in Central America. Their outreach goes beyond Central America. The last section of the chapter describes an increase in Garifuna organizations' exchanges with their Carib descendant communities in St. Vincent. Even as Garifuna groups engaged in their homelands, they remained active addressing social needs and participating in their New York City communities.

The conclusion highlights the diversity of the Garifuna population in terms of generation, nationality, and language proficiency (Garifuna, Spanish, or English). I also note some popular Garifuna sports figures, rappers, and hip-hop artists, many of whom have assimilated into African American society. This is similar to the experience of other Black immigrants' subsequent generations who also identify as African Americans. In addition, I highlight challenges to the development of a comprehensive Garifuna community in New York City, basing my observations on my experiences associating with Garifuna organizations. I outline the group's potential for advancement in the city, where a growing cadre of young professionals offers hope that they will connect with their Garifuna community.

The different Garifuna groups and their functions presented in each chapter support the book's argument that as a Black immigrant group, Garifuna contribute through their organizations to upholding their culture, subsistence, and participation in New York City as well as tending to issues in their home countries. The book follows the ethnic group's trajectory in the city, led by their organizations, evolving to becoming politically oriented. Since early times, as a Black ethnic group also experiencing discrimination, Garifuna associated with Black Americans. They also engaged with Latinos, West Indians, Africans, and other minority groups in their communities. This continues in the present with civically engaged Garifuna organizations establishing alliances with these groups' organizations in the city.

Chapter 1

Origins, Surviving, Ensuring Subsistence, and Culture

Yurumei giñeru nege wayuna,
Ñeiba bagüra bügüra wabu,
Warúeite ///
Waluahenañanu Garinagu waladi,

Liyumoun chururuti duna //
Ragübei benehene wabu,
Warúeite ///
Ragübei benehene wabu //
Waluahenañanu Garinagu waladi.

Our ancestor is arriving from Yurumei,
There you are going to tie your hammock with us, our king/queen,
We are looking for Garinagu like ourselves,

The mouth of the shallow river,
Grab your paddle with us, our king/queen
We are looking for Garinagu like ourselves.

"OUR ANCESTORS COME from St. Vincent" (*Yurumein giñeru nege wayuna*) is the Garifuna anthem. The song recounts the history and struggles of the Garifuna beginning on the island of St. Vincent, known as *Yurumein* in the Garifuna language. The song is common at festivals, family gatherings, and political and cultural events. The word *Yurumein* is also widely used in the Garifuna community in the names of businesses and organizations.

A significant part of Garifuna culture involves paying homage to the land and ancestors, recognizing their sacrifices and struggles for the generations that followed. This chapter focuses on the Caribbean island of St. Vincent (the largest of the islands of the nation St. Vincent and the Grenadines), the beginning of Garifuna history, and the development of their African and indigenous identity. Their long history of displacement and resistance challenging colonialism in the Caribbean and Central America begins on St. Vincent. Garifuna experiences on the island shed light on similarities and differences with other groups in the Caribbean and in Central and North America. Highlighted also are Garifuna efforts to organize themselves and form alliances with colonial Europeans and island natives to ensure their subsistence. That such organizing is central to Garifuna survival is already evident in this early period.

Early Beginnings in the Caribbean

St. Vincent and the Grenadines is a country consisting of a group of small islands in the eastern Caribbean. The Arawak Indians originally inhabited the area until the Carib Indians conquered the region. In the 1600s, Africans were reported on St. Vincent (C. Taylor 2012). There are different versions of how the Garifuna population got there. In one popular account, the Garifuna originated from a maroon African population arriving in the Caribbean and settling with the native indigenous population of St. Vincent. The Garifuna—referred to as the Black Caribs—gradually increased in population, eventually dominating the Arawak-Carib inhabitants, described by Europeans as either Red or Yellow Caribs (Johnson 2007, 3).

In addition to the commonly accepted 1635 shipwreck and slave escape narrative, scholars have cited transatlantic voyages prior to that of Christopher Columbus as evidence of an earlier African presence in the Americas. For example, Abu Bakari II of the African empire of Mali is believed to have traveled to the Americas in the 1300s. Christopher Taylor (2012) presents an alternative to the shipwreck narrative in *The Black Carib Wars*. According to Taylor, the shipwreck narrative was constructed to validate British goals of expanding and establishing sugar plantations on the Caribbean island of St. Vincent. He maintains that the British sought to delegitimize the "Black Carib" as runaway slaves who had no rights to freedom in the lands or the islands they inhabited (20). Taylor argues that the British goal was to usurp the Black Caribs' land in the island, so the

British ignored accounts that the Black Carib were present on the island of St. Vincent before European arrival. Taylor questions the authenticity of European writers' shipwreck story because, despite many shipwrecks occurring at that time, the dates in other accounts do not align with the Black Carib shipwreck in St. Vincent (16).

Another argument in favor of the Garifuna's pre-Columbian presence in the Americas is Ivan Van Sertima's 1976 *They Came before Columbus*, which describes the existence of the Olmec civilization (1200–100 BCE). The African phenotype of the large Olmec head statue in southern Mexico is cited as evidence of an African presence in the Americas before Columbus and has been used to draw conclusions about the Garifuna's early presence. In any case, the Garifuna evolved into a group of mixed indigenous and African heritage on St. Vincent, where their culture developed.

European settlement began in the early 1600s in the Caribbean islands, and for more than one hundred years the native Caribs engaged in trade and warfare with the British, Dutch, French, and Spanish. They used different strategies to stop the colonization of neighboring islands in the Lesser Antilles, allying with rival European factions. The Caribs also raided enemy European settlements, capturing and harboring African slaves, despite agreements to the contrary (Wilson 1993). In 1676 an estimated three thousand Blacks resided on St. Vincent with the natives. The mixed African and Amerindian population increased with the growing runaway African slave population and natural births. By the mid-1700s, the Amerindian African population surpassed the Amerindian population on St. Vincent, as acknowledged by French and British documents. To distinguish the two groups, the Europeans started referring to them as the Black Caribs and the Yellow Caribs (also known as Red Caribs), fomenting division (Beaucage 1970; Beckles 1992; J. Palacio 2005).

Several European countries, including the Netherlands, Spain, France, and England, sought control in the Caribbean. Early government exchanges between the Caribs and the Europeans began as early as the 1600s. One of the earliest accords was the Treaty of 1660, signed at Basse Terre, Guadeloupe, with Britain and France. It gave the island dwellers perpetual ownership of Dominica and St. Vincent, and they agreed not to raid European settlements (D. Taylor 1963, 19). Eight years later, the British broke the treaty and waged several wars to conquer the island dwellers' territory (S. Cayetano 1993). The British forced the island leaders of St. Vincent and Dominica to sign a new treaty in 1668 (initiated by Lord

Willoughby), which promised the return of escaped slaves to their masters and the acceptance of English sovereignty (D. Taylor 1963). During this period, the Caribs, fugitive African slaves, and Blacks from the Spanish ship lost in 1635 lived and collaborated with one another on St. Vincent (D. Taylor 1963, 18; C. Taylor 2012).

In 1700 a dividing line called Barre de l'isle was drawn on the island of St. Vincent, giving the western portion to the Red or Yellow Caribs and the eastern portion to the Black Caribs (Johnson 2007). The Yellow Caribs had sought assistance from the island's French governor to keep the Black Caribs from invading their territories. The French official's solution was the dividing line. The Black Caribs' territory was protected from the Europeans, and they engaged in trade with European colonists, exchanging natural resources for manufactured goods. They were also introduced to the French and English languages and Catholicism. In turn, the Yellow Caribs benefited by having control of the western portion of the island, facilitating ties with the French in the neighboring islands of St. Lucia and Martinique. The French saw the division of the island as beneficial because the Yellow Caribs shared the French aspirations to displace the Black Caribs and control the entire island (Kirby and Martin 1997). In 1719, however, the French failed in their attempt to displace the Black Caribs. The Yellow Caribs, who had planned the attack, astutely pulled out, acknowledging that they lacked sufficient soldiers to prevail (C. Taylor 2012).

With their greater numbers, the Black Caribs eventually represented the island's entire Carib population. The earliest diplomatic exchange involving the Black Caribs occurred in 1722 when an Englishman, Captain Braithwaite, sought to settle in St. Vincent. An earlier Dutch attempt to settle in the region had been unsuccessful. The chief of the Black Caribs informed Braithwaite that they were ready to defend themselves and had arms and ammunition acquired from the French, whom they did not trust but with whom they had a working relationship. He noted their 1719 victory over the French and vowed that the Black Caribs would never allow themselves to be in a position where Europeans could harm them. The Black Carib chief diplomatically asked Captain Braithwaite to leave the territory, which he did immediately (Kirby and Martin 1997; C. Taylor 2012).

The 1763 Treaty of Paris ceded St. Vincent to the English, who assumed control over French industry (cocoa, coffee, cotton) on the island. A commission led by Sir William Young was sent to survey, sell, and subdivide the land in St. Vincent (Kirby and Martin 1997, 18). The treaty made no mention of the Caribs, and the commissioners were instructed not to tamper with or survey the Caribs' territory without permission from the British government. Nevertheless, the commissioners and settlers sought to circumvent that order. Young advertised that unused land was available for sale in St. Vincent, ignoring the Black Caribs' system of cultivation and their communal land tenure system, which included territorial boundaries and a hierarchical chiefdom. The commissioners employed various measures, including deceit, to obtain the Caribs' land. They even used a Jesuit missionary as a liaison, but the Black Caribs suspected him of subversion and dismissed his negotiating efforts (Kirby and Martin 1997; C. Taylor 2012).

The British commissioners and settlers made several attempts to acquire the Black Caribs' rich land. Their society was organized separately and united under a chief only during conflict (C. Taylor 2012). Europeans struggled to dominate them due to their decentralized governance structure. British settlers' efforts to expand their control of the island led to the First Carib War of 1769–73, resulting in the Treaty of 1773. In 1769, without any order from the British government, the commissioners attacked the Caribs and then retreated. The settlers used a different strategy, purchasing land from the Black Caribs despite knowing that the validity of their titles would be questionable given the communal land system. The Caribs, coming together under their chief, Joseph Chatoyer, repelled British attacks and refused demands to sell their land. Eventually, after a failed offensive against the Caribs and disagreement within the British government about the war, the British decided to cease hostilities. This resulted in the Treaty of 1773, which defined Carib and British boundaries and required the natives' acceptance of Britain's king and his representative authority in the island, as well as several other stipulations. The treaty reflects the Black Caribs' efforts to negotiate and seek territorial sovereignty with British leaders following the defense of their territory in the war. Even so, the Caribs' land was demarcated with boundaries and reduced (Kirby and Martin 1997; C. Taylor 2012).

As France and Britain were at war during the American Revolution, the Caribs took advantage and allied with the French to oust the British from control of the island. With French military support, the Caribs enjoyed four years free of British territorial control until the 1783 Treaty of Paris, under which the French agreed to withdraw from the island and British control was restored. Nonetheless, some Frenchmen remained in St. Vincent (Kim 2013; Kirby and Martin 1997). Conflicts continued as the Caribs objected to encroachment on their lands and their marginalized status. Uprisings were occurring in the Caribbean in response to the French Revolution's ideals of liberty, law, and equality. When the English governor in St. Vincent learned of a planned Carib uprising, he contacted the Carib chiefs, Chatoyer and Duvalle, to discuss the terms of the 1773 treaty. However, the meeting never transpired, leading to the Second Carib War of 1795–97. Chief Chatoyer drafted a 1795 proclamation calling on Frenchmen in St. Vincent to support the war against the British for freedom and territorial autonomy (Kim 2013). The Caribs and a coalition of runaway slaves and French troops went on the offensive, capitalizing on uprisings and defending their territorial sovereignty. This uprising was depicted in the play *The Drama of King Shatoway* by William H. Brown and James Hewlett, which was presented in June 1823 at New York City's African Grove Theatre. This performance is recognized as the beginning of Black theater in the United States. Chatoyer died in battle in 1795, and the war ended after a discussion of the terms of surrender. The British demanded unconditional surrender with no negotiations, supported by their greater military power. In 1797 an estimated 4,633 Caribs, including 102 Yellow Caribs, were sent to the island of Balliceaux and then to Roatan off the Central American coast. Some Yellow Caribs who had not participated in the war and Black Caribs who had not surrendered remained on the outskirts of St. Vincent. Eventually, these Caribs settled in Sandy Bay and Greggs reservation in the northern part of the island (C. Taylor 2012; Kirby and Martin 1997).

Early Settlement in Central America

The Spanish had established the fort of Trujillo in 1525, in the region where the Garifuna eventually settled on the northern Atlantic coast of Honduras (Gonzalez 1988; Centeno García 1997). Before the Garifuna arrived in 1797, a number of Blacks were already present in the region, including freed or escaped Blacks of French (Saint-Domingue) and Spanish (Granada) descent. There were also a few former British slaves in the Spanish region when the Caribs arrived in 1797. Some accounts state that the French Blacks were the former slaves of French refugees from Santo Domingue (Haiti) and other French colonies (Gonzalez 1988). The British had been present in the circum-Caribbean region of Central America as early as the 1600s. British pirates or buccaneers had settlements in Belize, the San Andres Islands, La Mosquitia, and the Bay Islands. African slaves labored for the British in their unsuccessful sugar plantations in the region. Eventually, the British pirates formed trade and political alliances with the indigenous inhabitants of the area, the Miskitos, who dwelled in the northern Central American La Mosquitia region (Gonzalez 1988; England 2006; Gullick 1976; Euraque 2004). The Miskitos gained dominance in the region for two centuries with the aid of the British, expanding their presence from Trujillo, Honduras, to San Juan del Norte, Costa Rica (England 2006). The British alliance with the Miskitos allowed them to challenge Spain's dominance in the circum-Caribbean region, facilitating their combined attacks on Spanish forts and settlements. For two centuries, Trujillo had served as a Spanish fort in eastern Honduras. A 1787 agreement between the British and the Spaniards gave the British permission to log in the area and maintain their settlement in Belize. This came after more than a century of conflict. The conflicts continued into the 1800s, influenced by the British desire to trade and exploit natural resources, Spain's lack of protection, and the Miskitos' claim of the circum-Caribbean territory as their own, regardless of European treaties (England 2006). These were the prevailing circumstances when the Garifuna arrived.

A total of 2,026 Garifuna survived the arduous journey from St. Vincent to Port Royal on Roatan island off the northern coast of Central America (Gonzalez 1988; Centeno García 1997). The British strategy was to round up the rebellious Caribs and send them to the Central American mainland, hoping to destabilize Spanish control there (Gonzalez 1988; Gullick 1976). Given the sparse resources in Roatan, most of the Garifuna migrated to the Spanish territory of Trujillo, in present-day Honduras, after negotiations with the Spaniards. Rivas (1993) explains that the Miskitos living in Trujillo initially developed positive relations with the Garifuna, supplying advice and assistance as they established themselves. Once the Spaniards learned that the Caribs had military experience and arms the British had left them in Roatan, they realized the Caribs could be useful in protecting Fort Trujillo. Gonzalez (1988) explains that the Spaniards' weak control of the region meant that they needed soldiers to help defend against the British and the Miskitos. The shortage of laborers and the need for soldiers led the Spaniards to welcome the Garifuna, despite a lingering fear that the presence of a large Black population would enable the Garifuna to ally with the British against the Spaniards (Gonzalez 1988).

Garifuna engaged in agriculture, growing plantains, bananas, manioc, and coconut and raising chickens and pigs. Women assisted on the farms and participated in wage labor, such as laundering and cooking, when it was available. Men built thatch houses and canoes and fished for subsistence. These fishers and farmers also provided goods for local markets. As early as 1799, Garifuna traveled to British Honduras (Belize) in search of employment and worked in the British lumber industry. They also smuggled goods, considered contraband, to sell in Honduras, using their wages to buy European goods such as tools and household items. Members of the ethnic group earned a reputation as independent, intelligent, and strong laborers. By 1802, the Garifuna had established a Carib town, initially called Stann Creek and later Dangriga, in present-day Belize. The same year, some Garifuna settled in Livingston (Guatemala) and other regions along the Mosquitia (Honduras) (J. Palacio 2005; Arrivillaga Cortés 2009).[1] After the end of the British slave trade in 1807, labor shortages led to employment opportunities at sugar plantations and mahogany logging camps in Belize and La Mosquitia.

When the British attacked Trujillo in 1799, Garifuna helped the Spaniards defend the region against British naval vessels. The Garifuna fighting in this war showed strong animosity toward the British, whom they held responsible for their conquest and deportation from St. Vincent. Despite the Garifuna's help in repelling the British attack, the Spaniards oppressed the Garifuna and called for their expulsion, along with other Blacks, from Central America. In 1804 Governor Ramón Anguiano, from Comayagua Spanish headquarters, pressed for the removal of all Blacks from the Honduran coast (Gonzalez 1988). The Haitian revolution that occurred the same year sparked this decision, explaining the call for the removal of all French-speaking Blacks (Centeno García 2001; Gonzalez 1988; Gullick 1976). Although some Garifuna were not happy with the Spaniards' initiatives and allied with the British and Miskitos who planned attacks on Fort Trujillo, local Spaniards encouraged the Garifuna to come back to the region, acknowledging the need for their presence. Terms used to describe the Garifuna at the time were *Morenos*, Spanish for "dark skin"; *Caribes* or *Caribes Morenos*; and *Morenos Franceses*, or "dark-skinned French." After the mid-twentieth century, *Garifuna* became the common term used to describe the ethnic group (Canelas Díaz 1999; J. Ávila 2021, 36).

In the nineteenth century, Spain's territory included parts of the present-day southwestern United States and extended to Central and South America. As Spanish colonies sought independence, the Garifuna strategized, trying to determine which alliance would be most beneficial in terms of retaining their freedom and autonomy. In Central America, Spain's central governing region was Guatemala, recognized as the Captaincy General of Guatemala. After French power ceased with Napoleon's fall in 1815, Spain shifted its attention to its rebellious colonies, inspired by idealism and the French Revolution. Revolutionary activities in the colonies intensified, with the Garifuna and fugitive slaves from British Honduras (now Belize) constituting part of the colonial military. According to Gullick (1976), the Garifuna were recruited by the Spaniards, but some sided with the colonial rebels. Independence from Spain was declared in 1821, with the Central American provinces annexing Mexico the following year. Although the Central American Federation of States abolished slavery in 1823, it continued to exist until 1838. Coelho (1981) explains that in the first Honduran constitution (1825), the Garifuna were considered free dwellers of the country's coastal region. This was compensation for the Garifuna's past participation in military efforts (Coelho 1981, 46; Centeno García 1997).

After independence, internal conflicts emerged within the Central American Federation of States. In 1829 the federation's elected president, Manuel José Arce, was overthrown, and Francisco Morazán assumed power, ruling until 1840. Disagreements occurred, and some states separated and created factions, resulting in war in the region. According to Gonzalez (1988) and Johnson (2007), the Garifuna became involved as soldiers supporting both Arce (Conservative) and Morazán (Liberal). Santos Centeno García (1997), a Garifuna scholar, agrees with Garifuna oral historians that the Garifuna had a tradition of supporting Morazán. A Garifuna leader in Morazán's army, Juan Francisco Bulnes "Walumugu," is recognized as one of the early outstanding military leaders supporting Morazán and the federation (Arrivillaga Cortés 2005; Johnson 2007; Centeno García 1997). For the Garifuna, Morazán represented the best option in terms of meeting the needs of the Garifuna and all oppressed populations, and many participated in the 1832 war (Centeno García 1997). Slaves were still present in Central America in 1838, even though slavery had been abolished in the new constitution, and the Garifuna weighed their options carefully (Centeno García 1997, 12). There is documented evidence of Caribs and other groups being registered in Morazán's army "Ejército Aliado Protector de la Ley" (Centeno García 1997, 12).

By 1838, five nations that were part of the Central American federation had dissolved into separate nation-states: Guatemala, Honduras, El Salvador, Nicaragua, and Costa Rica (England 2006; Gonzalez 1988). Morazán's reign came to an end in 1840, and his attempt to recapture political power and unite the federation failed, ending with his execution in 1842 in Costa Rica. The dissolution of the Central American federation resulted in the establishment of border custom houses, and free trade among Garifuna across borders became illegal. Dealing in contraband was a very lucrative business requiring exceptional navigational skills and shrewdness—qualities the Garifuna possessed. Although these activities were dangerous, the Garifuna benefited financially (Coelho 1981).

Cultural Attributes of the Garifuna

Knowing that Garifuna society began on St. Vincent and evolved in the circum-Caribbean helps in understanding their culture. Their unique identity and isolated populations sustained their culture in their respective countries. In Belize, it is estimated that Garifuna account for 7 percent of the population; Mestizos and Creoles are the dominant groups there, with smaller numbers of Maya, Mennonites, East Indians, Chinese, and Arabs. For the most part, the Garifuna reside in the southern districts (Toledo, Stann Creek) of Belize. Mestizos, a mix of European and Amerindian, are the dominant population in Honduras, accounting for more than 90 percent; Amerindians (Chorti, Lenca, Miskitu, Pech, Tawakas, and Tolupanes) make up the next-largest group, followed by Afro-Honduran (Garifuna and Black English) populations. Most large Garifuna communities in Honduras are in the north on the Atlantic coast. In Guatemala, the population is predominantly Mestizo (54 percent), followed by indigenous (44 percent) and 1 percent to 2 percent Afro-Guatemalans, consisting of people of American, Belizean, Garifuna, and West Indian descent (Opie 2009). The Garifuna population is concentrated in Livingston, although they also reside in other towns and cities such as Puerto Barrios and Guatemala City. In Nicaragua, they are one of six different ethnic groups living on the Atlantic coast. The Mestizo population dominates, accounting for about 81 percent; the size of the Nicaraguan Garifuna population is similar to that in Guatemala.

Although each Central American country has its own culture and traditions, Garifuna have maintained a distinctive culture. Typically, they are recognized as excellent musicians and athletes. Just as African Americans are identified with sports (particularly basketball and football), Garifuna are recognized in Central America as excellent soccer (*fútbol*) players. Garifuna music and dance traditions are also popular in the region.

Garifuna identity is a legacy of both their African and Arawak-Carib heritage. They have traditional dishes, artisanal work, attire, dance styles, musical instruments, folktales, language, traditional medicines, and religious ceremonies. A substantial component of their culinary traditions reflects their West African and Caribbean heritage. Many ethnic Garifuna dishes are coconut based and include manioc or cassava bread (*ereba*), plantain (*baruru*), and different types of fish (*uüdüraü*). *Hudut* (ground plantain) with coconut milk and fish is similar to Puerto Rican *mofongo*, Dominican *mangu*, Jamaican and Tobago *run down*, and West African *fufu*.

Garifuna music comprises African and Amerindian elements, featuring call and response, dancing, and instruments such as conch shells, drums, and maracas. Parranda is one of several Garifuna musical genres; others are wanaragua, chumba, sambai, guchei, punta, and hüngühüngü. Music is central to Garifuna culture and identity. Their music conveyed stories about life's challenges, historical occurrences, and political conditions—stories that are passed orally from generation to generation. Individual singers and the call-and-response chorus accompany the sounds produced by traditional Garifuna musical instruments. Before utilizing modern instruments, Garifuna in Central America created their own. As the Garifuna community became less isolated and many people moved to cities, Garifuna bands organized and embraced popular Western musical genres, such as rhythm and blues, and the musical instruments used by popular bands of the 1940s and 1950s. Although traditional Garifuna folk music continued, Garifuna bands also embraced English Caribbean and rocksteady and later reggae, Spanish Caribbean, merengue, salsa, French Caribbean, compa, and zouk. In Central America as well as in New York City, Garifuna bands became important in promoting Garifuna communities' identity and unity.

In addition to food and music, the Garifuna's folktales, funeral traditions such as nine-nights (*beluria*), and traditional medicines are part of the African heritage they share with Black Caribbean communities. Garifuna spiritual traditions such as *lemesi*, *dugu*, or *walagayo* and *chugu* ancestral veneration and revelation of dreams are significant parts of their cultural identity, with both African and indigenous components. The belief that the spirits of deceased ancestors continue to live is highly regarded, and families often travel great distances to attend the larger *dugu* ceremonies.

Craftwork and creating tools are part of the Garifuna culture. Garifuna artisans' drum (*garawoun*) making is just one example of the useful implements they create, along with their traditional thatch homes (see figs. 1a, 1b). Residential homes (*muna*), ceremonial temples (*dabuyaba*), and the *ruguma*, a snake-like woven basket which strains cassava juice, are some of many Garifuna craft works. As a result of their early isolation, Garifuna depended on their ingenuity to survive before many of them ventured outside of their communities.

Language is another significant part of the Garifuna identity and their Carib-Arawak heritage. These Caribbean natives and their culture were almost completely eliminated, but thanks to the Garifuna, the Arawak

Figure 1a. Garifuna tools and instruments used in Central America: calabash (*rida*), duster (*baisawa*), grater (*egi*), cups (*weru*), stick (*wewe*), plate (*asíedu*), and cassava sifter (*híbise*).

Figure 1b. Traditional Garifuna house (*muna*) in Central America constructed with *murisi*, cohune palm leaves, used for thatching.

and Carib languages have been preserved. This facilitates the acquisition of knowledge about the early Caribbean inhabitants as part of the global world. The Garifuna language is a combination of 45 percent Arawak, 25 percent Carib, 15 percent French, and 10 percent English. The remaining percentage differs by Central American region. In Belize, where the official language is English, English elements are added to the Garifuna language. Spanish is the national language in Nicaragua, Guatemala, and Honduras, which influences the Garifuna language in those places. In the Garifuna language, certain words and descriptions are assigned to males and females. Designated gender roles also exist in dancing, certain crafts, and mourning rituals, and both men and women have always played important roles in leadership in the community (Gargallo 2005; Greene 2018). Research continues to distinguish African and Carib-Arawak elements in the Garifuna identity (J. Palacio 2005).

Conclusion

Overall, the history of the Garifuna on the island of St. Vincent serves as the foundation for an understanding of the Garifuna community presented in upcoming chapters. Knowledge of their culture broadens with an awareness of their identity. In addition, this chapter shows the beginning of Garifuna organizing and forming alliances for their survival, which became common when they migrated to Central America and also the United States. The following chapter focuses on their lives in coastal Central America, the challenges they faced, and the foundations of their organizing, as well as the causes of their migration to the United States. Garifuna migrations, prompted by different circumstances, began with forced removal from St. Vincent.

Chapter 2

Livelihood on the Caribbean Coast

GARIFUNA ESTABLISHED THEMSELVES in Central America's coastal communities with clear blue water, white sand beaches, and coconut palm trees. They adapted to new challenges, an ongoing occurrence wherever they settled. This chapter continues their history in Central America and reveals that although dispersed along the Central American coast, Garifuna remained united and organized across borders to address difficulties they encountered. In their place of settlement, the challenges and discrimination they experienced led to their unity. Background about their customs, organizational structure, and social experiences in Central America sheds light on many aspects of their migrant community in the United States, especially New York, where most Garifuna settled. Their motivations for leaving their homelands are also considered.

Garifuna Life in Central America

Early on, the Garifuna established settlements along the Central American coast in the cities and towns of Livingston and Puerto Barrios in Guatemala; Tela, La Ceiba, and Trujillo in Honduras; and Stann Creek and Punta Gorda in British Honduras.[1] Between 1825 and 1870 they often traveled between coastal settlements by boat and canoe, exchanging goods and visiting family. In the early nineteenth century the Garifuna sustained an informal governing structure—a council of elders—in their communities, as confirmed by Garifuna historian Victor Virgilio López during a personal visit (Moberg 1996; Coelho 1981). Eventually, under the influence of the Roman Catholic Church, the *patronato* system of informal governance developed in each Honduran Garifuna village and was later re-created in New York City as hometown associations coordinated with their counterparts back home. In this system, each village had administrators such as a president, vice president, treasurer, and secretary. In addition, a Catholic saint was assigned to represent each village and was recognized in annual celebrations organized with the support of the patronato (Johnson 2007).[2] As borders became better defined, regulations increased, inhibiting Garifuna exchanges among their communities in Central America. By 1838, the five nations that had been part of the joint Central American Federation (formed after declaring independence from Spain in 1821) became separate nation-states: Guatemala, Honduras, El Salvador, Nicaragua, and Costa Rica. With these changes, Garifuna travel across borders decreased. Nonetheless, they adjusted to the new geopolitical circumstances, engaging in various forms of subsistence (N. Gonzalez 2008).[3]

In the coastal town of Tela, Honduras, several Garifuna owned land and sold agricultural products, including bananas. Garifuna had owned *ejidal*, or communal land, as early as 1900 in Tela. According to city records from the 1910s and 1920s, Garifuna resident Pascual Valerio owned vast tracts of land and was involved in the sale of bananas. Honduran scholar Dario Euraque confirms that in the 1930s the Valerios owned much of the land in Tela's "Barrio Las Brisas," populated by Garifuna and other West Indian Blacks. In the city of La Ceiba, banana-growing Garifuna were economically dominant as early as the 1870s, and in the 1910s and early 1920s, Garifuna in this urban center basked in the wealth derived from the banana industry (Euraque 2003; Centeno García 2001). Garifuna landowners established a self-sustaining economic system that involved trade across borders in Central America and the cultivation of bananas for commerce. However, circumstances arose that challenged their livelihood.

Eventually, the United Fruit Company (UFCO) emerged, leading to changes in the coastal region. In Guatemala UFCO obtained control of Puerto Barrios, and in Honduras it gained a monopoly of smaller agroexport companies that had once served as its intermediaries. Standard Fruit Company (previously Vaccaro & D'Antoni) had functioned since 1902 in La Ceiba, and Cuyamel Fruit Company (previously Hubbard-Zemurray) had been operating since 1904, using the port facilities in Omoa and Puerto Cortés, Honduras. UFCO shifted its focus with the 1912 establishment of the Tela Railroad Company and the Trujillo Railroad Company. With government concessions, the company gained land and built railroads to facilitate the transport of agro-exports. Honduran president Manuel Bonilla (1903–7; 1911–13), who was of Garifuna descent, was one of the country's first public officials to grant concessions to foreign exporters. Bonilla granted foreign industries tax incentives and access to and control over Honduras's natural resources; in turn, he used U.S. funds to develop the country's infrastructure. Interestingly, after his government was overthrown in 1907, he spent time in exile in the Garifuna town of Stann Creek, British Honduras (Bardales 1985).[4]

Development of the coastal region by agro-exporters eventually transformed the economic and social status of the Garifuna, as many were employed by these industries and became dependent on wage labor. This also occurred in other Garifuna communities in Central America. As Garifuna scholar Santos Centeno García explains, these changes led to the development of a social hierarchy among the ethnic group, with a large economically marginalized segment.[5] In Honduras the Garifuna moved away from some of their coastal settlements as they grew into towns and cities; in addition, Mestizos and Caribbean immigrants who were looking for work moved into the area. Although many Garifuna experienced social and economic challenges during this period, others prospered. The income they received from working for the transnational companies was higher than their previous wages. Railroads provided access to communities that had once been accessible only by canoe or distant overland travel (Centeno García 2001).[6]

Although they shared a racial heritage, conflicts arose between the Garifuna and their Black Caribbean counterparts working for the agro-export companies. This was more evident in the northern coastal region, except for Puerto Cortés. The Caribbean Black population in Honduras started to grow in 1903, when company owners complained about labor shortages. This led to the importation of Black laborers from the English Caribbean islands (Jamaica, Cayman), Belize, Panama, and Colombia in the early twentieth century. Later, the Honduran government passed discriminatory and restrictive measures due to the increased Black population. Conflicts between Garifuna and Caribbean Blacks were common. The Standard Fruit Company and Tela Railroad Company employed Caribbean Blacks but not Garifuna in leadership positions, creating class divisions among Blacks. English Blacks were favored for their language, literacy, and experience in the banana industry; they were also more accustomed to white authority and racism. The U.S. transnationals transferred a racial class system to Honduras, with Blacks at the bottom (Gordon 1998; Centeno García 2001).

This racial social stratification also occurred in Guatemala, British Honduras, and Nicaragua. In Guatemala, railroad construction initiated along the coast in the late 1800s (International Railroad of Central America) was followed by U.S. agro-export companies hiring foreign laborers and nationals. The U.S.-based rail company recruited U.S. Blacks to build its operations in Guatemala. They accounted for a substantial proportion of the migrant population, as it was an opportunity to flee lynching, post-slavery discrimination, and the 1893–97 economic crisis in the United States. In 1900 UFCO established banana-exporting operations in Livingston, and in 1920 the company opened its ports in Puerto Barrios. An estimated two hundred West Indians arrived in 1901 to work there (Opie 2009).

In British Honduras, a class structure developed earlier than in other Central American countries. Before the British entered the region, groups of indigenous Maya inhabited the area. The Garifuna presence in British Honduras has been documented as early as 1802. In 1779 slaves made up 80 percent of the population in this British territory. British settlers in the eighteenth and nineteenth centuries had children with their African slaves, creating the Creole population. British slave owners created a group called the "free coloured," who occupied an intermediate place between masters and slaves. The free coloured evolved and became the Creole elite, who later replaced the Europeans in positions of power. Slavery was abolished in British Honduras in 1838, and slaves were replaced by Maya, Mestizo, and Afro-Caribbean laborers from the islands; later, in 1860, indentured servants from India and China were imported. UFCO was present in Stann Creek by 1909. The colonial government made an agreement with the company, permitting it to purchase land for a banana plantation. In addition, UFCO installed a rail transport system to move the goods to the wharf (Moberg 1996).[7] As a minority Black population, the Garifuna historically faced discrimination in British Honduras, with its Creole Blacks dominating both economically and politically.

Similarly, UFCO was present in Nicaragua's Caribbean coast. Although they are not a substantial population in New York City, Nicaraguan Garifuna were marginalized by Blacks and others in their country. As they were in British Honduras, Nicaraguan Garifuna were a minority, with the larger Black Creole population enjoying a better economic, political, and social status. The Black Creoles arrived as slaves of the English settlers in the 1650s. As British control declined in the region, indigenous Miskito dominance decreased, and there was a shift in local control. Creole Blacks accepted the English language and used it to obtain a dominant social status over the indigenous population (Gordon 1998). So, overall, a social hierarchy based on ethnicity was present on the Caribbean coast. Whites, Mestizos, and Creole Blacks were in the upper ranks, while the Garifuna and indigenous populations were at the bottom.

Although divisions existed, there was also unity among Blacks in their Central American coastal communities. Jamaican Marcus Garvey established the United Negro Improvement Association (UNIA), dispersed throughout the Americas; it advocated for Black unity, racial pride, repatriation to Africa, and self-determination. The movement also inspired labor organizing and strikes against the agro-exporters, resulting in Blacks uniting and collaborating. Garifuna were involved in the UNIA alongside their Black counterparts. Retired seaman Victor R. Avila, a founding member of the first Garifuna organization in New York City in 1943, recalled that his father often went to the UNIA union hall.[8] Avila was born in Honduras and raised in British Honduras, where a UNIA branch was founded in the 1920s. There were also UNIA chapters in Tela, El Porvernir, La Ceiba, and Trujillo in Honduras. In Nicaragua, the Bluefields chapter was one of five UNIA branches. There was also a UNIA branch in Puerto Barrios, Guatemala (Hill et al. 2014).[9]

Foundations of Garifuna Organizing

Honduran-born Thomas Vincent Ramos settled in British Honduras in 1923 and was one of the first Garifuna involved with the UNIA branch in Stann Creek. Inspired by the Garvey movement, Ramos esteemed Garifuna history and culture and supported his ethnic group's integration into Belizean society. This was challenging because the Garifuna in Belize experienced discrimination and marginalization, and Ramos sought to address this issue by highlighting their unique culture and identity. He founded Carib Disembarkation Day, an annual celebration of the Garifuna's arrival in British Honduras; it is now a national holiday in Belize known as Garifuna Settlement Day, celebrated on November 19. Ramos also advocated for Garifuna rights, as illustrated in his writings:

> For that no one can gainsay the fact that Carib teachers have proven their worth in training the Indians and other elements in the out-districts, but in a town like Stann Creek, settled by our ancestors and where their influence could be utilized to a greater advantage for uplifting their fellows, they are debarred from this opportunity which seems to be specially reserved for the upper class from abroad, this is certainly unfair to a struggling race of people who desire to

succeed in life but the odds against their rise is overwhelming, and so well planned as to keep a despised race of people in perpetual humiliation, and that unless we cry aloud to heavens we shall forever be trampled under the heels of certain white people who already are holding prominent positions, this they can wield at any time as a piercing weapon to crush us out of existence, added on top [of] this they pay slavery wages to the black man for his labour contrary to democratic principles. We must continue to agitate in order to obtain more latitude and a greater measure of consideration. We also pray and hope that a Carib teacher will be afforded the privilege of taking advantage offered to teachers under the Colony's new training scheme now available in Jamaica, Teacher Cleofus Augustine of the New Town School could be considered a suitable candidate having qualified as [a] first-class teacher. (T. Ramos 2000)

In this piece, titled "Stann Creek Faces a Period of Economic Crisis," Ramos advocates for better wages, better schools, and better opportunities for Garifuna teachers (T. Ramos 2000). He takes a proactive social position as he advocates for equity, which was absent from the Garifuna organizations later established in New York.

In 1924 Ramos established the Carib Development Society, followed by the Carib Burial Society and the Carib International Society (at the time, *Carib* was a descriptive term corresponding to *Garifuna*). These organizations supported the Garifuna in various ways, such as lending money to recently arrived Garifuna from Guatemala or Honduras and collecting funds to pay for medical treatment or burial. Members of the Carib Development Society (CDS) were dispersed in various Garifuna communities. Its affiliate, the Carib International Society (CIS), worked to unite the Garifuna across national borders. In 1931 the CIS met in Barranco, British Honduras, with Garifuna delegates representing various Central American countries.[10] Like the UNIA, the CIS had a flag. That CIS flag evolved into the present Garifuna flag of black (*würiti*), white (*haruti*), and yellow (*dumari*), which is evident in all Garifuna communities. The flag's meaning and symbols are complex, but in general, black at the top represents the people, yellow at the bottom represents the Amerindian heritage, and white in the middle represents peace, which the Garifuna continue to seek, and their past colonial exchanges with whites.[11] After the CIS dissolved, the CDS continued to use the flag; its successor, the National Garifuna Council in Belize, adopted it as well (Izard 2005).[12] The previous Garifuna flag shared the colors of the UNIA flag: red (blood shed for liberation) and black (the race of the people). However, instead of the UNIA flag's green, representing the wealth and rich land in Africa, the Garifuna flag used yellow (UNIA-ACL 2019). The yellow corresponded to both the Garifuna's indigenous heritage and the color of cassava, the foundation of their diet (Garifuna Nation, n.d.; S. Cayetano and E. Cayetano 2007).

Ramos's Carib Disembarkation Day, accepted in 1941 in Stann Creek, was also acknowledged in 1943 in Toledo district, the other center of Garifuna population in British Honduras (Izard 2005). Overall, as they were influenced by the UNIA, the Garifuna established their own organizations in British Honduras. This, in turn, inspired the Garifuna seamen who settled in New York to establish their own group in Harlem.

Although separated by national borders, the Garifuna remained connected, traveling to one another's communities for organized events or family functions. In Central America, some Garifuna even resettled in neighboring countries, as in the case of Thomas Vincent Ramos, who was born in Honduras and moved to British Honduras. Garifuna also supported migration between their communities when faced with political challenges. For instance, Catalina Clotter Avila told me about an event she witnessed as a teenager. One evening in 1937 the Honduran national army was sent to capture fifteen men from the Garifuna coastal community of San Juan. The soldiers executed the men on the nearby beach as the residents watched (Arrivillaga Cortés 2005; Euraque 2004).[13] Women were raped, and homes were ransacked. With help from a navy captain, some of the men, women, and children managed to escape to the Garifuna village of Hopkins in British Honduras. Although stories about the causes of this incident vary, it is agreed that the repressive regime of Honduran dictator Tiburcio Carías Andino (1932–45) committed various human rights violations. Garifuna relationships persisted despite national borders in Central America, and they continued among migrants to New York City, where they later established their first organization inspired by Ramos (Arrivillaga Cortés 2005).

Economic Changes Motivating Migration

UFCO influence expanded into Puerto Cortés, Honduras, by 1929. Garifuna men worked as longshoremen, haulers of bananas and other goods, maintenance men at agro-exporters' laundries, train operators, machinists, and utility workers. I learned about their experiences by speaking with Garifuna seamen who knew individuals from this era. Retired seaman Noe Francisco Caballero shared details about his great-grandfather

Figure 2. Identification card for Tela Railroad Company employee Hermenegildo Clotter, born April 13, 1896.

Hermenegildo Clotter, who worked as a laborer hauling bananas for the Tela Railroad Company (fig. 2). Ursulo Martinez, the grandfather of retired seaman Margarito Alvarez Martinez, also worked for the same UFCO affiliate in the Tela region. Banana production and exportation dropped between 1937 and 1939 due to agricultural disease, affecting the coastal economy. The decline in production and exportation continued into the 1940s and 1950s, along with a decrease in wage labor, due to World War II. The decline in agricultural exports also occurred in other Central American ports (N. Gonzalez 2008; Coelho 1981).

Fortunately, other types of employment became available during World War II with the resulting demand for laborers on ships. According to Clotter (as told to Caballero), U.S. ships docked in the Gulf of Honduras between Guatemala and Honduras to train seamen as part of recruitment initiatives. Many Garifuna men from other regions arrived in Puerto Cortés looking for employment because it was one of the leading departure points for Garifuna seamen. The Garifuna communities of Tulián, Cieneguita, Masca, Bajamar, and Travesía were also in the vicinity of the Honduran port, and many seamen were recruited there as well. Seamen from these regions and the department (province) of Colón eventually were among the first group of Honduran Garifuna settlers in New York. Records show that Garifuna seamen from British Honduras and Guatemala also departed from Puerto Cortés, Puerto Castilla, and Tela, located along the Honduras coast (Selected Passenger and Crew Lists). Honduran Caribbean Blacks worked as stationmasters, granting working papers to Garifuna and other Blacks. In Puerto Cortés, Martin Avila Reyes recruited Garifuna men to work as merchant marine seamen. Abraham Moreira, Pepe Mariano, and Matias Bernardez Nunez were among the many seamen recruited. Family connections also led to the recruitment of seamen. Pablo Arzu Sr. worked for the Tela Railroad Company's tugboat *Chamelecon*, along with Garifuna Marcos Lambert, Candido "Tormenta" Martinez, and Andres Avila. Arzu helped recruit many Garifuna from other Honduran departments, and his children Francisco "Don Paulito," Ines, Alonso, and Marcello all became seamen. Hermenegildo Clotter believed that the generation working for the agro-exporters and hauling bananas encouraged the next generation to jump on the opportunity to become seamen.[14]

Sigatoka banana disease and interruptions in the world market during World War II disrupted the fruit business along the Honduran coast and threatened Garifuna subsistence.[15] Toward the end of the 1930s, UFCO allied with the Cuyamel Fruit Company and pulled out of Trujillo, Honduras; Livingston, Guatemala; and British Honduras. However, it continued to ship fruits from Puerto Cortés and Tela in Honduras and Puerto Barrios in Guatemala for another generation. The Standard Fruit Company continued in La Ceiba and evolved into Castle and Cook and eventually into present-day Dole (N. Gonzalez 2008; Coelho 1981). Nevertheless, many Garifuna men capitalized on the opportunity to become seamen to improve their families' and their communities' economic circumstances. Their Black counterparts in Central America did the same, as many migrated to New York City to improve their economic conditions.

Three of Ursulo Martinez's sons became seamen. Ursulo's oldest son, Isabel Martinez, became a shipboard laborer during the 1940s. His second son, Juan Martinez, began his career as a seaman on December 1, 1945, at the age of sixteen, working as a utilityman on the tanker *Francis R. Hart*. Juan left extensive records of his ships and voyages. For example, the *Francis R. Hart* was registered and sailed under the flag of the Honduran company Empresas Hondureña de Vapores and operated from 1938 to 1958. It was one of several vessels associated with UFCO. Juan spent 1,256 days on the *Francis R. Hart*—more than any other ship—from December 1, 1945, to May 10, 1949. Ursulo's third son, Angel, sailed later. According to Angel, during Juan's early years as a sailor, the family often did not know his whereabouts. The family assumed that Juan's lack of communication was due to his need to adjust to life as a seaman.[16] Juan's log indicates that the tanker arrived several times in Tela but left again within a day. Most of the ships Juan worked on between 1945 and 1958 traveled along the U.S. East Coast and to Gulf ports such as New Orleans, Louisiana, and Mobile, Alabama, as well as the Caribbean, Central America, and Colombia. Between 1945 and 1958, other than the *Francis R. Hart*, Juan sailed on the *Toltec, La Playa, Almirante, Argual, Iriona, Aragon*, and *Orotava*. Later, he sailed primarily for North American and European vessels as a U.S. merchant marine seaman. Records show that many other Garifuna seamen from Guatemala and British Honduras had careers like that of Juan Martinez (Selected Passenger and Crew Lists). During their furloughs on land, especially in New York City, these Garifuna seamen gathered to socialize and support their existing organizations.

Conclusion

This chapter began by presenting Garifuna early settlement and their society structure in Central America's circum-Caribbean, which later influenced their organizing. An organization Garifuna established to promote their culture later played a role in the formation of different groups once in New York. Also presented are motivating factors causing Garifuna men to become seamen and leave their countries. Garifuna experienced agrarian extractivism, effects of neocolonialism, and racism challenging their subsistence in Central America. The next chapter follows Garifuna seamen settling in Harlem during the 1940s segregation period and establishing their first organization.

Chapter 3

Early U.S. Garifuna Communities

NEW YORK CITY sustained a vibrant social life in the 1940s, despite racism, segregation, and war. Black migration from the U.S. South to Harlem in upper Manhattan increased the city's Black population. Another Black group migrating from even farther south was the Garifuna from Central America. Black immigrants from Cuba, Panama, Puerto Rico, West Indies, Honduras, British Honduras, and Guatemala, including the Garifuna, moved into established African American neighborhoods in the 1930s and 1940s. Garifuna were among the Black Latinos and West Indians barred by racism and rejection from white areas of the city. These early Garifuna settled in Black communities in Harlem; later, many established themselves in the Bronx and Brooklyn. De facto segregation in housing meant that Blacks and Latinos were not welcome in some areas (Opie 2014). Like African Americans during the Great Migration, Latinos and Garifuna migrated to northern cities seeking better economic opportunities. However, whereas most southern Blacks migrated north by land, most Garifuna arrived on ships.

The New York passenger ship travel logs show that British Honduran Garifuna Peter Ellis arrived in the United States on April 9, 1924, from Puerto Castilla, Honduras, on the *Saramacca*; Ines P. Martinez arrived on August 17, 1931, from British Honduras on the *Turrialba*; and Andrew Zuniga arrived in New York on March 5, 1924. Other Garifuna men who settled in Harlem were Honduran Timothy Martinez, who arrived on September 22, 1931, on the *Toltec*, departing from Puerto Castilla, Honduras;

and his fellow countryman Gregorio Nunez, who left from Puerto Cortés, Honduras, on the *Choluteca* and arrived in New York City on September 9, 1926 (Selected Passenger and Crew Lists). These men and several other Garifuna seamen living in Harlem founded the city's first Garifuna organization, the Carib American Association, in 1944. According to passenger ship logs, Victor R. Avila arrived in New York City on January 13, 1945, aboard the *John Mitchell*, and his cousin Vincente Avila arrived December 22, 1946, on the *America* (although I was told they both arrived earlier). Victor Avila, a Honduran Garifuna, had close ties with many Garifuna from British Honduras, having spent his youth there. Avila was also one of the founding members of the first New York City Garifuna organization.[1] Documents I obtained list British Honduran Anthony Liston Ogaldez, another founding member, as present in New York in the early 1940s.[2] During one of his later voyages, Ogaldez arrived in New York City on September 12, 1961, aboard the *Queen Mary*. Several other Garifuna seamen who arrived in this early period settled in New Orleans, Louisiana, and others later relocated to New York City (Selected Passenger and Crew Lists).

These Garifuna seamen arrived in the United States during the turbulent Jim Crow period. Since the Civil War, the few vessels that carried both Black and white seamen were called checkerboard ships, and Blacks (known as Negroes at the time) worked only on the worst ships and received inferior jobs, such as galley crew. There was discrimination in hiring, and ship quarters were segregated (Horne 2005). However, at the first convention of the National Maritime Union (NMU) in 1937, the group declared its intention to organize all seamen "without regard for race, creed and color" and not to tolerate discrimination. The NMU's first vice president was Ferdinand Smith, a former ship steward of Jamaican descent. His powerful position as one of the NMU's cofounders and second in command to union president Joseph Curran made Smith one of the leading Black figures of this period. He stood strongly against all forms of racism and had connections to prominent leaders such as public officials Adam Clayton Powell Jr. and Benjamin J. Davis, A. Philip Randolph of the Brotherhood of Sleeping Car Porters (a majority-Black labor union), and Lester Granger of the National Urban League (Horne 2005). The NMU challenged companies on discriminatory practices, and discrimination was not allowed in union halls or on ships. Some commented that the NMU contributed to the Black civil rights struggle, supporting changes toward desegregation that were later implemented nationally. In addition, in the 1930s and early 1940s, Black churches and NMU halls were the only places Blacks and whites could meet (Horne 2005). Smith was actively engaged in advocating for seamen's rights outside the United States as well. For instance, he demanded that the U.S. State Department investigate the repatriation rights of Garifuna seaman Andres S. Martinez. Martinez was a crew member of the SS *Yaque*, owned by the United Fruit Steamship Company. The vessel had left him behind in Puerto Barrios, Guatemala, and local authorities denied him customary repatriation rights to return to Honduras (Horne 2005). Smith's position in the NMU and his efforts to ensure that seamen's rights were upheld led to less discrimination both on and off vessels. Seamen who experienced racism now had somewhere to direct their complaints (*On a True Course*).

Garifuna seamen had many experiences with racism and discrimination aboard ships and especially on land in U.S. cities north and south. For instance, Rufino Arzu initially settled in Harlem but later sought to buy a home in Westbury, Long Island. Certain whites tried to prevent him and his wife, Dora Hughes, from purchasing a home in the neighborhood. They eventually became homeowners in 1955—the first Black family to integrate the community. The family had to overcome ongoing discrimination by their neighbors as well as by their children's classmates. Another Garifuna seaman, Juan Martinez, objected to having to sit in the back of the bus when he lived and traveled in New Orleans and Mobile in the late 1940s and 1950s. One day, he expressed his displeasure by cursing at the bus driver in Spanish as he exited the segregated bus.[3] Despite decreasing discrimination on ships, Garifuna seamen continued to endure racism on land.

The shared experience of discrimination that encouraged the association of Garifuna and African Americans during this period in Harlem is explored in this chapter. At the same time, Garifuna began forming their organizations in the United States and groups to foster their social and cultural traditions. This chapter also shows Garifuna establishing their communities in the Bronx and Brooklyn, reflecting settlement patterns of other Black immigrant groups in New York City, beginning in Harlem and then moving to other boroughs.

Harlem, New York

The early Garifuna immigrants to New York experienced the later part of the Harlem Renaissance. This expression of African American culture, identity, and life challenged the negative stereotypes of Blacks that were common in the Jim Crow South but also existed in the North. In photographs, these Garifuna men look well dressed, with well-groomed hair, formal suits, and polished shoes, reflecting the popular Black culture of the period. Although there were some prosperous Blacks at this time, many in Harlem were economically impoverished and faced discrimination, especially during and after the Great Depression. For example, the 1934 Harlem Jobs for Negroes boycott targeted white business owners who controlled the community's commercial center (Muraskin 1972). Blacks organized, and after several months, some white-owned businesses conceded and hired Blacks. Another event was the 1935 Harlem race riot after a Black Puerto Rican teenager was falsely accused of robbery and brutally beaten. The rioting destroyed mainly white stores and resulted in three deaths and more than a hundred arrested and injured. Politician Adam Clayton Powell, who was also the reverend of the Harlem Abyssinian Baptist Church, led another boycott in 1941 against two private bus companies that refused to hire Blacks for other than janitorial jobs. After about a month, the companies agreed to hire Black bus drivers and more Black maintenance workers.

Another Harlem riot occurred in 1943 when a white police officer shot and wounded a Black soldier following a conflict. The two-day riot began after false reports circulated of the Black soldier's death. The result was vandalism, property destruction, and theft of white-owned property; six people died, and six hundred were arrested. Black residents' resentment over their poor social and economic status, as well as the discrimination and brutality they experienced at the hands of the city's majority-white police force, prompted these reactions (Swan 1971). Mayor Fiorello La Guardia called on Ferdinand Smith and other Black leaders for help in quelling the riot. Smith assumed leadership in this effort and worked tirelessly, using local radio stations to broadcast his message or riding around in a sound truck through the streets of Harlem to restore order (Horne 2005).

Garifuna and other Central American Blacks lived in Harlem during this period, but the extent of their political involvement in efforts to combat racism is unknown. However, in the same year as the 1943 riot, the Honduran American Association was registered in New York, led by Black, English-speaking Honduran immigrants from the Caribbean coast. It is interesting that this English-speaking population from a majority Spanish-speaking country established a group to represent all Hondurans. Its goals were to sponsor social activities, provide voluntary assistance to members and their families in case of sickness and distress, and contribute toward burial expenses for members who died. Listed on its New York State certificate of incorporation are the names Arthur S. Taylor, Edgar V. Hewlett,

Arthur P. Reynolds, Owen E. Hyde, and Clyde E. Vincente (a Garifuna). Important details about the organization's goals are included in its registration document:

(2) To take over, carry on and continue the affairs, property, obligations, business and objectives of the unincorporated association known as The Honduran American Association.

To secure as members of this corporation loyal citizens of the United States of Honduranian origin as well as native Honduranians residing in the United States, the members of their families, their relatives and their descendants, and to renew the association which may have been lost through their separation following their departure or that of their ancestor of relatives from Honduras, and to create among them a more cordial relationship and better understanding.

To promote friendship among its members; to inculcate in them a high sense of loyalty to each other; to stimulate their intellectual and cultural advancement and to hold meetings and social gatherings for the better realization of the aforesaid purposes.

To provide voluntary assistance to its members and their families in case of sickness and distress; to contribute, voluntarily, to the decent interment of its members in case of death. (New York State Department of State, Division of Corporations: Honduran American Association, Inc., January 2, 1943)

Carib American Association

In 1944, only a year after the Honduran American Association was founded, the Garifuna established the Carib American Association.[4] Perhaps differences with their Black Central American counterparts motivated the Garifuna to create an independent organization to promote their unique Black culture and identity. During my conversation with Angel Martinez, he showed me photographs left by his father, Pedro Martinez, who was part of the association's administrative body.[5] Written in ink beneath a group photo are the names of the founders of the Carib American Association. The names match those listed in several documents contained in the files of Timothy Martinez. The handwritten caption identifies Honduran Garifuna Victor R. Avila and Timothy Martinez and British Honduran Garifuna Martin Ciego, Andrew E. Zuniga, Liston A. Ogaldez, Willie Diego, and Clyde E. Vincente. Vincente's name was also listed on the incorporation document of the Honduran American Association. According to New York

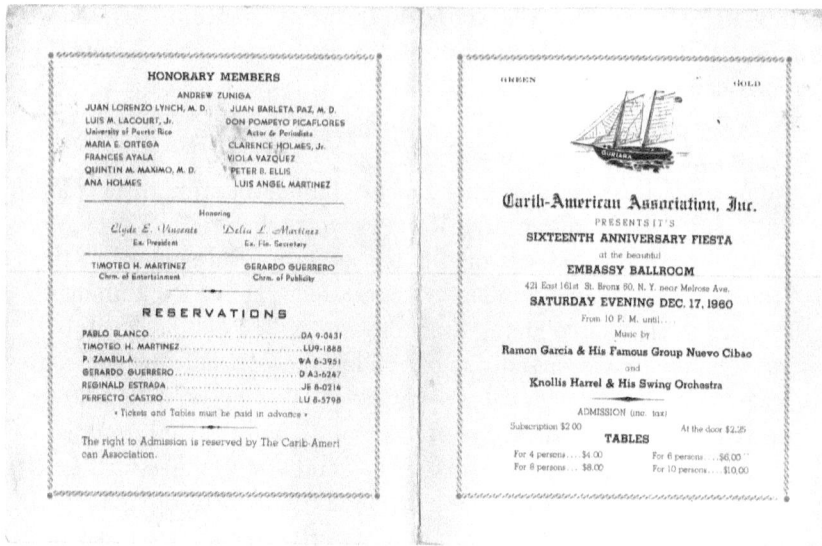

Figure 3. Program for the Carib American Association's sixteenth anniversary celebration, held December 17, 1960.

State's immigration and naturalization records, Clyde Ellis Vincente was born in the Garifuna town of Stann Creek, British Honduras. He was a seaman who departed from Omoa and Puerto Castilla, Honduras, as early as 1921 and arrived in New Orleans (Selected Passenger and Crew Lists). Vincente played a significant role in the ethnic group's early organization; his name appears in other documents, and he served a term as president of the Carib American Association (see fig. 3).

The Carib American Association was officially registered in 1946, listing Timothy Martinez's wife, Delia L. Martinez, as financial secretary, Ines P. Martinez as president, Andrew Zuniga as vice president, Liston A. Ogaldez as treasurer, Percy Vera as recording secretary, Peter Ellis as chaplain, and Jeff Thompson as sergeant at arms. The incorporation document included their addresses, all of which were in Harlem. The organization's stated goal was to promote friendship among its members through voluntary aid for individuals' advancement in areas such as business and social welfare.[6] Most members of the organization were Carib, meaning that they belonged "to the Carib Indian Tribe of Central America." (As noted earlier, Garifuna were known as Black Caribs, or in Spanish, *Negros Caribes*. The group was also commonly described as Carib in Central America, especially in British Honduras. This may explain the use of *Carib* in the organization's title.)

The founders of the organization from British Honduras and Honduras had ties with groups back home such as the Carib Burial Society, Carib International Society, and Carib Development Society, as well as with Carib Disembarkation Day celebrations. In addition, they may have kept in touch with those groups' founder, Thomas Vincent Ramos, who was still alive when the Carib American Association was established in New York.[7]

The Carib American Association in New York was founded in 1944, one year after Carib Disembarkation Day was established in the Toledo district of British Honduras. Thomas Vincent Ramos, Pantaleon Hernandez, and Domingo Ventura successfully lobbied the government to acknowledge this day, which later became a national holiday. In November 1945 the Carib American Association commemorated this day at a Harlem UNIA Liberty Hall (fig. 4), one of many Garvey facilities still functioning after his passing (A. Ramos 2000; UNIA 1945).[8]

As is evident in figure 4 and other photographs from this period, African American women were prominent social partners of the Garifuna seamen residing in Harlem. At the time, there were hardly any Garifuna women in the United States, as they did not migrate in significant numbers until after the 1960s (Jones-Correa 1998).[9] As a result, many Garifuna seamen established relationships and had families with African American women.

Figure 4. Celebration of Carib Disembarkation Day held at a UNIA Liberty Hall in Harlem on November 18, 1945. Among those present are Ines Martinez (*far left*), Liston Ogaldez (*seventh from left*), Timothy Martinez (*tall man with mustache*), and Victor Avila (*second from right*). This event was a precursor to Garifuna Settlement Day, a national holiday in Belize.

Timothy Martinez, Calixto "Don Paco" Colon, Manuel Herrera, Liston A. Ogaldez, Rufino Arzu, Juan Martinez, Victor R. Avila, and Julio Clotter all had non-Garifuna partners.[10]

The United Negro Improvement Association, newly organized as the UNIA and African Communities League (ACL), continued to function after Garvey's death. It also continued to be active in British Honduras, with an office in the Garifuna town of Stann Creek. Records show that in 1922 British Honduran member Isaiah Morter traveled to New York for the UNIA convention (UNIA 2020). I suspect that exposure to the UNIA and its ideals in Central America motivated the Garifuna living in New York to establish the Carib American Association. In addition, the presence of Black culture resonating in the community after the Harlem Renaissance may have prompted the ethnic group to embrace and take pride in their unique Black culture. Unfortunately, back in Central America, the Garifuna were discriminated against, and their culture was marginalized, a stark contrast to the celebration of Black culture they witnessed in Harlem.[11] Converging in one location in Harlem, New York—the cultural capital of Black America—facilitated ethnic solidarity among Garifuna from different countries, encouraging them to coalesce and establish their own group. Garifuna from Belize, Honduras, and Guatemala came together in appreciation of their unique culture.[12]

Conversations I had with several Garifuna who knew the founders of the Carib American Association provided more insights into the organization's history and functions. Belizean Garifuna Catherine Thompson (née Zuniga) knew most of the individuals in the Carib American Association and has family ties to one of the organization's founders, Andrew Zuniga. She was a teenager when the organization was developing in the late 1940s and 1950s. According to Catherine, there were not many Garifuna in New York City, and the meetings were held at the Harlem home of Liston A. Ogaldez. She recollected that all the organizers were men, and women were not present at these meetings. I also spoke with Angel Martinez, the son of one of the association's administrators, Pedro Martinez. Angel recalled that the Carib American Association rented locations in Harlem around Lenox Avenue for social functions and celebrations it hosted. During the early days, African American women were usually the members' guests at these social gatherings. I also learned that due to their employment as seamen, the association's administrators changed frequently. However, Timothy Martinez became one of its permanent managers when he transitioned to land-based employment; he worked as an elevator operator in a Manhattan office building.[13]

The founders of the Carib American Association were among the early seamen who immigrated to the United States before the extensive recruitment of sailors from Central America during World War II. Eventually, war demands prompted U.S. president Franklin Delano Roosevelt to ask Central American countries to recruit men to work on merchant ships, which increased the number of Garifuna seamen. These men were exposed to danger as their ships navigated perilous paths through war zones. Julio Clotter shared with me his wartime experiences as a seaman. He recalled that he found it difficult to sleep, as the ship's emergency sirens often woke the seamen to warn them of imminent danger from Japanese or German bombs or air attacks. Fortunately, Clotter's ship was never struck. Interestingly, he said he was grateful for the war, despite the risks, and even expressed "thanks [to] Hitler" because the war changed his economic status. He was able to build a two-story concrete house in his hometown of Puerto Cortés, Honduras—an improvement over the thatch-roofed houses in the village.[14]

Many merchant marines died during the war when their ships were sunk by Japanese kamikaze pilots in the Pacific. According to the National Maritime Union, 5,579 U.S. seamen died, and 733 American ships were lost (*On a True Course*). Though the number of Garifuna deaths is unknown, several Garifuna seamen risked their lives to improve their families' economic status, and many of them were members, administrators, or patrons of the Carib American Association. Association members who served as seamen during the war (and their dates of service) include Victor R. Avila (1944–45), Joaquín Nuñez (1944), Alfonso Ellis (1940–44), Pedro Martinez (1944), Nicasio Reyes (1944–45), and Raimundo Reyes (1944) (Selected Passenger and Crew Lists).[15] Merchant marines' wartime contributions were not acknowledged until many years later. A 1988 court decision found that U.S. merchant seamen who served between December 7, 1941, and August 15, 1945—the period of armed conflict—were eligible for veterans' benefits. The Merchant Mariners of World War II Act of 2005 also acknowledged their contributions to the war, compensating several Garifuna men who had applied for benefits.[16] One of those benefits was full access to medical services at Veterans Administration hospitals. Although some Garifuna applied and qualified for benefits, many who were eligible never applied, and others died before the legislation was passed.

According to former Garifuna seaman Rufino Arzu, during the war the seamen were permitted to apply for U.S. citizenship, which was granted automatically. Arzu stated that many Garifuna did not take advantage of this opportunity, even though many had settled in the United States. Some

Garifuna seamen went back home to Central America after the war. Others stayed and got jobs on land, planning to return to Central America later.

With the end of World War II, several Garifuna seamen advised their sons to follow in their footsteps and become merchant marines. Three sons of Honduran Garifuna seaman Maximo Lambert Arzu—Justo Lambert, Froylan Lambert, and Teodoro Lambert—became seamen and eventually settled in New York. Their younger brother Alejandro Lambert eventually immigrated to New York City after living in Belize with family. Angel and Alonzo Martinez, sons of retired Honduran Garifuna seaman Pedro Martinez, also worked as merchant marines. Their brother Jorge Martinez later moved to New York City, but he worked on land.

This new generation of Garifuna seamen participated in the social life of the city and attended Carib American Association functions. In interviews with me, Alejandro Lambert and Angel Martinez shared their experiences from the 1950s and 1960s. Alejandro temporarily served on the Carib American Association's finance committee, managing member dues. He was one of the younger individuals in the organization, having immigrated to New York in 1957 at age eighteen, following his older brother Justo, who had arrived in 1949. Alejandro recalled that Guatemalan Garifuna attended the association's events in the late 1950s, but Hondurans and British Hondurans dominated the leadership. He said Timothy Martinez wanted to help financially marginalized areas of the Garifuna community in Honduras, but he advised Martinez to focus on supporting the ethnic group's development in New York City. Some of the older members of the association when Alejandro arrived were Liston A. Ogaldez, Andrew Zuniga, Percy Vera, and Pedro Martinez. Pedro's son Angel Martinez arrived in the United States in 1963, following his brother Alonzo, who had immigrated in 1959. In our conversation, Angel admitted that he did not enjoy being a seaman and later looked for work on land. He attended only a handful of Carib American Association events, which he disliked because they involved heavy drinking and sometimes brawls. Both Angel and Alejandro stated that some locations refused to rent their auditoriums for Garifuna social functions because of the roughhousing that occurred. Retired Honduran Garifuna seaman Marcello Arzu expressed similar sentiments about this bad behavior, which caused him to distance himself from Carib American Association activities.[17] Around this period, Arzu was working aboard the SS *Smith Voyager*, which sank in the Atlantic on December 27, 1964. Fortunately, most of the seamen were rescued, including Marcello; however, four crewmembers lost their lives (Investigation Report 1966).

As time progressed, more Garifuna migrated to the United States, and the Carib American Association gained more supporters. Apparently, the organization's activities fluctuated over time. Although some members have unpleasant memories of the association's social functions, photographs and films depict these events as formal, calm, and congenial.

New Orleans, Louisiana

One of the other U.S. cities the Garifuna settled in after the mid-nineteenth century was New Orleans, Louisiana. Some say that New Orleans was the Garifuna seamen's first port of arrival. Records show that Carib American Association member Clyde E. Vincente arrived there in 1921; others followed in the 1940s, such as Raimundo Reyes, Nicasio Reyes, Alfonso Ellis, and Isabel Martinez (Selected Passenger and Crew Lists). Honduran ports had ties to New Orleans through agro-exports, primarily bananas, since the 1920s. According to scholars, Garifuna and other immigrants began to settle in New Orleans as early as the 1950s (Chaney 2012). Juan Martinez (the uncle of retired Garifuna seaman Margarito Alvarez Martinez) initially settled in New Orleans before moving to New York. There he met a Creole woman from Lake Charles, and they became involved in a relationship. The woman already had a son, and she and Martinez had a daughter who was born in March 1964. Throughout most of the 1960s, New Orleans was his primary place of residence when he was not at sea, and Martinez shared stories of racial discrimination, including separate public bathroom facilities, harsh treatment by whites, and restricted bus seating for Blacks.[18]

Juan Martinez's father-in-law, Francisco Lambert, and his uncle Urbano Martinez also lived in New Orleans when they were not at sea. I discovered their names listed in passenger and crew databases. Francisco Lambert arrived in New Orleans on July 30, 1953, aboard the *Eros*. Urbano Martinez arrived in New Orleans on October 15, 1945, on the *Atlantida* (Selected Passenger and Crew Lists). Records also indicate that Urbano arrived at and departed from the port of New York, where he no doubt contacted family and friends during his stay, such as Timothy Martinez. Urbano offered hospitality to many seamen both in New Orleans and in Puerto Cortés, Honduras, a common departure point. Many Garifuna had to travel long distances from their townships to Puerto Cortés (some trips took eight hours or more), and they would stay at Urbano's home while waiting for their ship assignments or departure times. Juan Martinez and many others slept over at Urbano's home before beginning their journeys overseas.[19]

Once they made it to the U.S. Gulf coast, the Garifuna seamen found that New Orleans and Baton Rouge were vibrant places with the popular music, culinary traditions, and nightlife they enjoyed. Seaman Juan Martinez spent time at various ports in Louisiana, including Ostrica. He claimed to be personally acquainted with rhythm-and-blues artist Fats Domino, and when sharing stories about Mr. Domino, Juan might sing the chorus of "Blueberry Hill."[20] Records show that Martinez initially arrived in New Orleans for a November 23, 1961, departure date on the SS *Atlantic Victory*, a steam vessel, for a short voyage along the U.S. coast and his discharge in New York City on December 4, 1961. After that voyage, all his arrivals and departures were concentrated in New Orleans (Selected Passenger Crew Lists). Like many others, Martinez eventually migrated north and settled in New York City, where he married and started a family. Some Garifuna remained in New Orleans, although there is no evidence that they established a strong, cohesive organization there. Urbano Martinez retired and eventually returned to Honduras. Francisco Lambert had similar plans but died unexpectedly and was buried in New Orleans.

Move to the Bronx

By the early 1950s, many Garifuna had moved to the outer boroughs of New York City, mainly Brooklyn and the Bronx. Garifuna and African Americans were among the Black working-class families moving from Harlem to the Morrisania neighborhood of the Bronx after the 1940s, where housing was better, rent was cheaper, crowding was less severe, and there were more parks. Urban planning also pushed many poor Black and Puerto Rican families from Harlem to the Bronx (Caro 1974). Morrisania's population was mixed working class, with union members and organizers; its diverse residents included Jews, Caribbeans, Irish, Puerto Ricans, and African Americans. St. Anthony of Padua Roman Catholic Church was the home parish of many African Americans in Morrisania, and its congregation increased as Garifuna and other immigrants arrived. In proximity to the church was the Forest Houses public housing project, built in 1956 as one of several urban renewal projects in the city; it became home to many Garifuna families (Selected Passenger and Crew Lists). Other areas, such as the Arthur Avenue section of the Bronx and northeastern Manhattan, were Italian-only zones where nonwhite visitors were in peril. According to Alejandro Lambert, Blacks were likely to be chased down and beaten by white mobs if they entered these neighborhoods. Timothy Martinez moved to the Morrisania section of the Bronx, and the Carib American

Association established a clubhouse in the same neighborhood. It was located on Boston Road, in an area where African Americans also had several social clubs (Naison and Gumbs 2016).[21] The Carib American Association hosted dances featuring popular Latin American bands that played salsa and merengue. The famous Cuban band La Sonora Matancera performed at the association's events. Alejandro Lambert recalled that some Garifuna residing in Brooklyn, especially those from British Honduras, traveled to the Bronx to attend these events. I learned through my interviews that Jamaicans and Puerto Ricans also attended some of these social gatherings.

The Belize Honduran Association of New York was established in 1956. It was described as a nonpolitical group aimed at supporting the social welfare of its population both in the United States and at home, as well as promoting the culture. The Belizean Creole Blacks on its board of directors were Charles B. Folks, residing in the Bronx; Ernesto Meighan and Herbert Gentle in Brooklyn; and Alvin Lightburn and Millicent C. Lamb in Manhattan. The group's stated purpose was

> (a.) To voluntar[il]y provides [sic] food, clothing and material assistance in case of need to people of British Honduran extraction, both in British Honduras, Central America, and in the United States in their own homes or in institutions conducted by other corporations.
>
> (b.) To promote the culture of British Honduras and to aid from time to time any worthy cause in such country. (New York State Department of State, Division of Corporations: Belize Honduran Association of New York, Inc., January 19, 1956)

Although some Belizean Garifuna may have supported this organization, many of them remained active members and officers of the Carib American Association. During a conversation, one Belizean Garifuna told me that this was because their ethnicity took precedence over their nationality. Honduran Garifuna felt the same way: ethnicity took precedence over nationality. The number of Honduran Garifuna in the city increased significantly during this period, and so did the activities of the Carib American Association. The organization participated in an outdoor event at Central Park's Theatre-in-the-Park in August 1959. The Hudson Celebration Folk Song and Dance Program featured folk songs and dances from Latin America. Groups from Haiti, Trinidad, Bolivia, Venezuela, Puerto Rico, Peru, and British Guiana also performed. An article about the event titled "Latin America Folk Dances in Manhattan" was published in the *Brooklyn Record*, a local newspaper (see fig. 5) (*Brooklyn Record* 1959). The Carib American Association presented the Black Carib, a traditional Garifuna

Latin America Folk Dances In Manhattan

A fascinating program of exotic folk songs and dances from Latin America will be presented as the seventh and the next to the last program of the Hudson Celebration Folk Song and Dance Program at the Theatre-in-the-Park in Central Park on Sunday, August 30th, at 3 p.m. Participating will be: Honduras, Trinidad, British Guiana, Bolivia, Perú, Venezuela, Haiti, Mexico and Puerto Rico.

The Carib-American Association representing Honduras will execute their traditional dance—the Black Carib. Trinidad will be represented by Mike uQashie and his Company who will perform the famous Limbo dance of Trinidad, derived from ritual dances of the Shango, Voodoo and Yanvelou peoples. Johnny Holder and Company will present a selection of typical folk songs from British Guiana. Exotic dances from Haiti will be rendered by Renee Moses and Joel Phillipi of the Haitian Folk Dance Society. Colorful songs will be offered as the Mexican contribution to the program. Puerto Rico will present exhilarating folk songs and dances.

From Bolivia come the native songs, Guapuru and Naranjita, which will be sung by Teresa Alexander and Jaime Zamorano, and Huayno — a mountain dance. The Bolivian portion of the program will be ably directed by Carmela Díaz. Miss Nelly Terrones will demonstrate the uHaynito, an Indian dance from the mountains of Perú. The Venezuelan members of the program, under the direction of Bertha Escalona, will offer a variety of authentic songs and dances. Alicia Mikuski, outstanding soloist, widely acclaimed in Venezuela for her interpretation of Indian and Venezuelan folk legends in songs and dances, will sing Tay, son from the musical drama Guaicaipuro, and Oración Negra. She will also dance Sombra en los Medanos, a waltz, with Angel Oscar Lugo. Mercedes Rincón will serve as Accompanist.

The final offering of the Hudson Celebration Folk Song and Dance Program will be from Africa, the Orient and the Far East, on Sunday, September 6th, at 3 p.m., in the Theatre-in-the-Park.

Free School

Two municipal and two New York State employees are among the eight recipients of full-tuition evening scholarships to New York University's Washington Square College of Arts and Science.

Figure 5. Article in the *Brooklyn Record* advertising a scheduled event at Central Park on August 28, 1959. *Source:* New York Public Library Research archives

dance. Garifuna music was appealing to the folk music audience, and in 1952 an album called *The Black Caribs of Honduras* had been recorded in the city.[22] Folkways Records recorded folk music from around the world, and Garifuna music was a part of its collection (Smithsonian 2020).

In general, although Garifuna continued to reside in Harlem and other locations in Manhattan, such as Washington Heights, much of the growing immigrant population opted to settle in the Bronx. As social functions continued in Harlem, Garifuna activities increased in the Bronx, especially when the Carib American Association established its clubhouse in that borough.

Transitions and New Organizations

Eventually, with the arrival of the Garifuna seamen's families, the Carib American Association expanded its activities beyond social dances and musical and cultural performances. Changes in the immigration law in 1965, as well as recognition of Central American seamen's service to the United States during World War II, allowed the men to apply for their families to join them (England 2006). With this new Garifuna population, the Carib American Association added family-oriented activities, such as hosting summer trips to beaches in the tristate area. Outings to Long Island, Heckscher State Park, and Orchard Beach in the Bronx were popular. Future Garifuna organizations in New York City would sponsor similar outings and trips, which continue today.

I also learned that the Garifuna experienced discrimination and racism during this period. Alejandro Lambert recalled that members of the Carib American Association were prevented from going to certain beaches and parks in New Jersey and Connecticut (Crawford 2018). On one occasion, the group's chartered bus arrived at a public state park in New Jersey, only to be denied access. The white park officials were apparently startled to see a bus full of Blacks, and they offered excuses for not allowing the bus to pass through the gateway to the beach, but all the passengers understood that it was because of their complexion. Eventually, the organizers instructed the bus driver to turn around and head back to Orchard Beach in the Bronx.[23] Perhaps members of the Carib American Association were not familiar with "Chicken Bone Beach," located in the northern section of Atlantic City. There, Blacks were allowed—one of the few beaches that welcomed Blacks before the 1964 Civil Rights Act opened the beaches to everyone (Duhart 2021; Goldberg 2016).

Alejandro Lambert also experienced discrimination in the South. He was attending City College in New York when he was drafted during the Vietnam War. While traveling to New York from Fort Benning, Georgia—wearing his army uniform—he was not permitted to eat at the restaurant in one bus station and had to wait until he arrived at another station. Alejandro found the experience especially disheartening after he had served overseas in the U.S. military. He reacted by writing a letter of complaint to government officials.

Lambert's friends and Carib American Association colleagues Victor R. Avila, Angel Martinez, and Juan Martinez also experienced racial challenges and witnessed the activism that took place during the civil rights era. Both Victor and Juan heard Malcolm X speak in the streets of Harlem at the corner of Lenox Avenue, along with many other people who stood and listened. Juan found the message of Malcolm X and the Nation of Islam—about white oppression and the lack of Black rights in America—appealing, but the dietary restrictions deterred him from joining the organization.[24] Malcolm X's assassination was tragic news that resonated around the world, but especially in New York City. Angel was living in an apartment close to the Audubon Ballroom where Malcolm X was killed, and he recalls Malcolm X being transported to Columbia Presbyterian Hospital, located on the same block as his apartment. Angel witnessed firsthand the commotion outside as he watched television coverage of the event.

Over time, the Carib American Association gradually shifted from Belizean (British Honduran) leadership to a majority Honduran Garifuna administration. The Honduran Garifuna population increased, and they became the majority Garifuna group in the city, concentrated in the Bronx. Because Honduran Garifuna are primarily Spanish speakers, the association's events promoted Latino music and bands, which facilitated the Garifuna's ties to the growing Latino population in their communities. The Belizean Garifuna became concentrated in the borough of Brooklyn, but during the 1960s, most of that ethnic population clustered across the country in Los Angeles, California. Honduran and Guatemalan Garifuna also immigrated to Los Angeles.

Despite the Carib American Association's Honduran majority, Belizeans, Guatemalans, and other ethnic groups continued to be members and supporters, as evidenced by the diverse membership list on the program for its sixteenth anniversary celebration (see fig. 3). The event was held at the Embassy Ballroom in the Bronx in December 1960. The musical performers catered to both Latino and non-Latino guests: Ramon Garcia and His Famous Group Nuevo Cibao, and Knollis Harrel and His Swing Orchestra. For other events, advertisements and tickets were written in both

English and Spanish (see figs. 6a–d). An example of the increased Honduran Garifuna presence in the Carib American Association's administration is a letter written in Spanish dated September 15, 1962, encouraging Hondurans in New York City to honor and celebrate the independence of their country and not to forget their homeland. The names included in the letterhead were primarily Honduran Garifuna, except for Delia Martinez, who was Afro–Puerto Rican.[25] This reflected a significant change, as in the association's 1946 registry, the administrators' names were primarily British Honduran (Belizean) Garifuna.

The Carib American Association remained active during the civil rights movement, but it is unknown whether and to what extent the Garifuna participated in or supported the movement. However, it appears that the historic March on Washington in August 1963 captured the attention of Carib American Association business manager Timothy Martinez. His files contained parts of Martin Luther King Jr.'s "I Have a Dream" speech translated from English to Spanish.

The formation in 1969 of an affiliate group, the Honduran Social Circle club, marked the end of the Carib American Association. After 1969, most of the flyers in Timothy Martinez's files were associated with the new organization. This includes an advertisement for an October 1969 event at Club Cangrejeros, located at 108 West 112th Street between Lenox and St. Nicholas Avenues, Manhattan. Timothy Martinez, Abelardo "Caramelito" Flores from Santa Fe, Honduras, and Jorge Gil from Trujillo, Honduras, are listed as sponsors of the event, and the Honduran band Coca y sus Exploradores was the musical guest (see fig. 6d).[26] Many of the Garifuna I interviewed stated that Club Cangrejeros was a popular dance club they frequented on weekends. I also learned that the bandleader Coca (or Coqui) was Jorge Gil, a popular Garifuna singer-musician at the time.[27] His band performed on Friday, July 25, 1969, at Club Cangrejeros to raise funds for the Honduran armed forces; included in the invitation to the event was a request to bring clothes for children and adults to donate to the people of Honduras. The fundraiser was a response to the so-called Soccer War between Honduras and El Salvador, July 14–18, 1969 (Jones-Correa 1998). Tensions between the two countries sparked during a FIFA World Cup qualifier game, leading to rioting. The Salvadoran army then attacked Honduras, but fortunately, the short war ended in a cease-fire. As part of the Honduran army, Garifuna soldiers and officers were used as radio operators and played a key role in the war, communicating in the Garifuna language, which was unknown to the enemy (Euraque 2004; M. Gonzalez 1969).

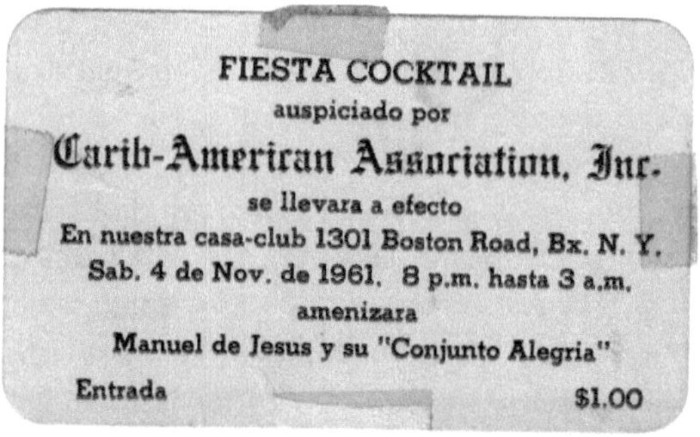

Figure 6a. Ticket for an Easter dinner event at the Carib American Association clubhouse, April 17, 1960.

Figure 6b. Ticket for a cocktail party at the Carib American Association clubhouse, November 4, 1961.

Figure 6c. Invitation to attend an event featuring radio and television artist Candy Frye at the Carib American Association clubhouse, September 21, 1963.

Figure 6d. Advertisement for a Honduran Social Circle club event at Club Cangrejeros, October 11, 1969.

The establishment of the Honduran Social Circle club, which publicized its events mostly in Spanish, indicated the growth of Spanish-speaking Garifuna in the city. As a result, the Carib American Association faded away, and new Garifuna organizations developed that focused on the nationality of individual home-country communities.

Two Garifuna social clubs were founded during the latter part of the Carib American Association's existence. The first one, the Fenix Social Club, registered in the city in 1959. Members Modesto Gil Jr. and Victor L. Blanco resided in the Bronx, and Victor Arriola, Bennette Herrera, and the president and founder, Juan Marin, resided in Harlem. The club's stated goals included

> To establish, own and maintain a place of reunion, clubhouse or club rooms by lease, purchase or otherwise, for the use and benefit of its members. To promote and inculcate a hearty interest in the civic and political affairs of the community; to encourage among the members the practice of civic virtues and the respect for law and order; to develop good citizenship; to cultivate among them the spirit of brotherhood and human understanding, political and racial tolerance; to promote friendship among the members of the organization; to foster loyalty and cooperation and mutual assistance among its members and to stimulate their cultural and social developments.
>
> To stimulate the members of the organization [to participate] in all types of civic, social, cultural and sporting activities; to awaken their interests in the arts and sciences; to inculcate in the members' [sic] the value of human association as means to a better understanding among them.
>
> To provide for recreational and social activities for its members and foster friendship and mutual respect; to advance the cultural development of its members and to promote their physical welfare by encouraging them to partake and compete in healthful indoor and outdoor sports and athletics.
>
> In order to carry on the foregoing objects this organization shall hold and participate in meetings, forums, panels, round table discussions, and all types of civic, artistic, cultural and sporting events. (New York State Department of State, Division of Corporations: Fenix Social Club, Inc., August 31, 1959)

The Fenix Social Club was short-lived, but many of its objectives were fulfilled in the next century, including Garifuna participation in civic affairs and community involvement, participation in the sciences, and the holding of forums and panels on a wide range of issues. The club's articles of incorporation mention "racial tolerance," acknowledging the racism that many experienced.

Led by Honduran Garifuna Juan Marin, the Fenix Social Club was the second known Garifuna organization established in New York City. Alejandro Lambert, Jorge Martinez, Jimmy Cordova, and René Mena told me that they attended Fenix Social Club events. One such event held on December 25, 1960, paid homage to a famous Garifuna artist in Latin America: Juan J. Laboriel. The advertisement, written in Spanish, invited "individuals and family to attend the homage and honor of the actor, composer and Honduran singer Juan J. Laboriel . . . at the American Legion at 108 West 112th Street, Manhattan, New York" (see fig. 7a). Laboriel, born in the town of Trujillo, Honduras, on July 13, 1906, became famous during the period known as the golden age of Mexican cinema. He appeared in at least twenty-eight Mexican films (Wilkinson 2013; J. Ávila 2020). Whenever the name Laboriel is mentioned, Garifuna elders always react with pride, knowing that someone of their ethnicity achieved fame in Latin America. However, the Fenix Social Club did not last long because of its leaders' poor management skills.[28]

The other Garifuna organization established in this period was the Honduran Football and Social Club, officially registered June 11, 1965. According to its founder, René J. Mena, he started the organization years earlier, and it held combined social events with the Fenix Social Club and the Carib American Association. At the time of its incorporation, the club's directors were René J. Mena, Mike B. Smith, Justo Lambert, Rod Padilla, and Luis Alvarez. All resided in the Bronx, except for Smith. This reflects the Garifuna population shift from Harlem to the Bronx. The organization's purpose was to "provide for the mutual assistance, enjoyment, entertainment and improvements of its members socially and physically by encouraging them" to participate in athletics or physical recreation.[29] But its name reflects the club's twofold purpose: in addition to being a soccer club that organized and participated in tournaments, it sponsored concerts by well-known Latin bands.[30]

Community Involvement

Contrary to the conclusions of previous studies that cited the Garifuna's limited language ability, the early Garifuna immigrants engaged with African Americans because many of them spoke English (Walker and

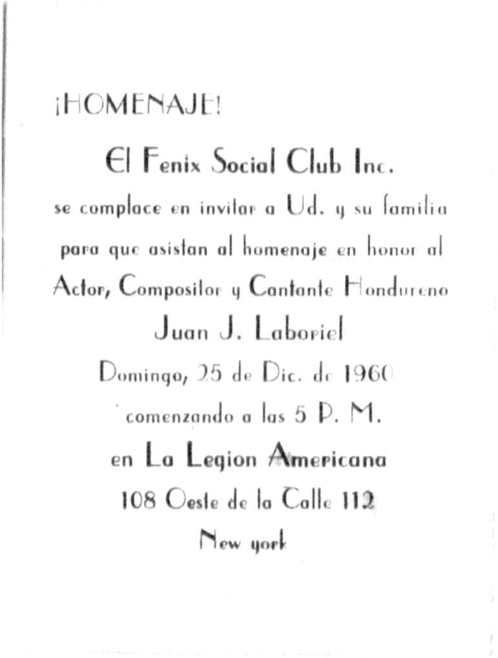
¡HOMENAJE!

El Fenix Social Club Inc.

se complace en invitar a Ud. y su familia
para que asistan al homenaje en honor al
Actor, Compositor y Cantante Hondureno
Juan J. Laboriel
Domingo, 25 de Dic. de 1960
comenzando a las 5 P. M.
en La Legion Americana
108 Oeste de la Calle 112
New york

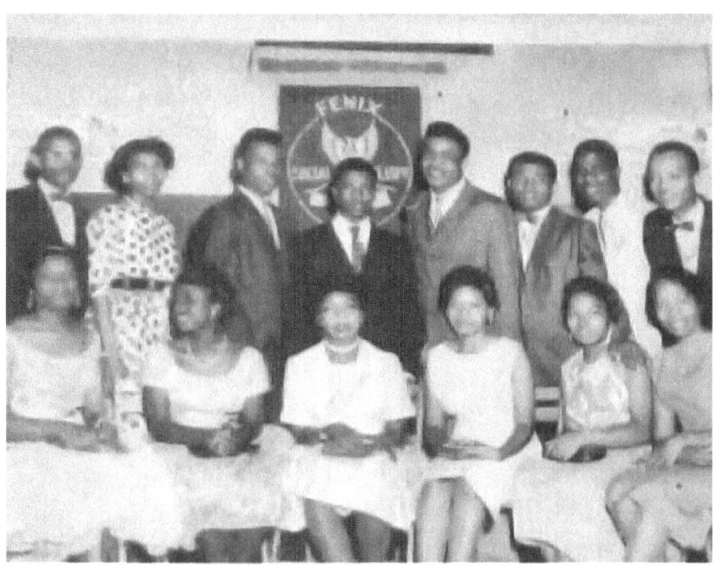

Figure 7a. Advertisement for a Fenix Social Club event, December 25, 1960.

Figure 7b. Fenix Social Club members in a group photo: Juan Marin (*standing in center*), Aida Lambert (*sitting in center*), René J. Mena (*standing second from right*). Photo courtesy of René J. Mena

Reyes 2017). Seamen and family members I interviewed explained that it was common for them to go to spend time in Belize with family and also attend schools where they learned English.[31] Garifuna established ties with African Americans and identified with them because of their race and the discrimination they experienced during this turbulent period of racial inequality.

In addition, the growing population of Honduran Garifuna, who were Spanish speakers, led to increased associations with Latinos in their Bronx communities, owing to their similar language and customs. The Garifuna became part of the population transition in the Bronx, with the influx of Puerto Ricans and the gradual outward migration of Jewish, Irish, and Italians by the late 1960s in the southern part of the borough. Salsa music became popular in the city, and the Garifuna frequented dance halls such as the Hunts Point Palace, Tropicana, and Club Cubano Inter-Americano (Naison and Gumbs 2016).[32]

As Garifuna social organizations developed, it became clear that these groups were open to the entire population. Membership was not limited to those from specific communities or villages, as described in prior studies (England 2006). For instance, the Fenix Social Club and Honduran Football and Social Club held events at some of the prominent dance halls in the city, and these events were attended by diverse guests, including Latinos.[33]

The demographic changes in the Bronx resulted in Black and Latino candidates assuming local political positions. In districts where the Garifuna resided, Blacks (mostly of Caribbean heritage) and Puerto Ricans representing the Democratic Party alternated in winning local elections. Walter H. Gladwin, born in British Guiana, became the first Black from the Bronx elected to the Assembly; he represented the Morrisania district from 1953 to 1957. He was followed by Ivan Warner, son of immigrants from the Caribbean island of St. Kitts, who was elected in 1958. In another district, Puerto Rican–born Felipe N. Torres became the first Latino elected in the borough; he represented the South Bronx in the Assembly from 1953 to 1963 (BHS, "Notable Bronxites"; Jonnes 2002; Naison and Gumbs 2016; Felipe N. Torres; NYS Legislators of Color; Cruz 2017).[34] It would be several decades before the Garifuna became civically engaged in collectively supporting one of their own as a political candidate representing the district.

Conclusion

Garifuna seamen immigrants settled in Harlem, New York, during a period of racial tension. Many experienced racism and discrimination during the civil rights period. As their population grew, they established social organizations focused on culture, dance, and music activities to bring them together. Leaders stated that they established the organizations because they wanted Garifuna to engage with one another as their population increased in the city. Over time, many settled in the Bronx, establishing several other social organizations that engaged with the community through various events. Garifuna early exchanges with the community reflect social networking that is positive for society. Such networking allows diverse groups to learn about each other, creating opportunities to collaborate in advancing their communities' well-being through civic engagement and other means. The next chapter shows increased Garifuna immigration and greater awareness and expressions of their culture in the post–civil rights period.

Chapter 4

Identity and Cultural Growth: *Garifunadao*

"THE BRONX IS BURNING": this phrase was uttered during the 1977 World Series and referred to a fire (attributed to arson) that could be seen raging behind Yankee Stadium while a game was in progress.[1] Landlords setting their buildings on fire to collect the insurance, and what to do with the displaced tenants, were just a sample of the borough's many problems. The city's financial crisis led to cuts in school programs. Gangs were active, and the crime rate was high. Rap music lyrics and graffiti art on the street reflected these circumstances. Beginning in 1969, many factories and other service industries moved from the Bronx to the suburbs and even out of state. As most of the ethnic whites moved out of the borough, Caribbean and Latino immigrants replaced them in the South and Central Bronx. Garifuna made up part of this incoming population. Although the economy had declined, low-wage jobs were still available, and Garifuna women were employed as home health care aides, cleaners, and factory workers. Garifuna men, many of whom were moving away from the seafaring life, took jobs on land in cleaning, building maintenance, and construction.

Despite the challenging environment, the Garifuna population in New York City grew during this period, as many sought better economic opportunities that were unavailable back home in Central America. Garifuna women and families were part of the second wave of migrants in the late 1960s, contributing to community organizing and the preservation of cultural practices (Johnson 2007; Fadahunsi 2003). Although there were

Garifuna communities in New Orleans and Los Angeles, New York City still had the highest U.S. population of Garifuna. They lived primarily in the Bronx and were concentrated in the Morrisania section; however, they also settled in other parts of the Bronx such as Melrose, Mount Eden, Marble Hill, Mott Haven, Longwood, Hunts Point, Crotona Park East, West Farm, and East Tremont. The Garifuna population also grew in Brooklyn, particularly in the Brownsville, Bushwick, and Bedford-Stuyvesant neighborhoods.

In the 1970s Blacks and Puerto Ricans reached new political milestones, securing local elected positions during the post–civil rights period. The Democratic Party in the city changed, accepting pro–civil rights and minority candidates. African American Wendell Foster became the first Black elected city official in the Bronx, representing the Morrisania, Highbridge, and Crotona neighborhoods on the New York City Council from 1978 to 2001 (NYS Legislators of Color). Puerto Rican Herman Badillo became the first Latino from the Bronx elected to the U.S. House of Representatives (1971–77), after being the first minority borough president (1965–69).[2] For the most part, throughout the latter half of the twentieth century, the Morrisania district assembly seat alternated between Blacks and Puerto Ricans Manuel Ramos, Edward A. Stevenson Sr., Louis Niñe, Estella Diggs, and Gloria Davis. Black and Latino officials elected in the Bronx presented opportunities to address the concerns of their population. Two decades later, Garifuna became directly involved in local politics through their organizations.

During this period Garifuna also integrated into their New York City communities. They expanded their networks with other ethnic groups, while nonetheless sustaining their unique Garifuna culture. Throughout this time, they continued to identify with their Central American communities and provided outreach support. Two periods divide this chapter by decade. Starting with the 1970s, focus is on Garifuna cultural awareness during the post–civil rights period, which also influenced their community. Several Garifuna organizations, such as sports and religious associations, provided opportunities for exchanges with other minorities experiencing similar socioeconomic challenges. These exchanges reflect fundamentals of social capital growth that strategize seeking to improve conditions. The decade of the 1980s highlights Garifuna cultural pride, music, and identity, as well as the significance of Garifuna women's contributions to their society. Garifuna groups throughout these two periods sustained their culture and provided for their communities' social development needs.

Garifuna Men's Labor Transition

The west Brooklyn piers, through which many Garifuna seamen passed, experienced a decline in the 1970s. There was a shift to containerized cargo, and a new transport center was built. Commercial freighters were now loaded and unloaded at shipping facilities in New Jersey's Port Newark and Port Elizabeth. With new shipping technology and economic decline came changes to local harbor businesses, and as shipboard employment opportunities decreased, many Garifuna men had to take jobs on land if they wanted to remain in their communities (Webster and Shirley 2016; Horne 2005).

Nevertheless, Garifuna continued to be active and engaged in the National Maritime Union (NMU). In 1976 Perfecto Castro, an administrator in the Carib American Association, was a New York delegate at the NMU's seventeenth convention (held every three years). For the most part, at least one convention delegate was elected by each ship's crew, except for larger vessels. Castro, chosen to represent the SS *Santa Isabal*, was accompanied by fellow Garifuna seaman Juan Martinez. Discussions at the convention covered the failure of the 1970 Merchant Marine Act to expand U.S. cargo ships and employment, support for Jimmy Carter and Walter Mondale for president and vice president, and recognition of the NAACP's Roy Wilkins prior to his retirement (SIU 2001).[3] Prominent guests included the Reverend Martin Luther King Sr., who delivered the invocation; Congressmen Andrew Young from Georgia and Herman Badillo from New York also spoke at the convention (*NMU Pilot* 1976; Horne 2005).

Juan Martinez was well known among the Garifuna seamen, having spent years working and socializing in the community.[4] After a total of 7,297 days on ships since 1945, Martinez took his last voyage in February 1982 and retired. For the most part, Martinez embarked and disembarked in New York City, but he sometimes had to travel to other ports to board his assigned vessels, such as Baltimore; Beaumont, Texas; Tampa, Florida; New Haven, Connecticut; Bayonne, New Jersey; Searsport and Portland, Maine; and Philadelphia. When returning from foreign trips, he would bring souvenirs for the entire family. His wife recalled that he brought home small pieces of furniture, leather slippers, and shoes from Ghana; small marble sphinx statues from Egypt; and T-shirts from Greece and Aruba.[5] His onboard jobs included wiper, oiler, engineman, and steward, but he worked most often in the ship's engine room, which exposed him to asbestos. He led a group of Garifuna seamen who demanded—and received—monetary compensation for asbestos exposure.[6] Unfortunately, he was later diagnosed with leukemia (possibly due to asbestos exposure), and he died shortly thereafter.

Another danger faced by the Garifuna seamen was shipwreck. Garifuna Julian Reyes and Prisciliano Avila were rescued from the SS *Texaco Oklahoma*, a tanker that wrecked off Cape Hatteras on March 27, 1971, on its way from Port Arthur to Boston. Among the thirty-three casualties was Garifuna Lorenzo Tifre, who saved many others by directing their construction of makeshift floating devices.[7] Garifuna seaman Catarino Blanco was lost at sea in another tragic accident (SS *Texaco Oklahoma* 2005).[8]

The 1970s: Cultural Awareness and Organizational Development

Many of their new Garifuna migrant population were influenced by the rise in cultural awareness back in their Central American communities. Garifuna who had already settled in New York continued to have contact with family and friends back home, and they embraced the cultural renaissance promoting their identity. In Belize, *Garifunadao*—exploration of the culture's origins and attempts to revitalize it—consolidated in the 1970s. Garifuna cultural recognition was also taking place in Honduras. Garifuna researched their roots, and some sought to communicate more in the Garifuna language and continue their culinary, artistic, and spiritual traditions. One change embraced the term *Garifuna* rather than *Carib* to describe the ethnic group (J. Palacio 2005, 182–83; Canelas Díaz 1999; J. Ávila 2021).[9] The influence of the 1960s Black civil rights movement ("Black is Beautiful and Black is Proud") and the 1970s Native American movement encouraged Garifuna communities to self-identify and promote themselves as Garifuna (Tuttle 2012; N. Gonzalez 1988).

These changes related to cultural awareness took longer to be accepted in New York (increasing in the 1980s) than in Los Angeles. The first Garifuna organizations developed in Los Angeles in the 1970s. For instance, two early organizations in Los Angeles were called the Garifuna Settlement Day Committee and the Preservation of Garifuna Culture and Society, Inc. (registered in 1980) (Swain 2000; Defay 2004; J. Palacio 1992).[10] Although Garifuna settlements were generally dispersed there, many resided in predominantly African American South-Central Los Angeles. Belizean Garifuna arriving in Los Angeles in the mid-1960s at first depended on established Belizean organizations for their educational, employment, and legal needs, but they eventually organized their own group to promote and sustain the culture, facilitate social engagement, and adapt to life in the United States. Honduran Garifuna also formed their organization in Los Angeles in the late 1970s. Both Guatemalan and Honduran Garifuna supported all their ethnic group's early organizations in Los Angeles (Defay 2004; Matthei and Smith 1998).

In New York City, Garifuna cultural consciousness grew in the 1970s through their music. Although Latino and Caribbean music was popular at social gatherings, music performed in the Garifuna language developed in the city. Social activities increased as their population grew. Photos and videos from this time show Garifuna men with Afros wearing polyester suits and bell-bottom pants and women with Afro puffed hair or feathered-style perms enjoying the social life in their communities. The Honduran Social Circle club continued to host events at Club Cangrejeros in Harlem, which became a popular destination for both Garifuna and Central Americans. Another popular location was a rented dance hall on 174th Street in the Bronx, near the Southern Boulevard and Boston Road area. Parties fostering communal closeness also thrived in private basements and garages. For many, these gatherings answered a sense of nostalgia, reminding the partygoers of being together back home (Fadahunsis 2004).[11]

Music

Several Garifuna bands formed in the city and performed at social gatherings. Many of the band members had been musicians back home and continued to showcase their musical talents after immigrating to New York.[12] Bands such as Los Tropicales, Los Bravos, Los Juniors, and Los Sicodelicos thrived during this period, playing merengue, salsa, bolero, and sometimes reggae.[13] Honduran Garifuna Agustin Martinez formed his band, Los Sicodelicos, in 1971. It became one of the first popular, all-male Garifuna bands, with keyboard, saxophone, trumpet, and drums; Los Sicodelicos performed with the famous Puerto Rican salsa orchestra El Gran Combo de Puerto Rico at the 34th Street Manhattan Center. Established in 1975, Los Satelites was led by Bernardo Guerrero and Pantaleon Hill Lambert and performed songs in the Garifuna language, such as "Nari Nati and Nitu-Chila" (My Brother Nati and My Sister Chila) (see fig. 8). Lambert shared pictures and song recordings and told me that the band practiced at his home.[14] According to elders in the Garifuna community, Santos Batis wrote music in the Garifuna language in Honduras and had a band in New York (J. Ávila 2018a).[15] When he immigrated from Honduras, he brought

IDENTITY AND CULTURAL GROWTH: *GARIFUNADAO* · 79

Figure 8. Los Satelites, an early band that sang in the Garifuna language, pictured ca. 1975. Individuals identified are Alejandro Martinez (*front row, second from left*) and Pantaleon Hill Lambert (*back row, second from left*). Other band members are Benny Guerrero, Jimmy Sambula, Mr. Laboriel, and Black American musicians from the Brooklyn Academy music conservatory Pantaleon Hill Lambert was enrolled in.

not only his musical talent but also his entrepreneurship skills; he had two nightclubs in the Bronx.[16]

For large-scale events involving the general community, organizations sometimes collaborated. The Bronx-based Honduran Football and Social Club (also known as the New York–Honduras Soccer Club) partnered with the Honduras Imperial Social Club (a Black Honduran group like the earlier Honduran American Association) to celebrate the 149th anniversary of the country's independence. The 1970 event was held in the Grand Ballroom of the Riverside Plaza Hotel at 253 West 73rd Street, Manhattan (see fig. 9). Invited musical guests were the famous Cuban band Sonora Matancera with Alberto Beltran and Norman Yzaguirre and His Soul Band.

Through their organizations' activities, the Garifuna increased their contact with others in their communities. West Indians, Puerto Ricans, Cubans, and other Latinos attended the dances and concerts hosted by groups such as the Honduran Social Circle club and the Honduran Football and Social Club. Garifuna musicians were also featured at many events

Figure 9. Program for the event cosponsored by the New York–Honduras Soccer Club and the Honduras Imperial Social Club to commemorate the 149th anniversary of Honduran independence, held at the Riverside Plaza Hotel on Saturday, September 12, 1970.

attended by the general public. Rented dance hall space in Manhattan and the Bronx was common, with Latin music (merengue, salsa) that drew many non-Garifuna to their events. René Mena, founder of the Honduran Football and Social Club, connected the Garifuna with the greater community through his promotion of social events and sports activities.[17] Santos Batis and Aida Lambert were among several Garifuna who had social clubs in the city that were patronized by the general Latino community.[18] Club Cangrejeros, rented by Timothy Martinez, was another popular place for Garifuna gatherings, but it had a diverse clientele, including non-Garifuna.[19] Aida Lambert's social club, La Lampara (The Lamplight), was open to all nationalities; it featured Garifuna bands and sought to introduce the culture to the larger community (Lambert 2010). Lambert was also one of the founders of the annual Hispanic Day parade (Desfile de La Hispanidad) to promote Garifuna culture. Aida migrated from Honduras in 1964 and associated with several Garifuna organizations during this early period. She noticed that the Garifuna had challenges organizing collaboratively, so she joined a diverse, inclusive national Honduran organization. As a member of the Sociedad Honduras New York, Inc., she ensured Garifuna representation in activities and invited Antonieta Maximo, René J. Mena, and other Garifuna to join.[20]

Community Associations

While the Bronx-based Honduran Garifuna were hosting their events, the Belizean Garifuna in Brooklyn also organized and sponsored social functions. British Honduras had not yet become independent (that took place in 1981), but it was a self-governing colony and was renamed Belize in 1973. Because many of the new Honduran Garifuna immigrants spoke Spanish rather than Garifuna—the language they had in common with their English-speaking Belizean Garifuna counterparts—separate Belizean Garifuna groups developed that were oriented more toward their hometown communities. Ines P. Martinez, who was involved with the Carib American Association, registered the Carib Community Association, Inc., in March 1974 to support the economic and educational needs of its members. According to Wellington Ramos, this organization evolved throughout the years, changing its name to the Dangriga Development Association, then the United Garifuna, Inc., followed by the United Garifuna Association. The New York State registry lists the group's headquarters in Brooklyn and its president as Ines Ponciano Martinez; its other Belizean Garifuna members included Elsie Miguel and Joseph Miguel. Its goals were

> (3) To create, establish and set up scholarships, financial grants and free loans to be given, donated and passed on to those persons so designated or deemed entitled thereto by Carib Community Association, Inc., and further,
>
> To enhance, provide, administer, service, fund and acquire funding for the above specified purpose; and further,
>
> All such other lawful activities related to and effecting the fulfillment of the aforesaid purpose of Carib Community Association, Inc. (New York State Department of State, Division of Corporations: Carib Community Association, Inc., March 1974)

The Carib Community Association produced an album featuring traditional Garifuna musical genres (M. Cayetano and R. Cayetano 2005). Ines Martinez was listed as one of the singers on this album, titled *Drums of Love*. The production of Garifuna music became more common during this period of cultural consciousness. One member of the Carib Community Association told me that the group participated in many activities that drew the community together, and it was also involved in investment ventures.[21] Although a group called the Carib American Investors was incorporated in New York in 1977, it had no ties to the Carib Community Association.

The succeeding organization was the Dangriga Development Association, registered in April 1976. Dangriga (in the Garifuna language, "standing waters") is the Garifuna town in Belize formerly known as Stann Creek. From this period onward, the Garifuna commonly used words from their native language in their organizations' names.[22] The stated purpose of the Dangriga Development Association was to support Dangrigans living in the United States and to promote healthy exchanges and civic engagement in both communities. Specifically, its goals were

> To exercise, promote, and protect the privileges and interests of the residents of the nation of Belize and to otherwise foster a healthy interest in the civic affairs of both the United States and Belize by Dangrigans living in the United States.
>
> To own, operate, and maintain a membership club, club houses, club rooms, recreation centers, and reception and assembly rooms for the purpose of providing for the members entertainment, sport, recreation and amusement of all kinds; to furnish, equip, decorate, and fit up such clubs and club rooms to promote social and friendly intercourse among the members of such club or among their guests; to provide and supply any and all appurtenances that may be necessary, useful or convenient for the carrying on of sports, recreations and diversions of all kinds and description for the entertainment, welfare and convenience of the members and their guests and friends. (New York State Department of State, Division of Corporations: Dangriga Development Association, April 15, 1976, Brooklyn, New York)

Mary Petillo and her husband, Robert "Bob" Petillo, led Belizean Garifuna activities in Brooklyn through the Dangriga Development Association. Its social gatherings and dance events were attended primarily by Belizean Garifuna. Support of the annual Garifuna masses was also a function of the group. Mary Petillo and others were part of a new generation of young Belizean Garifuna who were active in replacing Ines Martinez and the Carib Community Association as the leaders of their community's social activities. The upcoming generation had newer ideas for the group.

Just as the Dangriga Development Association focused on Belizeans and their country and region of origin, Honduran Garifuna groups continued to form to serve their fellow nationals. For instance, the Frente Unido Hondureño Social Club (Honduran United Front Social Club, or FUH) was founded by Garifuna from Honduras in 1969 and registered in 1972 in Brooklyn. Its stated purpose was

To provide for the mutual assistance, enjoyment, entertainment and improvements of its members socially; to promote good fellowship and social activities among its members; to promote the friendship of its members; to stimulate their intellectual and social advancement and to hold meetings and social gatherings for the realization of the above purpose; all without pecuniary profit. (New York State Department of State, Division of Corporations: Frente Unido Hondureño Social Club, January 27, 1972, Brooklyn, NY)

I spoke with several individuals involved with the FUH and learned that although Hondurans founded the organization, its focus was the advancement of all Garifuna. Later, non-Garifuna Hondurans also joined the organization. According to member Celso Castro, the FUH was created to galvanize the Garifuna diaspora and address political issues in Honduras. According to Efraim Castro, one of the founding leaders, he and Amado Lambert established the group because there was no other Garifuna organization dealing with acculturation and racial discrimination; most Garifuna groups concentrated on social activities. Efraim heard Malcolm X speak numerous times in Harlem, and he also attended Stokely Carmichael's (Kwame Ture) speaking engagements in Brooklyn. The Black Power movement was part of his motivation in starting the FUH, in addition to helping the Garifuna uplift themselves. Efraim stated that the FUH provided tutoring services, and about fifty youths participated in the program (held in the basement of a home). Many of them were recent immigrants and needed help with English. Fundraising dances and summertime beach trips to Long Island helped raise money for their activities.[23]

The FUH had a float in the annual West Indian Day parade in Brooklyn in September 1971. This event was described in the FUH publication *Reflejos* (Reflections). The publication details the fundraisers that were held to subsidize the float, featuring Garifuna music and the election of the FUH queen from among several contestants.[24] FUH member Celea Johnson led registration and organization efforts for the West Indian Day parade.[25]

The December 1971 issue of *Reflejos* contains several articles written by FUH members. One article discussed the ethnic group's identity and the history of its members' different self-identifications as Carib, Moreno (dark skin color), and Garifuna. It concluded that although some people continued to use the term *Carib*, most preferred *Garifuna* to identify their culture. Another article covered the election of a new administrative body and Amado Lambert as president. Invited honorary guests to the installation of the new president included pioneering Garifuna community leaders René Mena (Honduran Football and Social Club), Timothy Martinez (Carib American Association), and Juan Marin (Fenix Social Club), who was unable to attend. Their work to unite the community was acknowledged, as well as their participation in and support of FUH functions.

Garifuna culture was also featured by the local Spanish-language television station, Univision, in the 1970s. The FUH was showcased in a segment where members presented Garifuna culture, music, and dance. According to one member, it was the first time the Garifuna culture was highlighted in a television program in New York.

Although the FUH's headquarters was in Brooklyn, it also held functions in the Bronx (see fig. 10), which was convenient for the many Garifuna living in that borough. The organization's Brooklyn headquarters was in the basement of a home, and it was also a popular Garifuna meeting place. Honduran Garifuna Cesar Johnson, his brother Florentine Johnson, and Modesto Harry registered the Brooklyn location as the Club San Antonio Deportivo, Inc.[26] Although the basement was designated a sports club, it also functioned as a dance hall and a meeting place for soccer teams and other organizations. Its stated purpose was

> To promote the friendship of its members; to inculcate in them a high sense of loyalty to each other; to stimulate their intellectual advancement, and to hold meetings and social gatherings for the better realization of the above-named purposes.
>
> To cultivate social intercourse among its members; to establish a center of work and interest for the members in order to improve their health, physical and s [sic] conditions; and to promote friendship, socializing [sociability], culture among its members. (New York State Department of State, Division of Corporations: Club San Antonio Deportivo, Inc., February 5, 1975)

Although the FUH met at the Club San Antonio Deportivo location, according to member Sandra Colon, it also met at Our Lady of Mercy Roman Catholic Church in Brooklyn. At the church, the group took steps to publicize in the United States the devastating effects of the Cold War throughout Central America. Colon was also part of the Solidarity Group for Honduras (Grupo Solaridad por el Pueblo de Honduras) in 1978, collaborating with other Honduran support groups in Boston (Garcia 2014).[27] An effect of the Cold War in Honduras was labor repression; the army massacred fourteen protesters in 1975. Colon was also part of the Black

Figure 10. Advertisement for the FUH's Second Reggae Festival, scheduled for December 22, 1973, at the Bronx Savoy Manor and showcasing many musical genres in addition to reggae. Photo courtesy of Efraim Castro

Fraternal Organization of Honduras (Organización Fraternal Negra de Honduras, or OFRANEH), founded in 1977; it established a branch in New York City in 1978. In Honduras, this organization initially addressed Black Hondurans' racial concerns; it then evolved to focus on Garifuna territorial rights. Colon's residence alternated between Honduras and New York during this period.

According to Colon, the FUH's formation in 1969 was a reaction to the civil rights movement and especially the assassination of Martin Luther King Jr. the year before. Colon and fellow FUH members Celso Castro, Fernando Castro, and Efraim Castro were Garifuna in college at the time, and they were conscious of the U.S. racial struggle.[28] Over time, new immigrants, such as Honduran Garifuna union activists, and Ladinos became part of the organization.[29] Differences in ideas and a lack of consensus over admitting Ladinos eventually resulted in the FUH's dissolution. According to Celso Castro, by 1975, when he returned to New York after serving in the army during the Vietnam War, the FUH was being phased out.[30]

The Committee for the Development of Honduras—Comité Pro Desarrollo de Honduras (COPROD) was founded in September 1974 to provide emergency aid following Hurricane Fifi. Listed in COPROD's articles of incorporation are the names of FUH leaders and other Garifuna who founded other organizations decades later.[31]

Hometown Associations

As the Garifuna population increased, several Honduran Garifuna hometown associations representing Garifuna communities back home sprang up in New York City.[32] A 2010 study showed that about half of the forty-eight Honduran Garifuna communities had corresponding hometown associations in the United States, and twenty-two were in New York. Most of these associations were unregistered; however, four did register with the state.[33] These New York City hometown associations, known in Spanish as *patronatos* (see Chapter 2), corresponded with their counterparts in Honduras (Endo et al. 2010). In New York, meetings were initially held in family members' homes; later, depending on the number of people attending, meetings were held in churches or community centers.[34] Hometown associations provided financial support for annual village celebrations and for infrastructure development in their Central American communities. Although these were positive functions, these groups may have divided the Honduran Garifuna in New York, as many exclusively attended activities associated with their own villages.[35] According to Alejandro Lambert, his brother Justo Lambert established a hometown association representing Travesía, Honduras, in the 1960s; it was one of the first in New York. Others were established in the 1960s to represent the Garifuna community of Limon, Honduras. The Corozal Hometown Association, founded in 1969, was officially registered in Honduras that year and had offices in San Pedro Sula and Tegucigalpa; it also functioned as an organization in New York City.[36] By the 1970s, there were hometown associations in the city representing the Honduran Garifuna communities of Triunfo de la Cruz, Santa Fe, Santa Rosa de Aguan, Masca, Sambo Creek, San Antonio, Cristales, Iriona, and Guadalupe (England 2006; Endo et al. 2010).

There were several hometown associations representing Limon, one of the largest Garifuna communities in Honduras. The Comité Pro Desarrollo Comunal de Limon (CPDCL; succeeded in 1977 by the Frente Social Limoneño) focused on issues affecting the New York City Garifuna community. Celso Castro, also a member of the FUH, was one of the cofounders of the group, which began sometime around 1969.[37] Castro also served as editor of its *Voz Garifuna* (Garifuna Voice) newsletter, distributed throughout the city's Honduran Garifuna community.[38] Its articles focused on preserving the Garifuna culture, language, and history, and it included advertisements of community events. In addition, it published articles about past land expropriations and mineral and lumber excavations in the municipality of Limon (England 2006; Fadahunsi 2003). Led by its president, Jacobo Ventura, the CPDCL also supported development projects in the Limon community and held events in New York City to raise funds. The Frente Social Limoneño continued these projects after the CPDCL disbanded.

Ismael Melendez, vice president of the CPDCL, recalled that the group held musical and dance fundraising events to contribute to the Honduras hurricane relief fund in 1974, and it supported the production of several albums of traditional Garifuna music.[39] Similar to their Belizean Garifuna counterparts, Honduran Garifuna grew conscious of their culture and started recording their traditional Parranda music. Parranda traditionally encompasses an acoustic guitar, maracas, and background singers and uses a call-and-response format to tell personal or historical stories. *Garifuna Su Musica y Su Cancion* and *Musica Costena de Honduras Garifuna* were two albums the CPDCL recorded in New York City. Traditional Garifuna music was popular, and several other Garifuna recorded songs representing their Honduran communities. Other albums produced during this period were *Club Lagrimas de Corozal*, corresponding to Corozal, Honduras; *Los Hits de Santa Fe*, corresponding to Santa Fe, Honduras;

and *Garifuna de Honduras DPTO [Departamento] Colón*, produced in 1975 by E. Bermudez, and *Mala Estrella: Club Mala Estrella Wanagas*, produced in 1977 by Braulio Ramos Morales, both from the Aguan township.[40] All the albums featured a variety of traditional Garifuna musical genres.

In addition to Honduran Garifuna hometown associations, separate committees were created to address problems back home. Committees to address such issues as electricity, water, and church restoration were common. The longevity of these committees varied (England 2006).[41] The city's smaller populations of Belizean and Guatemalan Garifuna also supported their communities back home. As noted earlier, the Dangriga Development Association supported its home community in Belize. Similarly, Guatemalan Garifuna groups emerged to assist their hometowns.

Religious Associations

Other voluntary associations that formed in this period were Garifuna Roman Catholic groups known in Spanish as *pastorals*. These associations also existed in Central America and likely developed in New York during the second wave of Garifuna migration (N. Gonzalez 1988). They played a significant role in sustaining Garifuna spiritual traditions, which are central to their culture. The incorporation of traditional spiritual practices within the Catholic Church is commonly known as folk Catholicism (Johnson 2007). In 1962 the Vatican authorized indigenous peoples to maintain their culture while syncretizing their faith (Clawson 2000). Garifuna Catholic associations took the lead in coordinating masses and other church services, featuring their language and traditional instruments in songs, as well as traditional attire and food. According to Belizean Garifuna leader Rosita Alvarez, the blended masses held in New York City's Roman Catholic churches were influenced by the Garifuna in Los Angeles, who were already incorporating their culture into church services. One of these early Garifuna groups started in the 1970s at a Brooklyn Roman Catholic church. Eventually, many Belizean, Honduran, and Guatemalan Garifuna were attending services at Our Lady of Mercy Church in Brooklyn, and they continue to do so.[42] Belizean Garifuna John Mariano and Randall Enriquez were among those involved in forming the group; women such as Lucia Mariano and Rosita Alvarez eventually assumed leadership.[43] Several years later, other Garifuna Catholic voluntary associations developed in the Bronx and collaborated with the Brooklyn group. In the following century, Garifuna Catholic pastoral groups (such as the Pastoral of St. Anthony of

Padua Church in the Bronx, Pastoral of St. Augustine Church in the Bronx, and Pastoral of Our Lady of Mercy in Brooklyn) assembled each year to celebrate a Garifuna mass led by a guest priest from Belize, Guatemala, or Honduras. The general public and Garifuna from other parishes attend these masses, which feature traditional Garifuna apparel, musical instruments, singers, and food. A missal written in the Garifuna language is used (T. Colon 2010a).[44]

Most of the Garifuna who belong to these Catholic associations also participate in traditional spiritual ceremonies, and some of those practices have ties to Catholicism. Many Garifuna believe that their ancestors are part of their lives and protect them from evil. Several of their primary rituals feature interaction between Garifuna and the spirits of their ancestors. Many believe that "the ancestors communicate with the living through dreams interpreted by the *buyei*," a Garifuna priest-healer or shaman (J. Palacio 2005). In the *amuyadahani* ritual—the "bathing of a spirit" who died a few years earlier—a ceremony is typically held early in the morning with only close relatives, followed by a Roman Catholic mass. The *chugu* is a propitiation rite; it involves many descendants of the ancestor being honored and lasts less than twelve hours. The largest Garifuna ritual is the *dugu*; it is held only in villages in Central America and lasts for six to nine days (J. Valentine 2002; J. Palacio 2005). Garifuna family members related to the ancestor attend this healing rite, conducted by the *buyei*, to "propitiate those ancestors regarded as afflicting the living" (J. Palacio 2005, 252). Families travel from far away to attend this ceremony, including many Garifuna New Yorkers who make the trip to Central America. To varying degrees, all three rituals involve food, singing, and dancing, and are all requested by the ancestors. Another religious tradition of the Garifuna is the *beluria*, or wake: nine nights of prayers for the dead, usually at the home of the deceased. It is a Roman Catholic custom that the Garifuna adopted; it is also practiced frequently in New York (J. Valentine 2002). During my visit to a Garifuna village, a *dugu* ceremony was in progress in the *dabuyaba* temple. The temple was made of *murisi*, cohune palm leaf used for thatching. This temple was a rectangular structure and stood out in the village adjacent to the beautiful blue sea. There were three entry points, two on the parallel east and west sides and one exit at the south end of the structure. At the exit there was a veranda/canopy structure. The exit door and surrounding area led directly to the sea. Inside the temple, with a beautifully kept mud floor, various activities were taking place. I noticed a section in the *dabuyaba*, restricted and partitioned, with a curtain across the entire upper segment of the temple. It was explained to me that only the *buyeis* healers, or priest representatives, have access to that specific room (*guli*, sacred area in the temple) and individuals seeking spiritual consultations may be invited. The male *buyei* frequently went in and out. Most activities occurred in the main central *gayunaru* section. Clusters of men and women were dressed in matching clothing. At times women danced syncretically, rocking side to side while singing, participating in the *abeimahani* solidarity dance. I noticed live chickens, most of them tied but some roaming. The chickens are sacrificed at specific times during the ceremony. Incense smoke was common in the *gayunaru*. Overhead, baskets, brooms, and many hammocks hung from the ceiling. The objects in the ceiling as well as the separate groups (families) of individuals dressed uniformly are connected to the ancestors associated with the ceremony.

Outside of Central America Garifuna continue their religious traditions. The practice of Garifuna spiritual traditions was important in consolidating the immigrant community in New York. Respect and reverence for their ancestors are at the center of Garifuna culture. Many Garifuna believe that without their spiritual traditions, their culture would cease to exist. The second wave of Garifuna migration that brought Garifuna women—the core organizers of these rituals—to New York contributed to the maintenance of the Garifuna culture (England 2006; Johnson 2007). Spiritual ritual ties to the Roman Catholic church continue in the city using relics, prayers, and offering masses for deceased relatives.

Many Garifuna spiritual traditions occur through their voluntary Catholic associations. These associations are also recognized as *pastoral* groups in Spanish. The emergence of these associations signaled the presence and importance of Garifuna women in their New York City communities. Prior to the second wave of Garifuna migration, organized groups carrying on Garifuna cultural and religious traditions were practically nonexistent. For the most part, women are involved in all aspects of the pastoral groups, such as preparing traditional foods, designing coordinated clothing, singing in the chorus, and participating in prayer chant groups. As they do in Central America, Garifuna women in New York City plan the annual celebration for their respective townships' patron saints (England 2006). This involves coordination of male and female youth participation and the selection of a queen.

In the Roman Catholic Church, Garifuna also associate with individuals from various immigrant groups and established Latinos. This enhances their social exchanges with non-Garifuna and involvement in other community affairs. For example, Garifuna participate in archdiocese events in the cathedral as well as forums supporting immigration reforms (England

2006; Johnson 2007). Their voluntary associations also serve as a point of contact with their community. Fortunately, in the Catholic Church Garifuna have been able to form their own ethnic-oriented groups, which sustain their identity while they continue to be part of the general church body.[45]

Sports

As women were preserving the spiritual traditions of the Garifuna culture, men were preserving its sports traditions. Soccer (*fútbol*) is the national sport in their home countries. Many of the prominent soccer players in Honduras, Guatemala, and Belize are Garifuna. Several Garifuna soccer clubs, both registered and unregistered, developed in the 1970s and played in New York City's parks. Two popular teams were the Garifuna Brooklyn Stars, led by Hondurans Alonzo Arzu and Froylan Mariano, and the Ubafu ("power" in the Garifuna language), led by Belizeans Wellington Ramos and Moises Colon.[46] Soccer matches became community events for Garifuna families. They are still common, with some Garifuna coming merely to socialize and drink; children run around and play, and women vendors sell traditional bread and other dishes. Linden Park in Brooklyn and Van Cortlandt Park in the Bronx were two popular gathering places for soccer games.

According to German Cayetano, Victor Fernandez and Mariano Gutierrez from the Garifuna community of San Antonio, Honduras, also organized sports events in the city during this time. In the Bronx, René Mena, leader of the Honduran Football and Social Club, organized soccer matches for his team in the United States and Central America (see fig. 11). The team included players from various countries, including non-Garifuna. Several soccer tournaments were held in Van Cortlandt Park. During this time, soccer was not popular in the United States, but Mena played a role in promoting the sport. He was also involved in the development of major league soccer in New York and with the international soccer association FIFA. Mena's team sometimes practiced with the New York Cosmos. In addition, Mena served as a guest sports journalist for New York City's Latino paper *El Diario/La Prensa* (1970–79). For his efforts in promoting soccer, New York City mayor John Lindsay (1966–73) awarded Mena a citation that he showed me during a visit to his home.[47]

Through soccer teams and leagues, Garifuna associate with other minority ethnic groups such as West Indians, Latinos and Africans. Volunteer soccer clubs are also essential to the ethnic group, facilitating their

Figure 11. René J. Mena and the Honduran Football and Social Club. Photo courtesy of René J. Mena

community gathering and networking opportunities for employment, housing, civic engagement, legal assistance, or other necessities. Later we learn of a Garifuna soccer organizer engaging with local officials seeking to improve field conditions for the athletes.

Another sport that Garifuna men participated in was boxing. The New York Golden Gloves match held on January 31, 1979, featured a Garifuna boxer. Honduran-born Francisco Rodriguez, a twenty-five-year-old construction worker and novice heavyweight residing in Middletown, New York, fought Francis Ricottilli from Beacon, New York. Rodriguez was winning the fight, but in the second round he complained of fatigue and the referee stopped the fight. Unexpectedly, he died early in the morning at the hospital and it was found that he had an enlarged heart and sickle cell disease (Alfano 1979). Interestingly, in the following century another Honduran Garifuna boxer, Eddie Gomez, emerged by winning the New York Golden Gloves boxing match and becoming a professional boxer in the welterweight division (Abramson 2015; Gomez 2011).

The 1980s: New Garifuna Immigrants' Cultural Pride and Women's Contributions

The South Bronx in the 1980s was plagued by economic decay, drugs, crime, and gang warfare. The New York City Housing Authority police protected public housing units from crime, and the Guardian Angels, an unarmed volunteer force noted for their red berets and jackets, patrolled the streets and the subways. Graffiti covered subway cars and stations, as well as the walls of empty buildings; businesses were locked up behind metal gates for protection. Drug use, especially of crack cocaine, increased, along with the associated criminal activity and prostitution that often accompanied the economics of addiction. The deterioration of living quarters, broken glass in the streets, and sense of general despair are described in the popular rap song "The Message" by Grandmaster Flash and the Furious Five. The local news highlighted the constant crime, and television commercials by celebrities ranging from rappers to First Lady Nancy Reagan told people, "Just say no [to drugs]" and "Crack is wack." It was not unusual to be offered crack or small ziplock bags containing cocaine, and it was commonplace to find syringes in the streets. Drug addicts with noticeable needle marks and scantily clothed crackheads (even in winter) were everyday sights. There were pockets in the neighborhood where drug addicts loitered in clusters, regardless of the season; they resembled zombies. In addition, the HIV/AIDS epidemic was claiming countless victims throughout the city and the nation, and many Garifuna became infected and died.

Despite the crime and the economic and health challenges, Garifuna continued to come to the city, and their population increased during the third wave of immigration in the 1980s. This wave was the result of political and economic destabilization in Central America, caused partly by civil wars and partly by U.S. Cold War policy in the region, which sought to contain political movements perceived to be influenced by communism. Although Honduras was spared the civil wars that gripped neighboring El Salvador, Guatemala, and Nicaragua, Honduran Garifuna were indirectly affected by the unrest, which motivated their immigration to the United States. Additionally, high external debt levels, poor economic policies, and unfavorable terms of primary exports trade resulted in low economic growth rates and a decline in living standards in Honduras. In fact, they accounted for large numbers of new migrants, many of whom joined relatives who were already established in New York.

A large migration wave left Belize in the 1980s as the country gained its independence. After 1980 close to 50 percent of Belizeans migrated to the United States. Its economy was challenged by the global economic recession, high oil prices, the increased budget deficit, and low sugar prices impacting Belize's mono-export of sugar. Although gradual economic improvements occurred, people continued migrating as high unemployment and indirect taxes persisted and government services decreased. Belizean investors primarily benefited from the economic growth (Straughan 2004).

Cultural Pride

Ethnic pride continued to be important among the Garifuna, and more organizations used the Garifuna language in their names, connecting them to their culture. This occurred as the Honduran government recognized the Garifuna culture by embracing Garifuna choreographer Crisanto Armando Melendez and the Ballet Folklórico Nacional Garífuna de Honduras as part of the country's tourism initiative. (Unfortunately, years later, acknowledgment of Garifuna cultural dance worked against the Honduran Garifuna as the government sought to usurp their coastal lands for tourism initiatives [López García 2006].) Thus, the new organizations emerging in the 1980s held their culture in high esteem and promoted themselves as different from other Black organizations. Cultural pride, in addition to language barriers (most of the newcomers spoke Spanish) and social biases, hindered the recently arrived Garifuna immigrants from establishing close ties with African Americans. This was also evident in Garifuna settlements outside of New York.

During the mid-1980s, the Garifuna population increased in Houston, Texas, where Garifuna clustered in the Fifth Ward area, generally recognized as a poor or low-income community. The mixed population of Blacks and Latinos facilitated the Garifuna's move into the community, where they faced less discrimination. In addition, rent was less expensive, and there were already Garifuna established in the area. Cultural and language differences resulted in minimal integration between Blacks and Latinos. African Americans were the original settlers of North Lyons, followed by Mexicans in two waves in the 1950s and 1980s. In the twenty-first century, the Garifuna population increased substantially in the Greater Houston area, with many migrating from Central America as well as moving from New York City (Rodríguez 1987; Hutchinson et al. 1996; Soto 2022).

Punta Music and Community Solidarity

The popularization of the punta musical genre in the 1980s was one sign of ethnic pride. It made the Garifuna a more close-knit community as they socialized among themselves, regardless of their countries of origin. Weekend social gatherings in basements and at rented dance clubs continued, but in addition to the reggae and Latin music enjoyed in the past, some artists and groups started to perform in the Garifuna language. Punta and punta rock gained popularity as several bands emerged. In addition to being a Garifuna musical genre, punta is a ritualistic dance symbolizing fertility and reproduction; it is often performed upon the death of an adult or to celebrate the anniversary of a death. Many believe that punta has African origins. Traditional punta music uses two wooden drums (*garaun*), conch shells (*wadabágei*), and maracas (*sisira*). Punta rock constituted a change in musical style and involved the addition of instruments such as keyboards, bass and electric guitars, piano, and synthesizers. Garifuna Pen Cayetano and the Turtle Shell band started punta rock in Belize in the late 1970s and later brought it to the United States. This was around the time of the *Garifunadao* cultural revitalization cited by Garifuna anthropologist Joseph Palacio (1992). Since the 1980s, keyboards, electric bass guitars, synthesizers, and other percussive instruments have been added; many punta rock bands also include piano and brass, string, and woodwind instruments (Servio 1996). The emergence of punta bands in New York City increased the Garifuna's solidarity, and the ethnic group gained recognition as it became identified with punta music. Although storytelling was featured in some punta music, it was more popular in another Garifuna musical genre, parranda, which gained popularity years later. Parranda music has a slow-paced rhythm that is suitable for lyrics (sung in Garifuna) associated with themes such as social criticism, life struggles, and love relations (651 Arts 2007).[48]

Garifuna punta artists and bands increased in number and gained popularity in their New York City communities. Some of them also performed Spanish reggae, as it was popular. Like the previous immigrant groups in the 1960s and 1970s, these Garifuna brought their musical talents to New York from Central America. Some of the early popular groups in the city were Grupo H, the Labuga Boys, Goubana, Fuerza Brava, and the Sea Boys.[49] The Sea Boys' song "Garifuna Wagia" (We are Garifuna) was very popular throughout the Garifuna community. Its musical source was the Garifuna anthem *"Yurumein giñeru nege wayuna"* (Our ancestors come from St. Vincent), a story of Garifuna origins. Another popular group that formed in 1988 was the Garifuna Kids, whose members were first-generation Garifuna in New York City. The group performed at civic centers, schools and universities, open-air park events, and large-scale social clubs in New York City that were patronized by many Garifuna and Ladinos (Perry 1999; J. Ávila 2014). Some band members later joined another group called Garifuna Legacy. Throughout the 1990s, these groups popularized punta music and toured North America and Central America.

Garifuna Women and Community Development

Newly arrived Garifuna youth benefited from services and activities available in their communities through cultural and educational organizations, some of which were led by Garifuna women. One registered organization was Mujeres Garinagu en Marcha Pro-Educación, Inc. (Garifuna Women for Progress in Education, or MUGAMA), which assisted new immigrants in making the transition to life in New York. Based in Brooklyn, MUGAMA helped individuals learn English, obtain U.S. citizenship, and earn general equivalency diplomas (GEDs). The organization also awarded academic scholarships. Among MUGAMA's founders were Honduran Garifuna women Dionisia Amaya, Lydia Sacasa Hill, and Mirtha Sabio; they started the organization in 1989 to recognize the accomplishments of Garifuna women (Avila and Avila 2008).[50] Amaya worked for the New York City Board of Education as a guidance counselor and became interested in the educational advancement of recent Garifuna immigrants. She had immigrated from Honduras in 1964 and went from working as a housekeeper to earning a masters' degree (Avila and Avila 2014). Amaya and Hill were both involved with the short-lived 1974 organization Comité Pro Desarrollo de Honduras (COPROD).

Another Garifuna woman who immigrated from Honduras in the 1960s and worked for the city's Board of Education was Manuela Sabio. In 1988 she founded the dance group Wanichigu (Our Pride) to teach Garifuna traditions and values to young people. This folkloric dance company brought the ethnic group together, entertaining as well as presenting its history and culture through song, dance, and drama (Newman 2011). Similar dance groups that formed in the 1970s and 1980s included the Honduran Garifuna group Ashanti and the 1986 Guatemalan Garifuna group Ballet Folklórico Garífuna Guatemalteco (Yurumein). Yurumein is the name for St. Vincent in the Garifuna language (M. Colón 2014, 2015). However, Wanichigu was the first such Garifuna group to gain significant notoriety, performing at many popular events and locations in the city such as Symphony Space and the Lincoln Center Outdoors Festival in August 1997.

Other contributions to the arts during this period included the Honduran American Cultural Association, founded by Garifuna Antonieta Maximo in 1984 to promote the Honduran culture. Maximo noticed there was a lack of awareness of Honduran arts in the United States. Her work involves all Hondurans, including non-Garifuna. Through the center a wide range of Honduran artists such as painters, musicians, dancers, and literary figures have been invited to present their work in different prestigious places. She is known in the community for painting, writing, directing, and performing. Maximo immigrated in the early 1970s and became active in New York City theater, performing in productions both on and off Broadway; she has also written plays and has appeared in Spanish- and English-language movies (Swain 2015). Maximo was also involved with COPROD in the past and various other organizations. She served as the consul general of Honduras in New York and was president of the Federation of Honduran Organizations of New York (FEDHONY) and founding member of the Garifuna Coalition USA. Details of these organizations and her role are provided in the following chapter.

Two other popular Honduran Garifuna women led groups in the 1980s with ties to their hometowns. As it is for other leaders, preservation of the Garifuna culture for future generations is a motivating factor for leaders founding their group. The Comité Pro Mejoramiento de Travesía (Committee for the Improvement of Travesia, or Prometra), led by Leslie Avila Lacayo, supported that Honduran Garifuna community. It eventually evolved into the Prometra Garifuna Society, with the goal of empowering young adults to lead safe and healthy lives in Garifuna communities. This group sponsors and supports annual hometown celebrations for the Catholic patron saint, Garifuna cultural events, and workshops for youth (T. Colon 2012; J. Ávila 2017a).[51] The other group, the Organización de Damas Limoneña de Nueva York (Limon Ladies Organization of New York), is led by Marcia Gomez. It is dedicated to supporting the development of Limon, one of the largest Garifuna communities in Honduras. Its activities include annual fundraising events and supporting other Garifuna organizations in the city. Although the group started in the 1980s, it was not officially registered until the twenty-first century (Ávila 2017b). Marcia Gomez is an active supporter of the Garifuna Coalition USA, Inc., attending meetings and events, and served on the Bronx Community Board.

Garifuna women also led the first voluntary Catholic organization established in the Bronx, which was similar in function to the one formed in Brooklyn earlier. The Pastoral of St. Anthony of Padua Church held masses incorporating the Garifuna culture. Eventually, other Garifuna voluntary Catholic associations developed in the Bronx. In addition, the New York Catholic Archdiocese officially recognized the Garifuna language in church missals, which the Garifuna used in their ceremonies and masses (Avila 2011).

Highlighting women's contributions sheds light on gender inclusivity in Garifuna society and the outcomes of male and female roles from the past. Garifuna women's role working the land allowed them more time in the household educating the youth, including in the culture, compared to the men who were away hunting and fishing. During the 1980s, for the most part, many women led in establishing organizations promoting cultural traditions. Nevertheless, further chapters show that over time leaders of Garifuna organizations included both males and females, demonstrating gender inclusivity in the culture.

Other Organizations Identifying as Garifuna

Guatemalan Garifuna Carlos Gotay, who led the effort to convince the Archdiocese of New York to recognize Garifuna culture, cofounded an organization with countryman Julio Arzu in 1985. The Guatemalan Garifuna Association Yurumein Incorporated of New York (La Asociación Garífuna Guatemalteca Yurumein incorporada de New York) was incorporated in 1987. Its goal was to support and encourage individual and collective progress in Garifuna communities in both New York City and Guatemala. Another organization, United Garifuna, Inc., grew out of the 1970s Dangriga Development Association, with individuals such as Joseph Miguel, John Mariano, Felix Miranda, and other Belizean Garifuna involved; it was registered in 1981 (Avila 2011; N. Gonzalez 1989). Its new name identified the ethnic group as being inclusive across all national borders; the name later changed again to United Garifuna Association (UGA). According to UGA member Wellington Ramos, the group's headquarters was in the Bushwick section of Brooklyn.[52] Functions of the UGA changed over time since its start in the 1970s. Support of other Garifuna organizations in the city, educational forums, and political gatherings addressing political issues of Garifuna in Central America are some of the UGA's functions in the present day.

A religious organization that started during this period was the Garifuna Evangelical Church.[53] The first church was established in 1985 in Brooklyn, and a church opened in the Bronx in 1987. Church services integrate the Garifuna language, praise music, and activities and uphold the culture's culinary and clothing traditions (Hernandez 2008a). Although most Garifuna are Roman Catholic, a growing evangelical population developed, influenced by the appeal of the evangelical movement in Central America and U.S. Latino communities. According to Belizean Garifuna Reverend Andrew Nunez, during the 1980s two Belizean Garifuna Mennonite pastors living in Los Angeles, California, Basil Marin and Stephen Garcia, contributed to the start of Garifuna Evangelical churches. The Mennonite denomination has historical ties with the Garifuna community in both Belize and Honduras, where Mennonite missionaries have lived and proselytized since the 1950s. Eventually, Garcia moved to New York City and established the Believers Mennonite Church in Brooklyn in 1985.[54] Reverend Garcia helped Honduran Garifuna Celso Jaime establish the Garifuna Evangelical Church in the Bronx.[55]

Conclusion

Many Belizean, Guatemalan, and Honduran Garifuna immigrated to New York City in the 1970s and 1980s, and the city eventually became an extension of their society back home (N. Gonzalez 1989). Several of the original Garifuna seamen took up other occupations on land in response to economic and technological shifts. Garifuna women who migrated during the second wave contributed to community and organizational development. As the Garifuna population increased in the city, Garifuna organizations continued to be the foundation of their communities. Catholic voluntary associations, hometown associations, soccer groups, and folk dance groups were among the Garifuna organizations that developed; these groups, nonexistent during the first wave, facilitated the extension of hometown society to New York. Sports teams and musical groups formed, and festive social events and traditional spiritual rites were some of the activities taking place in the city. These groups also supported infrastructure development in their homelands and provided hurricane relief when needed. The groups that formed contributed to Garifuna social exchanges and connections in their communities. Songs in the Garifuna language proliferated, and an increasing number of organizations included *Garifuna* in their names, reflecting an awareness of their heritage. This helped bring the ethnic group together, despite the differences associated with their respective nationalities.

The Garifuna also attempted to integrate into broader society in various ways. Because the majority of the incoming Garifuna immigrants spoke

Spanish, they tended to associate with Latinos, the dominant minority group in their communities. However, some also connected with the Caribbeans and African Americans who were their neighbors in various parts of the city. Through musical events hosted by Garifuna organizations and activities in their respective churches, the Garifuna associated with those outside of their ethnic group. Many of the events taking place in the 1970s and 1980s were significant in establishing the foundations of Garifuna culture and identity in the United States. The following chapter focuses specifically on the efforts of Garifuna organizations in continuing to promote their culture and identity from the 1990s to the present.

Chapter 5

Music, Dance, and Sports from the 1990s to the Present

Garifuna organizations in New York City experienced substantial growth as the new millennium approached, supported by their population increase during the third wave of migration in the 1990s. The ethnic group congregated at popular gathering places such as Bill Rainey Park in the Bronx, known as *Waporu* ("ship" in Garifuna); another favorite spot in the Bronx, especially during warm weather, was Crotona Park, known as *Trujillano* after the name of a Honduran Garifuna city (Johnson 2007). Soccer continued as part of the community tradition, and Garifuna leagues played in Brooklyn's Linden Park, Van Cortlandt Park in the Bronx, and Fort Washington Park in Manhattan.[1] Garifuna nightclubs drew crowds year-round, as many enjoyed the popularity of punta, a musical genre identified with their culture. In the 1990s punta music expanded to a broader audience and gained mainstream international recognition among Latinos with the rise of Honduran Mestizo bands such as Banda Blanca, Sopa de Caracol, Sensato, and One, Two, Three (J. Ávila 2016a; M. Cayetano and R. Cayetano 2005).[2] The popularity of punta music continued into the new century. Eventually, punta became the national music of Honduras, in addition to being popular among the Garifuna in New York City.

Continuing to explore the theme that Garifuna's establishment of different groups sustains their culture and subsistence, this chapter presents Garifuna soccer clubs, folkloric dance groups, and social organizations' cultural events, leading Garifuna functions in the city from the 1990s to the present. These groups evolved from the previous period. As some consolidated, these groups primarily led Garifuna in integrating in their communities. Garifuna integrated as a separate ethnic group, promoting their culture and identity.

Garifuna Musical and Cultural Events

On March 25, 1990, an arsonist set ablaze the Happy Land Social Club, a Bronx nightclub. Of the 87 people who died, 59 were Honduran, and 70 percent of the deceased were Garifuna (Li 2010; Garcia 2014). The television news stations broadcast details about the fire over several days, and the story attracted national media coverage. One of the unfortunate consequences of the tragedy was the city's crackdown on illegal clubs, which meant that punta rock bands had no place to perform, and the people had no place to socialize. However, after a while, the nightlife picked up again.

Although the Happy Land fire temporarily hindered Garifuna socializing, it soon resumed.[3] Despite new building regulations, nightlife continued at rented locations as well as in basements (Blumenthal 1990). In addition, formal gatherings became more frequent after the Happy Land fire incident, and Garifuna were granted permission to hold activities at several prominent venues, including schools and colleges. Guatemalan Garifuna Carlos Gotay, cohost of the *Lumalali* radio program, established Garifuna International Promotions (GIP) to uplift the culture through the performing arts, with the goal of promoting Garifuna culture outside the community. A GIP event held in August 1992 at the Red-Carpet Theatre featured punta musicians Marcony Star, Gadu Nunez, Victor Arzu, Tulio Laboriel, Garifuna Kids, Garifuna Power (Guatemala), and Mighty K from Belize; the folk dance group Hamalali Wayunagu (Voices of Our Ancestors) also performed. The BronxNet cable channel telecast some GIP events on the *Centro America Show* established by Garifuna Murphy Valentine. One Thanksgiving, GIP featured Garifuna musicians Chico Ramos, Thomy A, Marcony Star, Fuerza Brava, and Kaligar Band at a holiday celebration at the Yaucana Social Club in the Bronx. An organization called Garifuna Enterprises Entertainment held its first Thanksgiving dance at Parkside Plaza in the Bronx. It was a subsidiary of Garifuna Enterprises, Inc., registered in 1998 by Hector Vera, Jorge Marin, Benny Solano, and Raymond Martinez to create microbusinesses to sell goods and services to Garifuna (*Garinagu Quarterly* 1996).

Honduran Garifuna Murphy Zenon Valentine was part of the growth in the ethnic group's local media presence during this period. In 1993 he founded the *Centro America Show*, a local cable TV program he cohosted with Garifuna community leader and choreographer Luz Solis. Valentine had previously been involved with another Latino show on cable, *Abriendo Brecha*. The *Centro America Show* informed the Garifuna and the general public about Garifuna cultural and political events in the United States and abroad (Garinet 2003; J. Ávila 2017b). When it started, many older Garifuna were excited to see a Garifuna hosting a television show and conducting interviews. They saw this as evidence of the group's advancement from its humble beginnings in Honduras, where it had low visibility and was marginalized. Garifuna folkloric dance presentations and punta and parranda music were also popular elements on the show, which featured both local artists and those from Central America (*Garinagu Quarterly* 1996).[4]

During this period in their community, the celebration of Garifuna Settlement Day, November 19, gave rise to a series of events. Although this holiday had been celebrated in the past by the Carib American Association, it was different in the 1990s. Its theme in 1995 was *Wabunagua luagudu buhabunu wayunagu waba* (We are building on the foundations built by our ancestors for us). As part of the celebration, the Thomas Vincent Ramos memorial service was held at a United Methodist church in the Bronx, and the Garifuna cultural night and selection of the Garifuna queen were held in the auditorium of Our Lady of Good Counsel Church in Brooklyn—the Roman Catholic church where the annual Garifuna Thanksgiving mass was also held. Garifuna dressed in traditional attire, and folk dances, punta music, and traditional food were part of the festivities. The concluding event, coronation of the Garifuna queen at the Marc Ballroom in New York, featured the Sound City Band from Dangriga, with punta rock stars Chico Ramos, Mohobub Flores, and Marian Martin (*Garinagu Quarterly* 1996). Many of the artists from the 1995 Settlement Day celebration participated in the First Garifuna World Music Awards in June 1998. The community came together for this event held at Hostos Community College in the Bronx and organized by Honduran Garifuna José F. Ávila. It was well attended by Honduran, Guatemalan, and Belizean Garifuna who gathered to enjoy performances by artists from their respective countries. These types of events laid the foundation for Garifuna-American Heritage Month, which began in the next century.

Interest in Garifuna culture also grew as a result of presentations at schools and universities, such as the December 1996 performance by the folk dance groups Wanichigu (Our Pride) and Illagulei (Roots) at City College of New York and the presentation by Stephen Garcia's group Emmausu [sic] at the State University of New York at Cortland (*Garinagu Quarterly* 1996). Another event featuring Garifuna culture took place at

Charles Drew Intermediate School 148 in the Bronx in June 1994. Two Garifuna folk dance groups—Luz Solis's Hamalali Wayunagu (Voices of Our Ancestors) and Pablo Gomez's Iseri Imenigi—were the main performers. In addition to punta and parranda, several other dances were included in the program: *wanaragua*, a warrior dance originating in St. Vincent; *sambai*, a dance by men working on plantations; *gunchai*, a French-influenced dance; *chumba*, a women's dance reflecting housework; and *culliou*, a couple's dance.[5] Luz Solis's Garifuna Heritage Center for the Arts and Culture held another event in May 1999 at Richard Green Middle School in the Bronx. This event, titled Garifuna Expo '99, featured segments on Garifuna spirituality, art, music, history, and language and performances by musical groups and folk dance companies.[6] Through drama, music, song, and dance, the general public as well as Garifuna youth learned about the culture. These types of activities held by Garifuna organizations continued in their community the following century, upholding their culture.

Celebrating, Promoting, and Recognizing Garifuna Culture in the New Century

Hometown association events, Garifuna soccer club tournaments, and Garifuna Catholic association events continued in both Brooklyn and the Bronx. In Brooklyn, the Garifuna Settlement Day mass and memorial celebration for Thomas Vincent Ramos continued from the previous century, recognizing Ramos's many contributions to the Garifuna community in Central America and his influence in starting the first Garifuna organization. Although the locations and organizers of these events changed, they continued to be part of the community (T. Colon 2010a).[7] For instance, in November 1995 the annual Thanksgiving mass was held at Our Lady of Good Counsel Church in Brooklyn, with guest priest Father Calixto Cayetano (*Garinagu Quarterly* 1996). In November 2013, the event was advertised as the Garifuna Settlement Day cultural mass and was held at Our Lady of Mercy Church in Brooklyn, led by guest priest Father Lawrence Nicasio from Central America.[8] The Garifuna Settlement Day Committee organized the 2013 memorial for Thomas Vincent Ramos at Believers Mennonite Garifuna Ministries in Brooklyn, whereas in 1996 it was held at Intermediate School 139 in the Bronx.[9] The previous year it was also held in the Bronx at the United Methodist church.

A noteworthy event in April 2007 was the Garifuna American Heritage Foundation United (GAHFU) forum in New York. GAHFU, based in Los Angeles, had established a strong presence on the West Coast, like the Garifuna Coalition USA in New York. During this period, differences between Garifuna organizations based on their Central American regional communities and nationality were common, at times causing divisions. GAHFU's founders, Guatemalan Garifuna Cheryl Noralez and her husband Rony Figueroa, sponsored the community forum in the Bronx to foster unity within the ethnic group. The event, held at the Charles R. Drew Public School auditorium, brought Belizean, Guatemalan, and Honduran Garifuna musicians together to discuss the challenges they faced in recording, promoting, and distributing Garifuna music. Dr. Oliver N. Greene presented his study of the Garifuna wanaragua dance, and he compared traditional dance forms among the Garifuna with similar choreography in the Caribbean.[10] Despite some differences, Garifuna cultural practices also show similarities with certain Caribbean groups. For instance, wanaragua, also known as *jankunu* in many English Caribbean islands, is associated with war in Garifuna tradition. Wanaragua involves masked men dressed as women in colorful costumes dancing to drumbeats to evade British invaders. During performances, dancers step inside a circle or semicircle as two drummers lead them. A chorus singing in the background accompanies the dancers and drummers. Dancers respond to the beating drum *garawoun* through their moves. Calls and responses in the Garifuna language and the occasional sound of the conch shell *wadabágei* can be heard. Jamaicans and other British-based Caribbean immigrants are able to see parallels with the Garifuna dance tradition presented at Caribbean events. Though similar, the Garifuna dance presentation has different meanings and purposes in Caribbean communities (Green 2005). Green's presentation was followed by cultural dance and musical performances and a roundtable discussion of the future of Garifuna music.[11]

Garifuna cultural events in the new century were more extravagant, reflecting growing social mobility within the ethnic group. The first annual Garifuna Heritage Awards and Cultural Night was held on March 13, 2010, at the Hostos College Center for the Arts and Culture in the Bronx. Performances and awards entertained the audience at this well-attended event spearheaded by members of the Garifuna Coalition USA. Among the performers were the Chief Joseph Chatoyer Garifuna Folkloric Ballet of New York; Hamalali Wayunagu Garifuna Dance Company; Paula Castillo; and James Lovell. Prominent Garifuna throughout the diaspora received awards, including Pablo Roberto Mejia, community leader in Livingston, Guatemala; Crisanto Armando Melendez, director of the National Garifuna Folkloric Ballet of Honduras; Kensy Sambola, community leader in the Garifuna community of Orinoco, Nicaragua; David Williams and David Augustine Glasglow from the Garifuna Heritage Foundation of St. Vincent and the Grenadines; and Blanca Arzu, a member of the Garifuna Coalition USA (T. Colon 2010b).

Another event held the same year was New Horizon Investment Club's third Garifuna Food Expo at St. Martin of Tours Church in the Bronx. Established in 2001, New Horizon Investment Club attempted to empower the Garifuna economically. The club hoped to teach Garifuna about investing in the stock market and encourage them to pool their resources to reap financial gains. Traditional Garifuna foods such as cassava bread (*ereba*), a fermented drink (*hiyu*), ground plantains with coconut milk and fish (*hudut*), coconut bread (*bounu*), and green plantain stew (*darasa*) were available for purchase. For entertainment, the rap group Black Steelz performed, as did the Hamalali Wayunagu Garifuna Dance Company (T. Colon 2010g). In May, New Horizon's Blue and Silver First Decade Gala was held at Eastwood Manor Caterers in the Bronx to officially celebrate the organization's tenth anniversary. At the upscale venue, Garifuna entrepreneurship was recognized, with Casabe O'Big Mama (a cassava bread company) cited as an example. Although Garifuna food was not part of the menu, the entertainment featured punta music, in addition to rhythm and blues, reggae, salsa, and calypso (Garcia 2014). New Horizon's affiliate the Garifuna Coalition USA held its formal Yellow, White and Black Gunchei Fund-Raising Gala at the same location in November, with non-Garifuna in attendance as well. Choreographer Mariano Martinez's J Dove Productions Dance Company performed. Teofilo Colon, a Garifuna journalist and filmmaker who manages the *Being Garifuna* online archive, was recognized for his social media contributions.

José F. Ávila, who led the New Horizon Investment Club and the Garifuna Coalition USA, engaged in promoting Garifuna culture and arts by forming a new organization, Garifuna Afro-Latino Entertainment, LLC (GALENT), which hosted annual Garifuna artist tributes and music awards.[12] One of the company's objectives is to broaden the audience for Garifuna music, which potentially can bring more people to Garifuna musical events. In 2015 GALENT hosted a musical tribute to Garifuna musician Aurelio Martinez, and in 2017 it presented Mahogany Beatz, a hip-hop and R&B producer of Garifuna descent, with a lifetime achievement award.

An important event focused on Garifuna female youth continued from the 1990s. Honduran Garifuna Mirtha Colón's Casa Yurumein/Hondurans Against AIDS organization took over hosting the annual Miss Garifuna pageant, which had previously been sponsored by Belizean Garifuna organizers. More details about the organization are presented in Chapter 6. Young Garifuna women undergo weeks of cultural training before participating in the competition. In addition, Casa Yurumein acknowledges women's role in cultural preservation and community service with the annual Barauda Award ceremony. Barauda was the name of the wife of Joseph Chatoyer, who defended the Garifuna against the British on St. Vincent. As at other Garifuna cultural events, traditional folk dance groups and musicians perform, highlighting the ethnic group identity at an event that is also attended by non-Garifuna guests and public officials (Colón 2014, 2015; Walker and Reyes 2017).

Folkloric Dance Groups

Folkloric dance groups are common in Garifuna communities. They complement Garifuna music as part of the ethnic group's identity. In New York City, these dance groups uphold Garifuna identity, performing music, dance, and drama presentations. They hold multifaceted roles educating the Garifuna youth and the general audience about the culture. Folkloric dance groups demonstrate Garifuna integration in their community, presenting their separate cultural identity, with performances at various social and civic events in the city.

Garifuna folkloric dance groups are contracted to participate at local and international cultural festivals and events sponsored by public officials throughout New York City. They perform at Kwanzaa, Hispanic Heritage Month, Black History Month, and Garifuna Heritage Month celebrations and cultural events. Garifuna folkloric dance groups serve as ambassadors of the culture to their communities and to New York City public officials. The events present opportunities for Garifuna, Blacks, and Latinos to view their cultural similarities and differences. Garifuna folkloric dance companies have performed at New York Public Library's Schomburg Research Center, Fordham University, City University of New York (CUNY) Medgar Evers College in Brooklyn (for African American and Caribbean events), and City University of New York Hostos Community College in the Bronx (for Latino events). Since the 1990s, Garifuna folkloric dance groups have also performed at the Lincoln Center summer outdoor festivals before a more diverse audience.

A long-established institution mentioned earlier in the chapter is the Garifuna Heritage Center for the Arts and Culture, home to Hamalali Wayunagu Garifuna Folkloric and Modern Dance Company. It was founded in 1992 by Honduran Garifuna Luz Solis, a professionally trained choreographer and graduate of Bard College's dance and drama program. Solis was inspired by several dance teachers and by her friend Manuela Sabio of the Wanichigu dance group to establish her own dance company. Like Sabio, Solis's goal is to ensure that Garifuna maintain their heritage.[13] I attended an event where Solis was honored for her contribution to the community which goes beyond supporting Garifuna arts. At the event held in the Bronx at the Hostos Community College Repertory Theatre, it was expressed that the Garifuna music is part of the Bronx, like "kora" music from Gambia and "parranda" from Puerto Rico.[14] Solis is also involved in discussions of both local and Central American Garifuna social and political issues. As mentioned previously, in the past Solis collaborated as a cohost of the *Centro America Show* at the Bronx local cable network, and also hosted other programs. The event program listed the mission of her organization, Garifuna Heritage Center for the Arts and Culture, as being "to preserve the Garifuna Culture through dance, music, singing, drama, poetry, and other art forms" (March 23, 2019). At a local school in the Bronx on a Saturday afternoon it is common to see Garifuna, Latino, and Black youth engaged in drumming, dance, and other cultural activities. The heritage center and the dance company continue to be recognized as the longest-running Garifuna dance troupe in New York City. However, the dance company recently rebranded its name to Wabafu Garifuna Dance Theater, co-led by Luz F. Solis's daughter, Catherine Solis-Rey.

Another popular folkloric dance group, Illagulei (Roots) Garifuna Cultural Performance Arts, Inc., was officially founded in 1994 and registered in 1997. Its goal is to preserve and promote Garifuna culture and ensure the youth born in the United States know their roots. Early on the group held its auditions at local schools in both the Bronx and Brooklyn. It performed together with Wanichugu, as in their combined performance December 1995 at City College of New York Aaron Davis Hall, and with other Garifuna folkloric and music groups. In addition, Illagulei performs at different Garifuna community events such as the November 19th celebration, church-affiliated presentations, and other invitational events. Illagulei was led by Garifuna Lena Dorina Castillo and cofounders James Lovell and Eleanor Bullock. Its leaders were all born in Belize and have dedicated many years to teaching youth music, dance, language, and different aspects of the culture. They are also involved with different Garifuna groups in the city that support issues pertinent to the community advancement in New York as well as in Central America. Like Solis, Bullock used her formal training—she graduated from Syracuse University's visual performing arts program—and served as the group's choreographer (Folkfest 2013; Skelly 2013).

On a cold, snowy evening in January 2015, many of us Garifuna gathered at Casa Yurumein, where the topic of the event was Garifuna culture. Garifuna choreographer Crisanto Armando Melendez, visiting from Honduras, gave a presentation about the history of choreographed dance and music and the present status of Garifuna culture, with a focus on sustaining the culture and providing proper guidance for youth. Melendez talked about learning from elders and mentioned that some Garifuna songs, dances, and instruments had originated in Africa. He also acknowledged the UN's Decennial of Afro-descendants, authorized in 2014 to support those of African heritage. This caused debate among the Garifuna community over the use of *Afro-* to describe themselves in both New York City and Central America. Further details are presented on this subject later in the chapter. Melendez popularized and modernized the Garifuna dance form and promoted the group's cultural identity. He trained many Garifuna dancers and established Garifuna folk dance as an art form, designing much of the choreography. In 1976 Melendez's dance company (which had been founded as a social network in the early 1960s) was transformed into the Ballet Folklórico Nacional Garífuna (National Garifuna Folkloric Ballet) and acquired support from the Honduran secretary of culture, tourism, and information. Melendez toured throughout Honduras and internationally, gaining recognition and acceptance by promoting Garifuna culture.

Many dancers trained by Melendez immigrated to New York City and established their own dance companies. Those include the Budari Dance Company in New York City, formally established in 2011, as well as the Chief Joseph Chatoyer Garifuna Folkloric Ballet of New York, founded by Felix Gamboa (J. Ávila 2017a). Like other folkloric dance group leaders, Gamboa trained under Crisanto Melendez in Honduras. After the Wanichugu Dance Company he was part of ended, Gamboa formed the Nuwani Dance Company, which evolved into the group named "Bodoma and Budari Garifuna Cultural Group," then the present Chief Joseph Chatoyer dance ensemble. Chief Joseph Chatoyer performs at various public and civic events in the city and abroad, from hosting its own theatrical musical play at Symphony Space on Broadway to performing at annual Garifuna events in Belize and St. Vincent.

A current popular Garifuna folkloric group which was part of this cohort promoting and educating the young about the culture is the Bodoma Garifuna Cultural Band, founded in 2001 by Carlos Norales, nicknamed "Bodoma." Many of the group's performers are U.S.-born Garifuna learning and engaging in the culture through the arts (Lopez 2006; M. Colón 2014).[15] The dance company presents theatrical performances, call-and-response choral singing, group dancing, solo performances, and drama. The dancers in the company, for the most part, consist of young Garifuna men and women from Honduras, Guatemala, and Belize.

In New York City, Garifuna folkloric dance companies bring together the ethnic group. Not only do the Garifuna folkloric dance performances entertain audiences, but they also help sustain the history and the culture of Garifuna through song, dance, and drama. As Garifuna have increased their political visibility through New York City, with local and state governments formally recognizing them, the dance companies usually are the main performers promoting the culture at local and state-sponsored gatherings.

Soccer Organizations

In New York City, Garifuna soccer clubs continued to be significant during this period. Their soccer clubs, like their folkloric dance groups, bring Garifuna together in reflecting part of their identity. Although established New York City Puerto Ricans and Dominicans hold minimal interest in soccer, Garifuna soccer clubs in the city historically facilitate their community's integration with other incoming immigrant populations.

Garifuna in New York City in the 1990s continued congregating in several parks in the spring and summer for soccer games. The Garifuna soccer league, its players, and teams historically fluctuated in its duration. Garifuna leagues in the past decade have lasted on average an estimated three to four years before a new one emerges, with teams and players at times crossing over to the new soccer league and teams. In the Bronx, although some recreation facilities such as St. Mary's Park, Crotona Park, and Rainey Park traditionally facilitate outdoor Garifuna meeting grounds and small soccer scrimmages, Van Cortlandt and now Ferry Point Parks are established locations for the soccer leagues (Garcia 2014). Since the 1970s, Garifuna in Brooklyn congregate primarily in one location—Linden Park, Brooklyn—where they hold their soccer league games. Several soccer leagues led by Garifuna have progressed since Victor Fernandez established his Garifuna league that played in Linden Park in the 1950s. During the 1980s and 1990s, Honduran Garifuna Mariano Gutierrez was actively engaged in the Garifuna leagues that played in Linden Park. His team was part of the league. Garifuna soccer leagues also congregated for soccer games in other New York City parks during the 1980s and 1990s.

Honduran Garifuna Miguel Guity, an active member of the soccer league, led his teams in tournaments at Van Cortlandt Park in the Bronx and Fort Washington Park in Manhattan during the 1980s and 1990s.[16] During this period, Garifuna assembled in the Bronx, Manhattan, and Brooklyn to participate in and watch soccer games.[17]

At the turn of this century, several new Garifuna soccer clubs developed. Most recently, in 2003, Garifuna established a soccer league in the Bronx. However, it spanned only a short time, ending in 2006. In 2005, the Honduras Unidos Soccer League was established; and, in 2009, the New York Honduran Soccer League was established. Both are described as sustaining longevity in comparison to other leagues in the Bronx (Li 2009). "Honduras" in the league's title signifies that the ethnic population is from this country and is the majority of individuals associated with the league. However, there are Garifuna from other Central American countries, including Africans and Caribbeans, affiliated with the league as players. I learned that two Garifuna-based leagues existed in Brooklyn, with Garifuna (primarily from Belize) playing in the Caribbean leagues in Linden Park.

Garifuna Barbara Lopez established the Honduras Unidos League, a soccer entity, in 2005. Hondurans, Jamaicans, and people from other Latin American countries make up the players. They play from April to October. As of 2014, the league consists of eleven teams with each having an estimated twenty players. The league holds its games on the weekend afternoons at Ferry Point Park in the Bronx. At the end of the league year, an award ceremony and recognition are held for the players and participants. Four years later, another larger Garifuna soccer league developed sharing the playing grounds at Ferry Point Park with the Honduras Unidos League (Garcia 2014; T. Colon 2014b; Wall 2012a).

In 2009, Honduran Garifuna Xiomara Esmeralda Arriola founded the New York Honduran Soccer League, which was approximately 77 to 80 percent Honduran. Some of the other players were from Africa, the Caribbean, and Central America (Chukwudi 2014). The league functioned from April to November. This league consisted of two divisions, with youths and adults comprising eighteen teams. There are twenty players on each team with games held on weekends at the Bronx Ferry Point Park. Many teams bear the names of Honduran Garifuna communities; however, there is the "Communication" team of Guatemala and the Belize Honduras team, representing Garifuna from both countries (T. Colon 2014d). At the end of the year, an awards ceremony is also held recognizing the participants and winners.

Interestingly, Arriola has connected with local public officials in support of the soccer league's playing grounds. The same year Arriola founded the league, she lobbied the New York City parks department to build a soccer field at Crotona Park in the Bronx. The Bronx borough president Rubén Díaz Jr. appointed Arriola to Community Board 3 that includes the Crotona Park East community. Arriola made several presentations and met with members of the parks department regarding the proposed soccer field and its specific turf needs. In addition, soccer players came to the board meetings and the board members were led on a fact-gathering visit to Crotona Park. Unfortunately, after construction of the new park, the league was unable to use the facilities (Wall 2012a; Chukwudi 2014).

The Garifuna also participate individually and collectively as a team in other non-Garifuna leagues sponsored by Caribbean and Latino organizations. For instance, in Brooklyn there is the Liga Hondurena de Futbol, Honduras-Lempira Football League, which holds its games in Linden Park. Garifuna and English-speaking Caribbean teams are part of this league (T. Colon 2010f). Adjacent to the Bronx in Manhattan, a non-Garifuna Honduran, Elvis Garcia Callejas, a migration counselor for Catholic Charities, founded La Union, another soccer league, in 2014. This league sustains several youths who migrated undocumented from Central America to the United States. Garifuna are among the many players. There were more than fifty youths from Central America in the league that played in the Macombs Dam Park near Yankee Stadium in the Bronx. Garifuna made up a substantial number of the players in the league. The league received support from the soccer sports club, South Bronx United, which aids in various social programs the youth participate in (Associated Press 2017).

Traditionally, Garifuna family and friends support the players as fans, and engage with and socialize with others at weekend soccer games. Many of the fans are part of various Garifuna and non-Garifuna organizations in the city, thus providing the possibilities for networking and exchanging information for employment or social needs. Growing immigrant groups—such as Caribbeans, West Africans, and Central Americans in the Bronx, Brooklyn, and Manhattan—exchange with Garifuna during these outdoor sporting events. In these interactions Garifuna are identified with the game of soccer, representing their country. Soccer leagues continue to be important in the Garifuna community, facilitating their unification and providing a healthy activity for youth and young adults.

Garifuna Culture and the Central American Parade

Every year in September city residents and visitors view Garifuna culture during their annual parade and festival. Garifuna organizations citywide participate, some march representing their groups, and others perform. This takes place as vendors sell foods, clothing, crafts, and other items. Headlining the event, their folkloric dance groups and music bands perform before the diverse attendees, including non-Garifuna.

This annual event started with an organization seeking to promote Garifuna and Central American culture. The Honduran Parade Committee, Inc. (incorporated in New York as a domestic not-for-profit on June 18, 1997) originated in 1996 as the Central American Independence Parade and Festival, Inc., led by Honduran Garifuna Francisco Yoba Ruiz. The parade and festival are held on the second Sunday of September in observance of Central American independence. Several Garifuna collaborated on this project and obtained support from the Puerto Rican community and elected officials. Honduran Garifuna Pablo Gomez told me that he began the parade to promote Central American culture and to recognize its contribution to New York City. After noticing that Dominicans and Puerto Ricans had their own parades, Gomez was motivated to start one for the Garifuna. Initial meetings were held in Vamos a La Peña del Bronx, a Puerto Rican–based community center directed by Victor Toro, who supported the idea of a parade and allowed various Garifuna organizations to meet and hold their activities there (Johnson 2007).[18] City councilman Federico Perez, who represented the Mott Haven, Crotona, and Hunts Point sections of the Bronx in 1997, signed the necessary documents to initiate the annual event. With support from the Puerto Rican community and Latino politicians such as Perez and Bronx borough president Fernando Ferrer, the parade gained momentum. The parade route changed several times, initially starting at 149th Street and Prospect Avenue and ending at St. Mary's Park in the Bronx. City councilman Jose Rivera (1987–2000), who represented the Fifteenth District (which includes Crotona Park), convinced Gomez to change the parade route; it now starts at Southern Boulevard and Boston Road and culminates at Crotona Park, where the festival is held. Gomez's Iseri Imenigi Garifuna Cultural Dance Group, in existence since the 1990s, participated in the parade alongside other prominent Garifuna organizations. Although Garifuna are in the majority at the parade, Central Americans, Mestizos, Latinos (e.g., Puerto Ricans, Dominicans), African Americans, West Indians, and other ethnic groups attend, taking particular interest in the musical performances. Traditional Central American and Garifuna cuisine, music, apparel, artisanal handiwork, ornaments, and other items are sold at the concession stands (Gill and Valentine 2018; T. Colon 2014a). The parade organization evolved changing its title and gaining support of public officials in the city. This change occurred the new century. The annual Garifuna-led parade in the Bronx was now promoted as the Central American Independence Parade and Festival. On November 8, 2002, Pablo Gomez filed an amendment changing the name from the Honduran Parade Committee to reflect the inclusion of Garifuna from other parts of Central America. Gomez eventually took a leave of absence due to health issues, and committee member Evelyn Chamorro Arauz was designated leader of the parade in 2008. New articles of incorporation were filed on June 28, 2012, registering the organization as the Honduran and Central American Bronx Day Parade, Inc. Over the past years and up to the present, the annual parade has provided a high-profile opportunity for the New York City Garifuna community to emphasize its significance to the community as a whole. In addition to the parade and festival commemorating the countries in Central America gaining their independence from Spain, they also function as an annual Garifuna gathering. The Central American community participates with dignitaries from their respective countries and representatives from their consulate offices in New York. The parade exposes the general non-Garifuna community to culinary traditions, diverse music genres, and the culture of Garifuna and Central Americans. Additionally, it broadens Garifuna visibility in the city with the presence of local elected officials seeking to encourage the community's civic engagement (T. Colon 2014a; Gill and Valentine 2018).[19]

Afro-Latino, Indigenous, Black Identity

Music and dance in the festival parade, as well as sports featured in this chapter, reflect parts of Garifuna identity. Their organizations facilitated these events and many were also involved in the new century discussing their ethnic classification and origins. Garifuna identity and origin were popular topics at a 2013 meeting hosted by the United Garifuna Association (UGA) that I attended. Garifuna community members, organizers, and pastors attended the event and exchanged different views during the question-and-answer segment. There, the Garifuna Amerindian heritage was challenged, and Belizean Garifuna Dr. Theodore Aranda spoke about Garifuna origins in the Americas before Columbus. Aranda is a well-known political figure in Belize and was a candidate for prime minister. In his presentation he dismissed the common shipwreck story of the Garifuna's arrival in Honduras. Aranda made reference to the pre-1600s Garifuna presence, such as Mali ruler Abu Bakari's twelfth-century voyage to the Americas and the Olmec heads in Mexico presented in Ivan Van Sertima's book. Nancie Gonzalez, one of the pioneering Garifuna anthropologists who conducted extensive investigations of the ethnic group, joined the social media discussion to defend her findings of a dual African and Amerindian heritage. She provided listings of her research and emphasized the extensive Amerindian heritage as a significant part of the culture. Other discussions in Garifuna meetings and their social media networks focused on whether to reject or adopt the terms *Afro-Indigenous* and *Afro-Latino* to describe them.

Several Garifuna leaders and scholars addressed their viewpoints on this issue of their ethnic classification. Garifuna scholar Doris Garcia (2013) analyzed discussions among Garifuna to either identify the community as solely Garifuna or accept the title Garifuna American. This she presents as attempts by the Garifuna Coalition USA to redefine Garifuna identity. The Garifuna Coalition USA popularized using the "Garifuna American" term, which embraced other segments of the ethnic group. Garifuna leaders I communicate with often express that there are several second- and third-generation Garifuna who have never been to their family's homeland in Central America, don't speak the language, or are isolated from the community. For some, "Garifuna American" recognizes this population segment. In addition, the term is also used to connect Garifuna into the broader American society (Garcia 2013). Beginning in 2008, Garifuna Coalition USA has submitted proposals to local New York officials to recognize "Garifuna American" culture and contributions to society. Several organizations followed their lead, including "Garifuna American" in their title, and at public events held with local officials the term was commonly used. For example, in New York City the Garifuna American Law Enforcement Association and the Garifuna American Veterans Association embraced the title. During a recent conversation with José F. Ávila, I asked him about the concern some Garifuna I spoke with expressed about being omitted in his use of "Afro-Latino" to describe the ethnic group. His most recent book, *Pan-Garifuna Afro-Latino Power of Pride*, includes the term. Concerns were that both the Garifuna descendants from St. Vincent, now a part of the New York City community, and Belizean Garifuna are English speakers with Caribbean cultures different from Latinos'. His response was similar to the point he made in his book that an Afro-Latino(a) is anyone of African descent born in or whose parents or descendants are from Latin America and the Caribbean. In his book he also mentions that Afro-Latinos are from countries speaking romance languages such as French, Spanish, and Portuguese and include different ethnic groups (J. Ávila 2021, 369).[20]

In his study of the U.S. 2010 and Honduras 2013 census campaigns, López Oro (2016b) also addresses differences within the Garifuna community regarding their identification. Many Garifuna reject all inclusive terms such as "Afro-Latino" or "Afro-Honduran" out of concern about the loss of their culture and identity. Garifuna see themselves as different from other Black Latinos and other Black Hondurans. Many Garifuna reject the prefix "Afro," expressing that they were never slaves, differentiating themselves from other Blacks. In 2014 the UN General Assembly authorized a ten-year period of support for people of African descent, and there were concerns that some Garifuna groups were trying to capitalize on this declaration. For instance, there were accusations that Honduran Garifuna leader Celeo Casildo Alvarez, leader of the Central American Black Organization (CABO) and Organización de Desarrollo Étnico Comunitario (Organization for Ethnic Community Development, ODECO), was advocating use of the terms Afro-descendants and Afro-Hondurans. Casildo, who is now deceased, attended the 2001 World Conference against Racism in Durban, South Africa, and embraced the African heritage of the Garifuna, connecting the ethnic group with the Black diaspora. This, some believe, enabled Casildo to obtain increased financial support for his organization and international notoriety. He also successfully lobbied the Honduran government to pass antidiscrimination legislation and to include Afro-Hondurans in the 2013 census. Many Garifuna leaders were upset about being classified as Afro-Honduran in the census, which ignored their ethnic identity and included them with the country's other Black populations. This challenged OFRANEH land claims filed against the Honduran government, stating that Garifuna indigenous heritage was being threatened because of the government's long-standing denial of Garifuna Amerindian roots. The result was that several Garifuna activists and political leaders filed a lawsuit against the Honduran government, rejecting the use of "Afro-Honduran" of "Afro-descendant" in the 2013 census (López Oro 2016b, 73). Overall, Garifuna ethnic classification is an ongoing debate in their communities. In New York City, the FUH organization in the 1970s also discussed topics regarding Garifuna ethnic classification as either African, Black or Indigenous. Other than within their ethnic group, Garifuna racial and ethnic identity also continues to attract scholarly research on the topic. As such discussions continue on Garifuna origins and ethnic classification, soccer clubs, folkloric dance groups, and organizations' cultural events persevere in sustaining their identity and visibility.

Conclusion

In this chapter it is learned that Garifuna origins and ethnic classification are the subjects of ongoing debate in their communities. In addition, Garifuna organizations were listed as important in sustaining their unique culture and identity in New York City. After the Bronx Happy Land Social Cub nightclub fire, Garifuna organizations grew. Their music and cultural events increased, being held at community events and in colleges and schools. Other outcomes from the visibility Garifuna gained from the fire incident was the development of print outlets, a local radio program, and cable TV media for their community. In addition, they established an annual parade featuring their culture and music. Garifuna soccer clubs also continued and expanded during this period with various leagues. The next chapter presents Garifuna organizations managing their social issues, including becoming engaged politically in their community.

Chapter 6

Social Issues in New York City from the 1990s to the Present

Prospects for peace and averting a nuclear war were good worldwide entering the 1990s. The Cold War ended, and globalization of the economy was expected to increase opportunities for everyone. Among the high points in New York City were Nelson Mandela's visit in June 1990 and the end of apartheid in South Africa. The city elected its first Black mayor, David N. Dinkins (1990–93), and the Bronx had already elected its second minority borough president, Puerto Rican Fernando Ferrer (1987–2001).[1] In the neighborhood, many abandoned, boarded-up buildings were spray-painted with the letters "PDC"—People's Development Corporation, an organization that took over abandoned buildings and rehabilitated them. It was one of several grassroots community and local government organizations engaged in rebuilding devastated neighborhoods and supporting new housing developments (Waldman 2000; Museum of the City; Bronx Historical Society).[2] Though many residents continued to endure poor housing, some Garifuna families benefited from the rehab efforts and moved into improved units.

The new century ushered in changes. The South Bronx experienced an increase in white residents in the Mott Haven section, across the river from Manhattan (Jonnes 2002; Moss 2017). Yemeni-owned bodegas and Korean-owned supermarkets were among the signs of change in the community. The growing West African population in the Morrisania and Highbridge areas was manifest in their mosques, evangelical churches, butcher shops, shipping companies, restaurants, and mini markets. Puerto Rican

Latino dominance in politics was challenged by shifts in the city's demographics. Since the later part of the last century, Puerto Ricans constituted less than 50 percent of the Latino population in the city. The second-largest Latino immigrant population in New York City are the Dominicans, who challenged Puerto Rican political dominance with active political and electoral organization (Jones-Correa 1998).

This chapter shows how Garifuna organizations managed social issues in their communities from the 1990s to the present, addressing many issues challenging their community, and how they became civically engaged. The first chapter section, addressing issues in their community beginning in the 1990s, introduces the way Garifuna capitalized on both private and public support received after many died in one of New York City's worst fires. The next section focuses on the new century, showing a Garifuna organization leading the campaign for social services and calling for political engagement. This section illustrates how ties with a Latino leader prompted Garifuna participation, in addition to their organizations acquiring meeting spaces and discretionary and private funding support. The final chapter section features different Garifuna organizations active in local electoral politics. Details of their group's exchanges with public officials in recent election campaigns in New York City are presented, as are their different alliances with African American and Latino candidates and their organizations.

Organizations Addressing Social Issues in the 1990s

In the 1990s Garifuna organizations began attempting to address some of their community's needs. They sought a multipurpose center for social activities, education, and meetings; social and health services; English as a Second Language (ESL) and trades training; activities for youth; and services for undocumented immigrants, among other interests. Communication media to keep them abreast of their community activities and issues were also pursued. Their organizations also sought recognition of their culture and language, advocating its promotion and preservation.

Following the Happy Land Social Club fire, the Federation of Honduran Organizations of New York (Federación de Organizaciones Hondureña en Nueva York, or FEDHONY) was created. The City of New York fined the owner of the club and earmarked funds to build a Garifuna center, which were turned over to FEDHONY.[3] Other support came from the office of Mayor David Dinkins and the Catholic Archdiocese of New York. Honduran president Rafael Callejas's office also offered help toward purchasing land and building a Garifuna community and recreational center in the city. Non-Garifuna Honduran groups were also part of FEDHONY, which represented twenty organizations. Honduran Antonieta Maximo was president, Dionisia Amaya Bonilla (of MUGAMA) was one of the founders, and Mirtha Colón was a board member. Walter L. Krochmal, of Honduran heritage through his mestiza mother, was named executive director. The group provided community services, organized classes to teach English and computer skills, held reproductive health workshops for women, ran an entrepreneur training program, and supported the arts. During Hurricane Mitch in 1998, FEDHONY collected nonperishable items to distribute to the victims. The community center was never built, however, and FEDHONY was dissolved (Garcia 2014; England 1999; Li 2010; Dooley 1995).[4]

Another attempt to build a multipurpose community center followed when MUGAMA established the Garifuna House Committee. Its goals were to provide day care for children, an adult learning center, and several programs ranging from health education to economic development to cultural preservation. Although the organization was registered in 1999 as a nonprofit, the center never materialized (Li 2010; England 2006; Garcia 2014). Nevertheless, the Garifuna community holds a memorial on the anniversary of the Happy Land fire. Masses are held at St. Thomas Aquinas Roman Catholic Church, followed by a procession to the marble monument built to commemorate those who died.

After the tragedy, the Garifuna sought to capitalize on their greater visibility to benefit their community, and their leaders increased their contact with city agencies. In 1991 Mayor Dinkins signed the proclamation officially recognizing November 19 as Garifuna Day in New York City. This date corresponded with Garifuna Settlement Day, a national holiday in Belize. Also in 1991, Garifuna organizations advocated for New York City public schools to include the Garifuna language in districts with substantial Garifuna populations. The New York City Department of Education granted special Title VII funds to establish a bilingual education program for students of Garifuna heritage at PS 144 in Harlem. This effort, spearheaded by Felix Miranda, was approved in April 1999 and supported by City University of New York (CUNY) professor George Irish. Although the plans never fully materialized, the New York City Department of Education recognized Garifuna as a language of communication among students citywide (England 1999; John-Sandy 1997; T. Ávila 2017).

Local Garifuna media also developed during this period, as the ethnic group's notoriety after the fire disaster presented opportunities for networking. Murphy Zenon Valentine's *Centro America Show* on local

BronxNet cable TV, mentioned in the previous chapter, was part of the growth in the ethnic group's local media presence in this period. On the radio was the *Lumalali* ("Their Voice" in the Garifuna language) radio show, hosted and produced by Felix Miranda, was on WNWE 91.5 FM in New York. Miranda played Garifuna music, reported the news in the Garifuna language, and publicized Garifuna cultural and community events. Another Belizean Garifuna, Stephen Garcia, established *Garinagu Quarterly Magazine* in 1995, serving as its publisher and editor. Claudette Sacasa was the magazine's copublisher and coeditor, Gregorio Velez was the marketing director, Rejil Solis the director of finance, Antonieta Rochez the customer service director, and Victor Gutierrez the photographer. According to Rochez, although the magazine was short-lived, it circulated in Garifuna communities outside the city. During their existence, these media outlets served an important function, informing the Garifuna community about available resources as well as about upcoming social events.

Public Health Education, Youth Outreach, and Services for Undocumented Immigrants

Honduran Garifuna Mirtha Colón used her formal training as a social worker to support the Garifuna community, particularly in the area of public health. I first met Colón several years ago at Iglesia de San Juan Bautista (San Juan Bautista Mission) in the Bronx, the previous headquarters of her organization, Hondurans Against AIDS. Since our interview we have often crossed paths at Garifuna community events. Colón, who was a board member of FEDHONY, established Hondurans Against AIDS in 1992. Despite its name, the organization's activities and services are available to the entire Garifuna community in the city. This is true of several Garifuna organizations. Garifuna from Honduras are the majority population in the city, but their organizations serve Garifuna from other Central American countries as well the general community at large (Walker and Reyes 2017). Hondurans Against AIDS began providing HIV/AIDS education and support in both Central America and New York, targeting Garifuna. Since the 1980s, many Garifuna in both New York and Honduras died of AIDS, prompting Colón and others to address this public health issue. Eventually, Colón's organization evolved to support both community development and cultural awareness. It is affiliated with several other groups, including the Organization for Community Development (ODECO), based in La Ceiba, Honduras.

ODECO promotes the Garifuna community's cultural and political development and advocates against discrimination. ODECO, as opposed to OFRANEH, focuses on alliances with regional and international Black organizations and identifies Garifuna as Blacks to a greater extent than indigenous (Brondo 2006; Mark Anderson 2009).[5] Colón is also involved with Allianza Americas, the Central American Black Organization (CABO), and the Garifuna Coalition USA organization, both discussed in detail later in the chapter (López Oro 2016a; M. Colón 2015). During my visit to the Hondurans Against AIDS organization, I learned community concerns targeted by the organization included the AIDS crisis in the NYC Honduran communities and in their home country, the large undocumented NYC Honduran population, and the need to develop youth leadership programs organizing the young adults. A function of the organization, shared by Colón's colleague Tola Guerrero, is to assist in documentation, with goals leading to citizenship, and for this group to become politically active in the electoral process. In addition, the basis of the youth outreach efforts is to encourage them to become politically active. The AIDS crisis was expressed as contributing to the deterioration of many communities in Honduras and families in New York. The Hondurans Against AIDS organization confronted these challenges, sponsoring education awareness in NYC Honduran communities and in their country of origin.

Mirtha Colón and I also discussed the issue of race and that most Honduran Mestizos/Ladino distance themselves from associating with Garifuna. Colón expressed "that Garifuna as a minority struggle against political and economic injustices similar to other minority populations in both countries. Differences in race relations is a global phenomenon, and many Mestizos do not understand certain issues Garifuna address." Nevertheless, Colón agreed with Guerrero that there is evidence of improvement in relations. Colón sustains contact with local public officials, such as in New York State Assembly District 79, with an extensive Garifuna population. During the inauguration ceremony of former Bronx assemblyman Eric Stevenson (2011–14) I attended, Colón was an invited guest and was acknowledged before the audience as representing the Garifuna community. In 2014 when we met again, Colón mentioned the challenges in ensuring financial support for programs after her recent election as the president of the Central American Black Organization (CABO). Annual meetings of CABO occasionally are held in the Hondurans Against AIDS meeting place, "Casa Yurumein" in the Bronx. The organizations with representatives from Central American countries' Black population advocate for their unity and for tackling cultural, economic, and political concerns. Five years later, at another Garifuna community gathering I attended, Colón's

Hondurans Against AIDS organization partnered with other groups and local officials in addressing immigration concerns of the community. As a member of different organizations, Colón has been at the forefront advocating for Temporary Protection Status (TPS) and Deferred Action for Childhood Arrivals (DACA). During an interview she said, "We have requested DACA to achieve permanent residence for those who are here and are recipients of immigration programs" (Sierra 2021). Colón has long been involved with organizations such as Allianza Americas, advocating for immigrant rights and reforms.

In the current century Colón's Hondurans Against AIDS organization expanded, addressing other needs of the community. It adopted the name "Casa Yurumein" in 2009, tending to other community needs. Some of the many functions it assumed are collection for hurricane relief efforts in Honduras, offering Garifuna language classes, organizing youth agriculture projects in Honduran Garifuna communities, holding fundraisers (such as support for Garifuna land rights protest in Honduras), offering community food pantry services, running a COVID-19 vaccination campaign, and other activities. Its rented office/conference room space also served as a meeting venue for Garifuna and other groups to convene (Allen 2023; Castillo 2023).[6]

SHANY, ESL and Trades Training, Youth Activities, Local Media

After the Happy Land nightclub fire, many Garifuna sought to unify the community and better serve its needs. Another organization that grew out of the incident, and like Colón's organization referred to Honduras in its title, nevertheless serves the entire community. The Sociedad Hondureña Activa de Nueva York (Honduran Active Society of New York, or SHANY) was founded by Honduran Garifuna Cresencio Bulnes and registered in June 1994 in the Bronx. It provides multiple services to New York Garifuna as well as Blacks and Latinos in the community. Cresencio migrated early to the city and is a longtime member and listed among the officers and leadership of New York City SEIU 32J union. On his organization's storefront sign, an image of the Honduran flag appears, with SHANY's emblem on the opposite side, and several other mini flags from various countries. SHANY offers educational and cultural programs for youth and adults. In addition, SHANY obtains donations from local churches and hospitals and ships medical supplies (e.g., wheelchairs, crutches) to Honduras (SHANY 2021).[7] Many in the community at large including Garifuna benefit from the certification programs and classes offered at SHANY: English as a Second

Language classes; trades—building maintenance, electricity, plumbing, carpentry—and other certification courses (SHANY). During natural disasters in Central America SHANY actively engages in leading emergency support services, collecting and sending goods abroad.

Like Mirtha Colón, Bulnes corresponds with several local political officials. He is a longtime supporter of Rubén Díaz Sr., who served as a member of the New York State Senate from the 32nd District from 2003 to 2017, then joined the city council. Díaz's office has corresponded with Bulnes in planning events to gather Garifuna organizations and support the community. At SHANY graduation ceremonies for students completing maintenance courses, noted public officials and non-Garifuna community organizations are among the guests recognizing the organization's contribution. State Senator Gustavo Rivera; Assemblyman Victor M. Pichardo; New York City Council members Rubén Díaz Sr., María del Carmen Arroyo, and Fernando Cabrera; and Congressman Charles Rangel are among officials who have participated in SHANY's graduation ceremonies. At SHANY graduation ceremonies, Bulnes acknowledged Fernando Cabrera as a key supporter in sponsoring the events (Aparicio 2014, 2015). Fernando Cabrera, who has connections with other Garifuna organizations, recognized SHANY's contributions to the community. Cabrera credits Bulnes's leadership in getting the community together to provide supplies, canned goods, clothing, and other needs after the 2020 hurricanes (Eta and Iota) in Central America.

SHANY has also engaged in other humanitarian relief services in Central America, including food assistance support during the COVID-19 pandemic. In 2014 I took part in a SHANY internet radio program, on which local community issues as well as Honduran politics are common themes discussed. Bulnes invited me to share my travel experiences and observations in several Garifuna communities I visited. Julian Rochez, founder of *Puntalogy Internet Radio Show*, interviewed me. Rochez's *Puntalogy* show features primarily the entertainment segment of the radio station, presenting an array of Garifuna music (punta, parranda, etc.) to the public. The office is always active, with a diverse population (including non-Garifuna) from the community participating in its many services. Support of youth activities is also a goal, including team sports such as a young women's soccer team. SHANY also makes its conference room available for meetings of Garifuna hometown associations and other groups, and for fundraising events.

Garifuna Umbrella Associations, Consolidating to Address Social Needs

After FEDHONY's decline, Garifuna continued their efforts to establish umbrella organizations. They perceived that by uniting they would be more successful in supporting the rights of Garifuna immigrants, encouraging their civic participation, and advancing the Garifuna community's cultural, economic, and social status in the city. Evangelical Christian Garifuna sought to do the same in promoting Christian ethics through their activities. Two other important organizations with longevity in the community also began in the 1990s and acted as umbrella organizations for other Garifuna groups, but in contrast to Hondurans Against AIDS, SHANY, and the Honduran Parade Committee, these two groups promoted Garifuna culture and identity specifically in their organizations' names.

The Reverend Wilberto Oliva, a Honduran Garifuna, had a vision in the 1980s: he wanted to start a Garifuna parachurch organization. The result was the Evangelical Garifuna Council of Churches (EGCC), which Oliva and his Belizean colleague the Reverend Andrew Nunez established in 1995.[8] One of its primary functions is holding events and sponsoring activities that bring Garifuna evangelical churches together; it also holds conferences twice a year for church leaders and members. The council's goal is for secular and Christian Garifuna to work together for the welfare of their communities in the United States and abroad. Part of this involves supporting churches promoting Christian ethics through their youth groups and activities to challenge juvenile delinquency and other societal problems. As with other youth in their communities, young Garifuna are susceptible to drugs, crime, gang enrollment, teenage pregnancy, and other challenges.

One of the initiatives of the EGCC is preserving Garifuna culture and identity for future generations. The EGCC was central in promoting the incorporation of elements of Garifuna culture into the church, which was not readily accepted by many. Songs in the Garifuna language and traditional musical instruments such as drums (*garawon*), maracas (*sísira*), and conch shells (*wadabágei*) are now common at many church services (R. Cayetano 1993).[9] Another event that was not immediately embraced was the annual celebration of Garifuna Day, which is an open-air activity outside the church and includes nonevangelical Garifuna and the community at large. Streets are closed for the day, and vendors offer various items for sale while attendees enjoy music, drama, and traditional foods such as baked bread, pastries, and *hudut* (ground plantain) with coconut milk and fish. The EGCC also supported the Wycliffe Bible project, which translated the Old and New Testaments into the Garifuna language. Efforts initiated by the EGCC resulted in the establishment of a Garifuna church in 1997 in Miami, Florida, and another in 1999 in New Orleans, Louisiana.

The EGCC was one of several Garifuna organizations that sent food, clothing, and equipment to ravaged Honduran communities after Hurricane Mitch in 1998. The hurricane contributed to a substantial increase in the Garifuna population in the city, as many Hondurans migrated to and settled in New York. Like other Central Americans, they took advantage of U.S. Temporary Protection Status (TPS) to extend their residence. Most significantly, the EGCC established the largest network of Garifuna organizations throughout the United States and Central America. By the next century, Garifuna churches had been established in various Garifuna population centers in U.S. cities (Guzman 2018; Castillo 2022b). The Garifuna Mennonite Mission (GMM), a new group that grew out of the EGCC, furthered interconnections among Garifuna in U.S. cities. Led by Omar Guzman and Galileo Bernardez, GMM continued the church-planting initiatives of the EGCC. Churches were established in cities such as Wilmington, North Carolina; Boston, Massachusetts; Houston, Texas; Seattle, Washington; Miami, Florida; and New Orleans, Louisiana (Guzman 2018).[10]

The other umbrella group organized in the latter part of the decade was the Garifuna Coalition USA, created in 1998. (For the coalition's founders, see appendix E.) The motivation behind the coalition was the 1997 bicentennial celebration of the Garifuna's arrival in Central America. Members of the bicentennial planning committee established the organization, initially called the Garifuna Nation, to represent Honduras, Belize, and Guatemala. After years of living in the United States, these professionals in various fields (e.g., education, social services, health care) sought to advance their community as one entity. They decided to continue working together after the bicentennial. Bicentennial committee member Rejil Solis was the group's first president. Solis was also the director of finance for the *Garinagu Quarterly Magazine* and was involved with the Solis Mejia Family Foundation. Part of the Garifuna Coalition USA's objective was to serve as an umbrella for all Garifuna organizations in New York City. Its mission included supporting the rights of Garifuna immigrants, encouraging their civic participation, and advancing the Garifuna community's cultural, economic, and social status.[11] Garifuna Coalition USA members became involved in economic development projects and political events in Honduras (England 2006; J. Ávila 2021). Some of the organizations affiliated with the Garifuna Coalition USA were MUGAMA, Unificación Cultural Garifuna (Unification of Garifuna Culture, UNCUGA), Garifuna House, Guatemalan Garifuna Organization, Castro Family Foundation, Hondurans Against AIDS, FEDHONY, Bicentennial Committee, Santa Fe Women's Club, Hamalali Wayunagu, Garifuna Council of New York, ODECO, and Garifuna World (Endo et al. 2010). Through the Garifuna Coalition USA, headquartered in the Bronx, Garifuna organizations sought to achieve unity in their community.

There was a substantial increase in the number of Garifuna organizations from the 1990s into the start of the new century. For the most part the Garifuna organizations that were established following the Happy Land period were led by individuals who were part of FEDHONY. These Garifuna leaders sought the best way to serve their community with their own abilities and ideas, forming their own groups as FEDHONY declined. In the twenty-first century, Garifuna organizations gained recognition among local public officials and Black and Latino organizations for their various community endeavors.

Civic Engagement: The New Century Addressing Social Needs

Garifuna were also part of the growing new population in the borough of the Bronx in the new century. Many of the new migrants to the United States were undocumented. At Bill Rainey Park it was common to see Garifuna and their children—some wearing ankle bracelet tracking devices—as they waited for their hearing dates to determine whether they would be allowed to stay in the United States. Although the Garifuna population increased overall, many also left the city. Gentrification in the Bronx led to rent increases, causing many residents, including Garifuna, to move out. Employment opportunities motivated many to settle in New Orleans, especially after Hurricane Katrina in 2005. Houston, Texas, also became a popular destination for many Garifuna, offering better housing and a lower cost of living compared with New York. Crime increased in some areas of the Bronx, and gunshots became common at night, especially in the summer. The New York Police Department was a constant presence, with multiple police vehicles and helicopters, in certain parts of the borough (Bronx Historical Society; Moss 2017; Angotti 2008). With all the changes at the start of the new century Garifuna organizations continued to increase and represent their community.

Garifuna Coalition USA, Inc., Strategizing to Address Its Community Needs

Garifuna supported the Garifuna Coalition USA, Inc., which gained prominence in the twenty-first century as its many functions enhanced its visibility among local officials, colleges and universities, and public and private agencies. In New York City, officials recognized that the coalition represented all Guatemalan, Honduran, and Belizean Garifuna organizations. Although other Garifuna organizations sponsored and supported various activities, the Garifuna Coalition USA stood out and received more local media coverage due to its political contacts and civic engagement. Honduran Garifuna Rejil Solis had been president of the Garifuna Coalition USA since its establishment in 1998.[12] The organization now strategized to address community needs. On May 4, 2003, at the Templo nightclub in the Bronx, it held a meeting titled "Sustainable Development Master Plan for the New York City Garifuna Community." Later that year, it held a breakfast event on September 28 celebrating Honduran and Central American independence; attendees included Bronx borough vice president Earl Brown and guest of honor Antonieta Maximo, consul general of Honduras (J. Ávila 2006; Ávila and Ávila 2008). Maximo's involvement with many organizations in the city, including COPROD, Honduran American Cultural Association, and FEDHONY, was recognized especially in connection with achieving her new position with the Honduran government.

In the early part of the new century, another important initiative was the New Horizon Investment Club, an attempt to empower the Garifuna economically. The club, organized in 2001, hoped to teach Garifuna about investing in the stock market and encourage them to pool their resources to reap financial gains. José F. Ávila was one of the club's leaders during his leave of absence from the Garifuna Coalition USA, of which he was also a member (Endo et al. 2010; J. Ávila 2004).[13] He returned to the Garifuna Coalition USA in 2002, and the board of directors elected him treasurer. Ávila explored various other ways to help the community, and in 2004 he established the Honduran Political Action Committee (HAMPAC). During my meeting with Ávila in 2006, he explained that HAMPAC's primary goals were to register voters for presidential and citywide elections and to educate and inform New York officeholders about issues pertaining to Hondurans. The political action committee was also involved in naturalization drives to encourage Hondurans to obtain U.S. citizenship and thereby increase their voting potential.[14] Ávila shared with me that he was invited to Washington, D.C., by the Honduran embassy, representing HAMPAC, to lobby in support of the DR-CAFTA (Dominican Republic,

Central American Free Trade Agreement). The organization also participated in research projects to analyze the role of political action committees in the Latino community. This project was headed jointly by the Puerto Rican Legal Defense and Education Fund and the Columbia University School of International and Public Affairs.

Overall, Ávila said that the original idea for HAMPAC came from Ávila's brother Tomás, who had drafted a plan to form a Garifuna Political Action Committee (GAPAC) in 1999. HAMPAC was short-lived, and one of its problems was the need to broaden the political action committee to include all Garifuna, not only Hondurans. Nevertheless, Ávila transferred HAMPAC's goals to the Garifuna Coalition USA. Later in the chapter, his advocacy for the Garifuna in New York City is shown in his support of Garifuna participation in the political process. This he implemented through the Garifuna Coalition USA by supporting Garifuna political candidates, drafting bills and lobbying for legislation to recognize the ethnic group and culture, and engaging in voter registration.

When Hurricane Katrina devastated New Orleans in August 2005, many New York Garifuna had family residing in the area. Garifuna organizations in New York collaborated to gather supplies to help the affected communities. Garifuna Coalition USA leader Jerry Castro was among the organizers of New York fundraising efforts to support families and individuals affected by the hurricane in New Orleans. Castro also reported and announced events on the Garifuna web page networks. The post-Katrina period resulted in a new wave of immigration to New Orleans, as well as the relocation of many Garifuna from New York and other U.S. cities to take advantage of employment opportunities. Garifuna men capitalized on the availability of construction jobs, and women worked in the housekeeping and hospitality industry (Castro 2005; Chaney 2012).[15]

Meeting Space, Local Concerns, and Challenges

Garifuna organizations were accustomed to meeting in church auditoriums and community centers. In the past, any space they operated had primarily been for social and festive occasions, such as the Carib American Association clubhouse, Club San Antonio, and the United Garifuna Association meeting place in Brooklyn. However, this changed when two organizations acquired meeting spaces to address the needs of the Garifuna community. In 2009 Casa Yurumein opened in the Bronx and became a meeting place for Garifuna as well as the headquarters of Hondurans Against AIDS, which had received a Ford Foundation grant to expand its services.

The name Casa Yurumei is a combination of Spanish and Garifuna: *casa*, meaning "home" in Spanish, and *Yurumei*, the name for St. Vincent in the Garifuna language. In addition to functioning as a meeting place for Garifuna organizations, Casa Yurumei offers Garifuna language classes and other activities. Before Casa Yurumei opened, Garifuna organizations in the Bronx met at local community centers such as La Peña, Club Cubano Interamericano Social Club, or Protestant or Roman Catholic church facilities (Walker and Reyes 2017; Johnson 2007; López Oro 2016a).[16]

Also in 2009 the Garifuna Coalition USA received a grant to establish an advocacy center to provide social services to and advocate for community members.[17] The center, located in the South Bronx, provides translation services, networking opportunities, a Garifuna youth leadership program, community organizing, and cultural programs. For social services, referrals are made to the Phipps Community Development Corporation, which provides educational and vocational programs (López Oro 2016a; Small 2014; Walker and Reyes 2017).

As the new century progressed, a meeting was held on May 8, 2007, to discuss concerns of the Garifuna community and their status in the city's development plans. Those concerns included construction of Ferry Point Park in the Bronx, which was scheduled to open in 2009, and whether soccer fields were part of the local government's plans. The tenant status of many Garifuna was another concern, as public housing, where many of them resided, was being sold to private entities. Another issue raised was the proposal to change the name of Dawson Street to Chief Joseph Chatoyer Street (Caroom 2008; Castro 2007).[18] As mentioned in earlier chapters, Joseph Chatoyer was a Garifuna Carib descendant on the island of St. Vincent who had defended the ethnic group against European invasion (C. Taylor 2012). This section of the Bronx, near Bill Rainey Park, is a popular Garifuna meeting place. Many people signed a petition in favor of the name change, and it was submitted to city councilwoman Maria del Carmen Arroyo, but it never happened. A planned voter registration campaign was also discussed at the May 2007 meeting. Lack of Garifuna political participation was an issue, prompting leaders to start attending the monthly Bronx community board meetings. Guatemalan Garifuna Jerry Castro, listed as the Garifuna Coalition USA contact person in its newsletter (he also briefly served as its executive director), was very involved in the community and local politics and supported Garifuna advancement (Castro 2007; Chukwudi 2014).

Unfortunately, that same month a Garifuna man joined the list of unarmed Black males killed by police officers. A series of such incidents, including the killing of Amadou Diallou in 1999 and Sean Bell in 2006, exacerbated tensions within the Black and Latino communities. In this case, an off-duty New York City police officer shot forty-one-year-old Fermin Arzu five times and killed him after Arzu crashed his van in the policeman's neighborhood. Officer Raphael Lora claimed he fired in self-defense, as he thought Arzu was reaching for a weapon in his glove compartment; however, investigators found no gun. On behalf of the Garifuna Coalition USA, José F. Ávila and Mirtha Colón issued a press release denouncing the incident. The shooting made the front page of the Black newspaper *New York Amsterdam News*, and the *New York Times* and *Daily News* also reported the incident. Civil rights activist Reverend Al Sharpton of the National Action Network assisted the Arzu family and was present at the funeral, alongside members of Sean Bell's family (Fernandez 2007). A protest and rally were held at Sharpton's House of Justice headquarters in Harlem. The officer was fired; he was convicted at trial for fatally shooting Arzu and sentenced to serve time in prison. However, Lora was released on appeal and in June 2011 was acquitted by the appellate court, never serving time. Years later, in 2017, aided by attorneys, Arzu's family filed a wrongful death suit against the city, and a settlement was reached for $2 million (Moorer 2007; Block and Siemaszko 2009; Gardiner 2011; Carrega 2017).

Foundations of New York City Black and Latino Civic Engagement

Previous immigrants and minority groups, some participating in social movements, paved the path to civic engagement for Garifuna in New York City. Some background on that process will help in understanding how Garifuna in turn were able to become politically engaged in the city. During the 1920s West Indians and African Americans were drawn to the Socialist Party and the Communist Party in the city. Many were unhappy with the mainstream political parties. The Marcus Garvey Black nationalist movement was popular among Blacks and Caribbeans in New York City and their home countries. Some West Indians who became elected officials were Garveyites born in the Caribbean. Nevertheless, Black nationalism lost favor with the advent of New Deal economic reforms (1933–39). In addition, the New Deal reduced Black support of the Republican Party. In the past, African Americans had avoided the Democratic Party because of its traditional opposition to civil rights. West Indians capitalized on the shift in New York Blacks' political support from the Republican to the Democratic Party during the 1930s due to the New Deal. Ideological differences within the far left and the opening of elective opportunities also drew many Black immigrants to the Democratic Party (Kasinitz 1992, 215). Although West Indians registered in both political parties, they took advantage of elective and leadership positions open in the Democratic Party. In the 1940s and 1950s West Indians led the Democratic Party in the New York City Black community. In the Bronx in 1952, as in Brooklyn four years earlier, a West Indian became the first Black elected government official.[19]

Other transformations expanded opportunities for recent immigrants' civic engagement. One of the many changes in the 1960s with new civil rights legislation was the Supreme Court's 1963 ruling striking down partisan gerrymandering. This led to redistricting in the city's boroughs, enlarging district areas that opened opportunities for Blacks and Latinos. In the 1960s there was another West Indian migration wave, although the number of elected officials from that community nevertheless decreased during the next decade. In turn, the number of African American politicians in New York City increased during the post–civil rights period. By the 1970s African Americans obtained high posts in the Democratic Party, especially in Brooklyn, which overtook Harlem in Black population concentration. The African American political establishment in the Bronx was weak, compared to that in Queens and Brooklyn (Kasinitz 1992). Puerto Ricans obtained political power in the Bronx. The Bronx overall also has the largest number of Latino elected officials (Falcón 2017).

Puerto Ricans were the first Latino group to become involved in New York City politics. This group's advantage for participating in politics, compared to other Latino immigrant populations, is their automatic citizenship status due to Puerto Rico's status as a U.S. protectorate. Puerto Ricans gained political power in New York City by forming various electoral and political organizations, followed by capturing political positions in established Democratic districts during the 1960s. The extensive Puerto Rican population supported their political gain. However, Puerto Rican Latino dominance in politics is challenged by shifts in the city's demographics. As mentioned previously, shifts occurred with Puerto Ricans comprising less than 50 percent of the Latino population in the city (Jones-Correa 1998, 114–15). The second-largest Latino immigrant population in New York City is the Dominicans. Despite the increased influence of immigrants from the Dominican Republic, Puerto Ricans continue to dominate politics in New York. By 2000 they were an estimated 50 percent of the city's Latino population and more than 70 percent of Latino voters (Sales and Bush 2000). Puerto Ricans have dominated in many political positions, including borough president and Bronx Democratic County Committee members (Falcón 2005, 2017).

Puerto Ricans', African Americans', and West Indians' civic engagement provided the foundation for Garifuna participation. Since the latter twentieth century, Garifuna organizations engaged with local minority officials in the city. Garifuna share similarities in culture, economic status, and needs with many constituents in the Bronx. Their organization leaders' relations with minority officials continue to grow. Although New York has elected two consecutive Republican mayors (Rudolph Giuliani, Michael Bloomberg), the Democratic Party dominates the city politically. (Bloomberg was a lifelong Democrat; however, in the 2001 elections he ran on the Republican ticket. He switched from Republican to Independent during his second term in office. Since 2018 he has been a Democrat.) Like Puerto Ricans, many voters in the city are registered Democrats. In New York City, the Democratic Party holds most state and local elected positions. Democrats' powerful political organizations work to produce candidates for state assembly seats and city council positions (Wong 2003).

Gains of Blacks and Latinos in public office and government agencies since the postwar period aided Garifuna during this challenging time and simultaneously opened opportunities for them to engage with local officials. Blacks and Latinos in office helped address infrastructure development, community services (addressing drugs, delinquency, teenage pregnancy), education, housing, and other needs in the Bronx. The redistricting of the 1980s increased the number of Blacks and Latinos in the city council and state assembly, for the most part aligned with the Democratic Party. In addition, redistricting aided David Dinkins's election as mayor, as well as Jesse Jackson's campaigns for president (1984, 1988), increasing registration of Blacks and Latinos in the Democratic Party (Sales and Bush 2000). Many Blacks, Latinos, and Garifuna were inspired by identifying with Jackson's presence campaigning for the presidency. In the new century they also drew inspiration from the election of Barack Obama as the first Black president motivating their participation.

Civic Engagement and Garifuna Coalition USA, Inc.

What distinguished the Garifuna Coalition USA in the twenty-first century from other Garifuna groups was its role in initiating direct civic engagement.[20] The coalition began engaging with and lobbying local government officials to recognize the ethnic group. To a lesser extent, the Garifuna community had been connecting with local public officials since the Happy

Land fire in the 1990s and the initiation of the Garifuna-led Central American Day parade in the Bronx.[21] However, the Garifuna Coalition USA cultivated relations with local officials through several means. In 2008 its interim executive director, José F. Ávila, submitted a proposal to Bronx borough president Adolfo Carrion Jr. (2002–9) supporting the recognition of the culture and contributions of Garifuna Americans in New York City. Carrion issued a proclamation in 2009 designating March 11 to April 12 as Garifuna American Heritage Month in the Bronx, recognizing Garifuna Americans and commemorating their arrival on the island of Roatan off the coast of Central America from the island of St. Vincent (Walker and Reyes 2017; J. Ávila 2017b, 2021).

Next, the Garifuna Coalition USA sought recognition of Garifuna American heritage at the state level. Assemblyman Michael Benjamin (2003–10), representing District 79 in the Bronx (Morrisania, Crotona Park East, and East Tremont, with an extensive Garifuna population), was petitioned to introduce a resolution in the New York State Assembly to declare Garifuna American Heritage Month in the state. New York City mayor Michael Bloomberg (2002–13) was also asked to support the resolution to celebrate Garifuna American Heritage Month. At a press conference at the Bronx County building on March 11, 2010, a representative from the Community Affairs Office of the Mayor issued a proclamation celebrating Garifuna American heritage. Also present were Bronx borough president Rubén Díaz Jr. (2009–21), Assemblyman Michael Benjamin, and a representative of New York's first African American governor, David Patterson (2008–10). Since then, a proclamation is issued every year at the State Capitol in Albany, declaring Garifuna American Heritage Month in the state of New York (J. Ávila 2021).[22] During the month, the Garifuna Coalition USA posts activities being held in the city to celebrate Garifuna heritage. These activities represent a substantial change from past celebrations of Garifuna Settlement Day (November 19) in the city (J. Ávila 2017a; King 2018a). Since 2011, representatives of the Garifuna Coalition USA, along with delegates from its member organizations and partners, have visited the State Capitol in Albany each year for Garifuna American Legislative Day, in support of Garifuna American Heritage Month (see fig. 12). Assemblymen and state senators from all districts with a Garifuna population participate, led by those representing the Bronx, Brooklyn, Manhattan, and Queens. After concluding their work in the chamber, they participate in a brief social event and panel presentation (J. Ávila 2019b).[23]

Garifuna in other U.S. cities followed the New York model in their efforts to obtain recognition of their heritage with proclamations from their

Figure 12. Garifuna delegates and local elected officials participating in Garifuna American Legislative Day at the State Capitol in Albany, New York, May 15, 2018, a temporary change from the March–April schedule.

local governments. Houston recognized the Garifuna and their heritage in 2009, and the entire state of Texas followed suit in 2010. Famous Garifuna punta rock musician Andy Palacio was honored in 2009 when Houston declared December 2 Andy Palacio Day.[24] The City of Los Angeles proclaimed Garifuna Heritage Month in 2014, and the states of Illinois and Massachusetts did so in 2011.[25] According to Jerry Castro, who led several efforts to gain recognition for the Garifuna, the cities of Las Vegas, Atlanta, Detroit, and New Orleans have also acknowledged Garifuna Americans and their contributions to society (Thevenot 2012).[26]

Other civic engagement activities in which the Garifuna Coalition USA participated included the 2010 U.S. census. However, that was not the first attempt to get an accurate count of the Garifuna population. Prior to the 2000 census, Garifuna organizers Maria Elena Maximo and Francisco Ruiz established the nonprofit Jamalali Uaguacha, Inc. (The voice of our ancestors) in the Bronx to help Garifuna with health care education, GED classes, and preparing and filing immigration papers. Maximo, a retired teacher, was especially interested in addressing the high HIV infection rate and the lack of English-language skills in arriving immigrants (Henderson 2004; Zambito 2006).[27] Her political contacts and membership on the Bronx Community Board facilitated her organization's receipt of government grants and support from local public officials, who provided office space. Acknowledging the hurdles of obtaining an accurate Garifuna population count due to the many undocumented immigrants, she also saw the importance of an accurate census in terms of applying for grants and government funding. As part of a community census count, Maximo gathered names, birthplaces, and education and income levels of ten thousand Garifuna at Crotona Park in the Bronx, a popular hangout during warm weather (Glaberson 2007). The Garifuna Coalition USA went further in 2010 to obtain an estimate of the number of Garifuna participating in the census. It launched a campaign to encourage people to mark "Garifuna" in the "Other" space on the census form related to ethnic identification. Those efforts captured the attention of the mayor's office as well as the *New York Times*, which published a multimedia series on the Garifuna (López Oro 2016; Orr and Singh 2012). Once he knew about the coalition's census outreach campaign, Mayor Michael Bloomberg accepted an invitation to attend a town hall meeting in July 2010 at the auditorium of Lincoln Hospital in the Bronx. During his presentation, he acknowledged the Garifuna census work and answered questions. Questions covered the need for economic development and support for entrepreneurship, follow-up on an April 1991 study by the New York City Department of Education regarding the number of Garifuna students with English-language proficiency, and an inquiry about providing the Garifuna with a multipurpose building (Walker and Reyes 2017; T. Colon 2010i).

Although Jamalali Uaguacha's initiatives were outstanding in providing services to Garifuna, Black, and Latino populations, the organization was short-lived. Maria Elena Maximo was convicted of defrauding immigrants of more than $1 million. She was arrested in 2006 and accused of charging undocumented immigrants enormous fees to apply for work permits and green cards for which they were not eligible. State and federal prosecutors found more than one thousand fraudulent applications. Maximo pleaded guilty to two counts of mail fraud and was sentenced to seventeen years in prison. The arrest and court procedures were covered in the local media, newspapers, and cable networks, temporarily damaging Garifuna reputation in the community. Ávila has described his efforts to restore Garifuna credibility by meeting with local Bronx officials and apologizing, stating that the illicit actions were not representative of his community. Ávila mentioned that the results of his presentation to local Bronx officials representing the Garifuna Coalition USA led to closer relations with the policy makers in supporting his efforts (J. Ávila 2021).

The Garifuna Coalition USA was involved in a voter registration drive for the 2012 general election and the 2013 local elections in New York. Voters could register at popular Garifuna gathering places such as festivals, cultural events, sporting events, parades, and churches. In addition, registration tables were set up at Bill Rainey Park, Crotona Park, and Ferry Point Park in the Bronx and at Linden Park in Brooklyn. Voter education and registration workshops were also held at the Garifuna Coalition USA advocacy center, Casa Yurumein in the Bronx, and the Biko Transformation Center in Brooklyn (J. Ávila 2009; Colón 2010e; Walker and Reyes 2017).

As mentioned earlier, there had been discussions about the need for greater political participation among the Garifuna or even an official elected representative. As a result, Garifuna organizations agreed to support the candidacy of one of their members. By 2009, Jerry Castro was no longer executive director of the Garifuna Coalition USA, so he created an exploratory committee and raised funds, hoping to be a candidate for a seat in the New York State Assembly in 2010. He had previously worked as a legislative liaison for the 79th Assembly District, where the Garifuna population is concentrated, and served as director of community relations in the New York State attorney general's Harlem Regional Office. In addition, Castro was a member of the Bronx Planning Board 2 and was appointed vice chair of the New York City Department of Community Development Neighborhood Advisory Board 3 (J. Ávila 2017a; Garcia 2013). Although his political aspirations did not materialize, other Garifuna candidates would be supported by their community in the future.

Alliances with Representative Rubén Díaz Sr.

Beginning in 2011, Abrazo Garifuna was hosted each year by New York State Senator Rubén Díaz Sr. to recognize Garifuna contributions to their communities. As part of outreach efforts to his constituents in the Bronx, Rubén Díaz Sr. initiated annual events celebrating large ethnic and racial populations such as African Americans, Bangladeshi, Puerto Ricans, Dominicans, and the Garifuna (Walker and Reyes 2017). Garifuna organizations participate in this event, held at a prestigious ballroom in the Bronx. Each group (Belizean, Guatemalan, Honduran) invites guests to the event, which is attended by members of Garifuna soccer clubs, Catholic and evangelical groups, professional associations, health and education groups, investment clubs, and women's groups. Local public officials such as council members and the borough president also attend or send representatives. Garifuna leaders are honored for their contributions to the community, and the program concludes with entertainment consisting of traditional Garifuna folk dancing, musical selections from prominent Garifuna artists, and a DJ playing punta and other traditional music.[28]

At the 2017 Abrazo Garifuna, Guatemalan Garifuna Edson Arzu, a U.S. Navy veteran, was among the honorees (Wirsing 2017). Arzu, founder of the Garifuna American Veterans Association, is connected with more than two hundred active-duty service members and veterans of Garifuna descent through social media. Edson felt the calling to document Garifuna in the U.S. military and support those enlisted to ensure that they benefit from education and other opportunities the military offers. As of May 23, 2019, Arzu reported that there were over a thousand Garifuna active-duty service members, retirees, and veterans from all branches of the U.S. military. Thus far, he has uncovered approximately five hundred Garifuna veterans. Since 2013, the Garifuna American Veterans Association has bestowed the annual Core Values Award in recognition of past and present Garifuna service members (T. Colon 2014c; Duran 2019). Another professional Garifuna group, the Garifuna American Law Enforcement Association, was founded in 2017. The organization was motivated by Arzu's group and seeks to support the careers of Garifuna in various New York City agencies of law enforcement. Fundraisers are held supporting Garifuna community needs in the city and Honduras. The organization also established a partnership with Garifuna law enforcement officials in Honduras (T. Colon 2018).

Rubén Díaz Sr. has been central in expanding Garifuna political networks and the ethnic group's recognition among local public officials. This relationship started with members of the EGCC, with whom Díaz was able to establish connections. The Garifuna population is concentrated in Díaz's 32nd New York State Senate District, and Díaz shares a common ethnicity with the Garifuna, as he is an Afro-Latino of Puerto Rican descent. In addition, Díaz is a clergyman and held close ties with Reverend Isabel Sonia Fernandez, a former EGCC member and part of the New York Hispanic Clergy Association; Díaz also knows Reverends Wilberto Oliva and Andrew Nunez, EGCC leaders.[29] Díaz consulted Fernandez about starting Abrazo Garifuna, and according to Fernandez, she disagreed with the initial concept of its festive and secular nature, so Díaz approached SHANY, the Honduran self-help organization based in the Bronx.[30] At a meeting attended by Díaz and representatives of various Garifuna organizations, Díaz selected the Garifuna Coalition USA as a point of contact for establishing Abrazo Garifuna and other activities intended to increase the group's political participation, because of this organization's representation of the entire ethnic group in New York. At first, Díaz had assumed that the Garifuna were mainly Hondurans, owing to his many contacts with leaders from that country. After learning that the New York City Garifuna population also included many Guatemalans and Belizeans, he decided to call the event Abrazo Garifuna instead of Abrazo Hondureños.

Endurance and Change

As the Garifuna community underwent change in the early part of the twenty-first century, its organizations experienced transitions as well. As Casa Yurumein emerged as part of Hondurans Against AIDS, the functions of the Garifuna Coalition USA shifted. First, its leadership changed in 2011 when Sulma Arzu-Brown replaced José F. Ávila as chairperson and interim executive director. Arzu-Brown had been a volunteer for the organization since 2007. The Fund for New Citizens at the New York Community Trust allowed a one-year grant to be used to create the managing director position for Arzu-Brown (*Caribbean* 2011a). The following year, the Garifuna Coalition USA advocacy center began a program to help immigrant entrepreneurs in the Bronx start their own businesses.[31] Afro-Latin Publishing grew out of this initiative, publishing works by Garifuna artist Isidra Sabio as well as Sulma Arzu-Brown. Arzu-Brown's children's books focus on Garifuna culture, language, and Black girls' hair as part of their identity. By 2014, the Garifuna Coalition USA was transitioning again, as Arzu-Brown moved on to a position as director of events for the New York City Hispanic Chamber of Commerce.

Meanwhile, José F. Ávila established Garifuna Afro-Latino Entertainment (GALENT) in 2013 to assist in the marketing, production, and distribution of recorded Garifuna music. Although the Garifuna Coalition USA closed its office and ended its programs, Ávila resumed leadership of the organization, administering its web page and serving as a point of contact for various public officials on behalf of the Garifuna community (J. Ávila 2013). Ávila's new method of managing the Garifuna Coalition USA included accepting discretionary funds for youth programs. In 2014 Bronx council members Vanessa Gibson, Ritchie Torres, and Fernando Cabrera allocated discretionary funds to the Garifuna Coalition USA for Garifuna youth leadership and cultural awareness programs. Councilwoman Gibson (2009–21), now borough president, has been a leader in supporting the Garifuna community; she represented District 16, which has a substantial Garifuna population. On March 12, 2014, Gibson presented the first Garifuna American Heritage Month proclamation at the New York City

Council. On April 10, 2014, Congressman Jose E. Serrano (1990–2019), in a symbolic gesture of support, issued a tribute to the celebration of Garifuna American Heritage Month (March 11 to April 12) in the House of Representatives (Small 2014; King 2018a; J. Ávila 2017a). Serrano represented the 15th District, encompassing the South Bronx. Brooklyn borough president Eric Adams, now New York City mayor, also recognized Garifuna American Heritage Month, making the official announcement at a reception at Brooklyn Borough Hall in April 2014, with representatives from several Garifuna organization present (Barker 2014). Adams fulfilled his promise of hosting the first Garifuna American Heritage Month event at the mayor's Gracie Mansion residence in 2023. Representatives of various Garifuna organizations were present as Adams acknowledged their contributions to the city in many areas such as civil service, education, and business (King 2023a).

Acknowledging the recognition and support of local politicians, Ávila continued to pursue one of the Garifuna Coalition USA's goals: a Garifuna elected official. In the 2014 New York State primary elections, he supported Garifuna Rosemary Ordonez-Jenkins, who sought to represent the 87th Assembly District as an alternate delegate to the Judicial Convention and County Committee. Unfortunately, she did not win (J. Ávila 2016b).

Attending to New Undocumented Immigrants and Gun Violence

As the Garifuna Coalition USA underwent structural changes, a new Garifuna organization emerged in 2014. The Garifuna Community Services formed as a result of the wave of Central American immigrants in 2013–14, which included many Garifuna. Latino community activists and Garifuna organizers gathered to address these issues.[32] Migrant Garifuna were also featured in New York City's Spanish-language *El Diario* newspaper (Cortes de Solano 2015). Many of the Central American immigrants who arrived in the spring of 2014 sought economic opportunities and were fleeing from the gang-imposed extortion common in their home countries. Some of these migrants were granted temporary entry and were required to wear ankle bracelet monitors as they awaited their court dates to determine their status. Several sought legal counsel to determine their qualification for temporary protection status (TPS). At the Bronx Garifuna Church Community Center, Honduran Garifuna Gregoria Flores offered legal advice on immigration on a weekly basis. The New York City Mennonite Central Committee also helped many families. In addition, legal fairs were held to orient the Garifuna immigrants to U.S. immigration procedures

(Fretz 2015). This eventually led to the start of Garifuna Community Services, which is affiliated with the Garifuna church. It collaborates with city agencies in providing shelter, medical care, food, and legal counseling for recent immigrants (Valdés 2015). The group also engaged with the mayor's office and traveled to Washington, D.C., to protest the discontinuation of TPS for immigrants from certain countries. The Garifuna Community Services organization (registered in 2016 in New York State) grew, assuming other activities and gaining volunteer supporters. Garifuna Community Services organizes occasional events through which basic foods, children's clothing, school supplies, toys, and sweets are distributed. Other community service activities include fundraisers and sexual and reproductive health clinics.

Garifuna Community Services is affiliated with the Evangelical Garifuna Church and the Mennonite Garifuna Mission, which grew out of the EGCC. In recent years the church has shifted toward community involvement and political participation, thus reflecting their integration in the community. The Evangelical Garifuna church associates itself with city agencies and representatives in addressing policy issues impacting their ethnic group as well as the community at large. The Evangelical Garifuna Church in the Bronx has supported initiatives to curb gun violence, prevalent in its community, located in Mott Haven in the Bronx, at the heart of one of the most violent neighborhoods of the United States. Church members participated in the city crime prevention programs. In 2016 the Evangelical Garifuna Church participated in the gun buy-back program whereby individuals exchanged their weapons for cash in an effort to curb gun violence in the community. Garifuna church clergy collaborated with the police commissioner, the Bronx district attorney, the local council representative, and the Bronx borough president in promoting the event (McLaughlin and Rayman 2016; Small 2016). The Evangelical Garifuna Church leadership's social exchanges with local public officials demonstrate their engagement outside of their ethnic group and provides evidence of their civic participation in addressing an issue for their overall community improvement.

I met with Flores several times at the Bronx Garifuna Church Community Center, discussing issues in the Garifuna community. She is also present at Garifuna community gatherings I attend. During one of our meetings at the church community center, non-Garifuna also had their immigration needs attended to. Garifuna Community Services' significant role in the community is examined further in this and the following chapter.

Ongoing Civic Engagement

José F. Ávila, representing the Garifuna Coalition USA, supported New York State legislation to recognize Garifuna culture and language. In March 2017 the New York State Assembly presented bill 4925 (originally introduced by Senator Rubén Díaz Sr.), which would add Garifuna culture to the state's educational curriculum. (Years earlier, in 1991, initiatives to include the Garifuna language and culture had been presented to the Board of Education's Bilingual Department, with support from Dr. George Irish, a professor at Medgar Evers College.) The Garifuna American Leadership Alliance supported bill 3972, also introduced in January 2017 by Assemblyman Luis R. Sepulveda, which would amend the state education law to include Garifuna history.[33] Both Díaz and Sepulveda represented districts with large Garifuna populations.[34] Although neither bill gained traction, the Garifuna gained experience in the political process and lobbying (J. Ávila 2017a, 2021).

The Garifuna Coalition USA partnered with the NAACP for the September 2017 New York City Council District 18 candidates' forum, held in the Bronx. The nonpartisan forum allowed local candidates for office to voice their political platforms, giving the public an opportunity to engage with them and become familiar with their positions prior to the upcoming election. Isabel Sonia Fernandez ran in the 2017 primary for city council, hoping to represent neighboring District 17 in the Bronx (*Bronx Chronicle* 2017; Skurnik 2017). After receiving minimal support, Fernandez backed African American candidate Helen Hines. Fernandez once again aspired to be on the June 2020 ballot, this time as a candidate for the 79th Assembly District in the Bronx.[35]

Once again, the Garifuna community obtained discretionary funding from local public officials. For fiscal year 2017, councilman Rafael Salamanca Jr. allocated funds to the Garifuna community (through the Garifuna Coalition USA) to promote Garifuna cultural history and traditions in New York. In fiscal year 2019, Councilman Rubén Díaz Sr. allocated funding for the development of the Garifuna Renaissance Arts and Culture Center, led by José F. Ávila (J. Ávila 2018b; King 2019a; Small 2014).[36] Ávila and several coalition affiliates were present in April 2018 when Councilwoman Vanessa L. Gibson introduced the celebration of Garifuna American Heritage Month. The festive event included a performance by the Chief Joseph Chatoyer Garifuna Folk Dance Company and the national anthem sung by Garifuna artist Lucy Blanco. The following year, a follow-up event was held at the Bronx Museum of the Arts. This time, the

Wabafu (Our Power) Garifuna Dance Theater group performed, and four members of the community were honored for their contributions. The Garifuna Coalition USA was one of the program sponsors, and Ávila presented the opening and closing remarks. Councilwoman Gibson dressed in traditional Garifuna dress of yellow, white, and black, and she acknowledged her Garifuna staff (Minsky 2018).[37]

Networking with Local Officials and Engaging in Electoral Politics

Garifuna Coalition USA's liaison role between the community and local officials continued after GALENT was formed in 2013, and José F. Ávila used social media to provide updates on events in the Garifuna community, his networking with local politicians, and other pertinent information. For instance, he provided a detailed list of Garifuna appointed to the Bronx Community Board in 2019–20, as well as their participation in other political positions (see appendix D).

However, toward the end of the second decade of the twenty-first century, other Garifuna organizations began to network directly with local public officials. One of them was Garifuna Community Services. In April 2018, at the auditorium of Lincoln Hospital in the Bronx, Garifuna Community Services and several other Garifuna organizations hosted a town hall forum with Mayor Bill DeBlasio's office. (In 2010 an earlier town hall had been held at the same place with Mayor Michael Bloomberg.) In the lobby area, various agencies set up tables with representatives ready to assist people with questions related to health care, housing, small businesses, immigration, and senior citizen and youth issues. A Garifuna folkloric dance group performed before the primarily Garifuna audience, and representatives from the mayor's office spoke and answered questions. After the panel presentation segment of the program, there were separate workshops addressing issues such as health, housing, and youth development (Walker and Reyes 2017; Cosgrove et al. 2021).[38] The following year, the office of New York City comptroller Scott Stringer hosted a town hall at the Bronx Police Athletic League. Garifuna Community Services also organized other Garifuna groups in support of this event, where Stringer, Councilwoman Vanessa Gibson, and Assemblyman Marcos Crespo addressed the audience.

Garifuna Community Services also received funds from Mayor de Blasio's office as part of the Census Complete Count Fund to be used to ensure an accurate count of the Garifuna in the 2020 census. In previous years, the Garifuna Coalition USA had taken the lead in both organizing town hall meetings and collecting census data, so this was a change as new leadership engaged in activities on behalf of the community (Vad 2020; T. Colon 2019).[39] A previous task of the Garifuna Coalition USA, directing the annual Garifuna American Legislative Day in Albany, also temporarily changed leadership. In 2020 Casa Yurumein assumed leadership in directing Garifuna organization representatives' bus trip to the capital.[40] Mirtha Colón's Hondurans Against AIDS–Casa Yurumein increased its direct engagement with local officials. However, this time attendance for the Albany trip was low, as the start of the COVID-19 pandemic caused many Garifuna to abstain from going because of health precautions. Since the pandemic shutdown of services and meetings in New York City, this and other annual functions afterward were temporarily suspended.

2020–21 New York City Local Elections

For the 2020 presidential election, voter turnout was high as many were motivated in opposition to Donald Trump winning another term in office. Trump's immigration policies and divisive rhetoric aimed toward minorities motivated many to register and vote in local and general elections. One of the results was that Democrats won control of the New York State Senate in the 2018 elections and increased their majority in the State Assembly. That year voter turnout was historically high; however, it decreased afterward in local elections. The Bronx continued its trend of averaging the lowest voter turnout of the boroughs. Many residents of the Bronx do not see voting as essential to changing their socioeconomic status in the borough. Attempts were made to increase the number of voters in New York City. In 2022 the New York City Council voted in favor of allowing noncitizens to vote in local elections starting the following year. However, the state Supreme Court denied this attempt, ruling that it violated the state constitution. The Garifuna are among many noncitizens in the city, especially their new undocumented population (NYC Votes 2019; Ashford 2022; Mays 2022).

The 2020 and 2021 local elections in New York City were significant because a new mayor was to be elected. In addition, competition was close for local political positions, including in the Bronx. The election was also important because Garifuna community leaders sustained close ties with several aspiring political candidates competing for higher political offices. During this time several Garifuna organizations networked more with local officials, and politicians visited their functions while campaigning for office. Initially it was only the Garifuna Coalition USA representing the ethnic group, but now several groups interacted independently with officials when it came to electoral politics. However, the Garifuna Coalition USA was at an advantage, recognized for coordinating the annual Garifuna legislative trip to Albany and for the "Abrazos Garifuna" event attended by local politicians. Early on the Garifuna Coalition USA established alliances with the Bronx borough president's office and with local political representatives' districts where the ethnic group's population is concentrated. The organizational efforts were facilitated when Rubén Díaz Sr. established "team Díaz" bringing several local politicians in districts with Garifuna population concentrations together at the events (Díaz 2015).

Garifuna organizations made no substantial campaigning or lobbying efforts during the 2021 New York City mayoral elections. Garifuna groups engaged more with candidates for New York State Senate, Assembly, and City Council than with the mayoral candidates. This could have played a role in the low level of Garifuna collective organizational participation in the mayoral election. Also, the COVID-19 pandemic reduced campaigning efforts. Nonetheless, Garifuna are familiar with Mayor Eric Adams. As Brooklyn borough president, Eric Adams celebrated Garifuna American Heritage Month in 2015 and followed through on his previous promise, as the state senator representing Flatbush, Crown Heights, Park Slope, Sunset Park, and Prospect Heights, to recognize the ethnic group (J. Ávila 2017a; 651 Arts 2007; Minsky 2015; Barker 2014). Most likely Adams gained Garifuna support as name recognition of candidates is associated with increased chances of electoral support. Social media sites of several Garifuna political action groups also highlighted campaign advertisements of Adams's and other local political offices' campaigns.

Several Garifuna political action groups developed; some were registered and others not.[41] Two prominent Garifuna organizations registered their political platform group. For example, the SHANY organization registered the Garifuna Political Action Community Platform NYC (Plataforma Garifuna Accion Politica Communitaria NYC) in 2019. The Garifuna Coalition USA had the Garifuna Political Action Committee (Garifuna PAC) officially registered in 2016. Unregistered political and civic action groups also connected to their respective Garifuna organizations are presented later in this chapter.

Election Campaign for the New York 15th Congressional District

Noticeable in the 2021 elections was a contrast in Garifuna political engagement in deciding support for their congressional district representative in Washington, D.C. In the election for their new representative in the 2022 U.S. Congress, Garifuna organizations supported different candidates. There were fifteen candidates competing for the position in the Democratic primary. The question was which candidate the Garifuna would support: Black Puerto Rican Rubén Díaz Sr., who had long-standing ties to the Garifuna community; Black American of Jamaican descent Michael Blake, who had more recent connections to the ethnic group; or Black and Puerto Rican Ritchie Torres. The winner among these three was expected to be the Democratic primary winner. The majority of Garifuna and other people in the district historically align with the Democratic Party. In New York City most elections are effectively decided in the Democratic primary because of the political party's dominance in the region. But it was interesting to see whether race or ethnicity played a role in the election. Garifuna can claim both Black and Latino heritage. Being multiethnic, they tend to self-identify with whatever group will provide the best outcome when it comes to politics. This seat was also an important one because the winner could join either the Black or Hispanic Congressional Caucus in Washington, D.C. Representative Jose Serrano was retiring from Congress, so his seat in the 15th District was up for grabs in 2021. Then candidate Ritchie Torres was present at a Casa Yurumein event as he campaigned for Congress and continued strong ties with the organization and Garifuna community after the election. Friends associated with Casa Yurumein shared that although appreciative of candidate Rubén Díaz Sr.'s support in the past promoting Garifuna culture, more was expected. One of the many needs of the Garifuna was a permanent funded meeting space for cultural, educational, and other uses, which never came to fruition. Current meeting locations are rented, sustained through fundraisers and other means. Rubén Díaz Sr., who is also a minister, did gain the support of some Garifuna groups affiliated with their evangelical church community. The other candidate, Michael Blake, a front-runner, engaged with the Garifuna Coalition USA leader José F. Ávila at a campaign event.

Eventually José F. Ávila and the Garifuna Political Action Committee officially endorsed Michael Blake as their candidate for the U.S. Congress. Speaking to Ávila's supporters who aligned with his endorsement, I learned that Blake was seen as the best option for longevity in the position given that he was young and experienced in Washington, D.C. Blake worked as a campaign aide to former U.S. president Barack Obama, and in the administration served in the White House Office of Intergovernmental Affairs. Other Garifuna organizations might have been cautious about endorsing any candidate, considering leaders' close ties to many candidates. In addition, some organizations are continuing to grow in the area of lobbying and are not yet as widely recognized as the Garifuna Coalition USA, limiting their potential effectiveness in endorsing a candidate. Several of the local political candidates seeking to reach the U.S. Congress also supported the Garifuna community, granting funds through the Garifuna Coalition USA in their previous elected posts. Friends associated with SHANY and Garifuna Community Services shared with me that Afro-Latino Díaz was the candidate they supported. To what extent the Garifuna electorate align with their representative organizations is unknown; however, the groups mentioned have substantial followings. The outcome was that the candidate endorsed by the most recognized organization, Garifuna Coalition USA, did not win. Black and Puerto Rican candidate Ritchie Torres was elected to represent this district, considered one of the poorest in the United States. Torres thereafter joined the Congressional Black Caucus and the Congressional Hispanic Caucus, noting that both caucuses reflect his identity as well as that of his constituents in the Bronx.

Since his victory, Torres continues his connections with Mirtha Colón's Casa Yurumein organization, supporting immigration reform and TPS. In addition, Torres drafted a plan to make Garifuna Heritage Month recognized across the United States. He also established a U.S. Garifuna Caucus for legislators to address policy issues affecting the Garifuna community. This is significant because Garifuna can negotiate with members from both Black and Hispanic Caucuses to address their community needs in New York City as well as abroad in Central America. Haitian organizations in New York City successfully gained House and Senate support in addressing political challenges in their home country. Such action contacting local New York City organizations and public officials resulted in Haitian policy needs gaining national recognition supported by congressional representatives. Representative Torres's initiative allows Garifuna organizations the opportunity to lobby other members of Congress who represent Garifuna districts in U.S. cities to address their community's needs and the repression Garifuna face in their home countries in regard to land issues.

In May 2010, members of the U.S. Congress—Sen. Mike Honda (D-CA), Rep. Barbara Lee (D-CA), Rep. Raul Grijalva (D-AZ), and the late Rep. Donald Payne (D-NJ)—visited Honduras and noted the social, economic, and political concerns of the Honduran Garifuna. Rep. Donald Payne of the Congressional Black Caucus advanced the interests of African descendant communities, including those in Latin America, by introducing several bills. Of particular concern to the congressman was the plight of Afro-Colombians (Ribando 2007). Members of both the Congressional Hispanic Caucus and the Congressional Black Caucus traveled to Honduras on this trip guided by former CABO and ODECO president Celeo Casildo Alvarez. In April 2022, U.S. congressional representatives visited Central America, meeting with the Fraternal Black Organization of Honduras (OFRANEH), and learned about challenges Garifuna have experienced. Representatives Ilhan Omar (MN), Cori Bush (MO), Jamaal Bowman (NY), Jesús "Chuy" García (IL), and a representative from Jan Schakowsky's (IL) office visited OFRANEH at that time. The public officials, also members of the Congressional Black Caucus and Hispanic Caucus, joined U.S.-based organizations on a fact-finding mission to Central America (Guatemala, Honduras) to uncover the roots of migration. Upon their return they concluded that corporate interests and international institutions, as well as U.S. government policies, contributed to destabilizing the region (García 2022; Castillo 2022a; SOA Watch 2022). The representatives followed their visit by introducing to Congress House Resolution 1521, on December 14, 2021, to ensure the rights of the Garifuna. The resolution condemned the violence committed against the Garifuna, as well as calling for the accountability of international institutions and the Honduran government's role in the abuses. In the past, Representatives Janice Schakowsky and Henry "Hank" Johnson raised awareness of human rights and land abuses in Honduras. Representative Schakowsky's 2014 draft resolution highlights the human rights and land abuses that are being committed by the Honduran government against the Garifuna and other ethnic populations. In March 2021, Representative Hank Johnson from Georgia reintroduced the Berta Caceres Human Rights Act, to suspend U.S. funding of police and military operation until the Honduran government initiates investigations of law enforcement violations of human rights in Honduras.[42]

U.S. public officials' contacts, visits to Garifuna communities, and bill proposals raise the potential for the ethnic groups to coalesce and work with Torres representing their district of high Garifuna population concentration. Overall, Congressman Torres's initiatives signal progress in Garifuna political engagement with the potential to address concerns abroad and in New York. Fortunately, this time Garifuna organizations' lack of a unified voting bloc supporting a single candidate for U.S. Congress in the city resulted in a positive outcome.[43]

Local Election Campaigns in the Bronx

Another competitive local political post in the 2021 election was that of Bronx borough president. From 1987 to 2017 a Puerto Rican has consecutively been elected as the Bronx borough president, and the Garifuna community has sustained contacts with each one through their organizations. The Bronx has the highest Latino population (54.8 percent estimated) compared to the other races in the boroughs (NYC Planning 2021). It was expected that front-runner Latino Fernando Cabrera (Puerto Rican and Dominican) would be elected borough president in 2021; however, African American Vanessa Gibson won. Cabrera was interviewed on a popular online Garifuna program, *Conversing with Arnold Ciego—Garifuna Civic Action (Conversando con Arnold Ciego—Accion Civica Garifuna)*.[44] Guatemalan Garifuna Arnold Ciego is a Christian minister and community organizer whose multifaceted program includes interviews with Garifuna organizers and public officials from Central America. Ciego, Murphy Valentine, and Belinda Crisanto interviewed Cabrera, asking him his connections and how he would aid the Garifuna community. Cabrera mentioned his support through relief aid and travels to Honduras during the recent 2020 Hurricanes Eta and Iota disaster. He also mentioned his contacts with Garifuna leaders and measures he would implement to address economic development and immigration concerns if elected. During one of his responses, Cabrera noted factions that existed within the Garifuna community. He urged Garifuna organizations to come together as one voice to reap political and economic gains during this critical period of elections in the city where the ethnic group has an opportunity. Garifuna Coalition USA, Ávila, and Jorge Rochez, leader of the Garifuna American Law Enforcement Association, participated, acknowledging Cabrera's support of the community and being one of the first elected officials to hire a Garifuna on his staff (Ciego 2021). An official endorsement was not announced, and the extent of Garifuna support for each candidate is unknown. Most likely, Vanessa Gibson gained greater Garifuna support in winning the election as borough president. Gibson also has Garifuna on her staff, and her visibility is greater at Garifuna Coalition USA events. During the online Garifuna Civic Action forum, José F. Ávila had questioned Cabrera's lack of visibility at Garifuna events. Gibson spearheaded efforts recognizing the Garifuna culture in City Hall in 2014, 2018, and the Bronx in 2019 and sustains a working relationship with the Garifuna Coalition USA. During her campaign, Gibson and Ritchie Torres attended an event at Casa Yurumein (Castillo 2021).

Several local offices are important to the Garifuna in districts in the southern section of the Bronx, their population concentration. New York's 15th Congressional District (West Bronx, South Bronx), New York State Assembly District 79 (Claremont Village, Crotona Park East, Crotona, Morrisania), New York State Senate District 32 (Parkchester, Soundview, West Farms, Hunts Point, Longwood, Concourse, Melrose, Morrisania, Mott Haven, East Tremont, and Westchester Square), and New York City's 16th City Council district (Concourse, Morrisania, Highbridge, Morris Heights, and Tremont). However, there are several public officials in other districts with Garifuna population engaging and supporting Garifuna organization activities. For example, in the New York State Assembly District 87 (Van Nest, Parkchester, Castle Hill), Karines Reyes supports Garifuna activities. Reyes has led in sponsoring a bill in the State Assembly to declare Garifuna American Heritage Month. She also collaborated with Casa Yurumei, in 2021 hosting the Garifuna American heritage virtual lobby day with several public officials whose districts include Garifuna populations. Because of the coronavirus pandemic, the onsite annual event was held virtually. At a Garifuna town hall meeting Reyes expressed her connectedness with the Garifuna. She stated she is from a community founded by maroons in the Dominican Republic know as San Lorenzo de Los Mina.[45]

During the 2021 election campaign several seats in the New York State Legislature were open. Garifuna organizations' political engagement activity was minimal. One candidate was an incumbent the community knew and the other was endorsed by the previous officeholder with whom Garifuna organizations had close ties. For the New York State Senate District 32, Luis R. Sepulveda was reelected. At a recent 2022 Garifuna American Heritage Month event hosted by the Garifuna Coalition USA, Sepulveda and Bronx borough president Vanessa Gibson were present. It was acknowledged that Sepulveda introduced Senate Resolution No. 1802 "memorializing Gov. Kathy Hochul to declare March 11, 2022, to April 12, 2022, as Garifuna American Heritage Month in the State of New York." After incumbent Michael Blake declared his campaign for U.S. Congress, Chantel Jackson announced her candidacy for the 79th State Assembly District seat. Jackson, who was endorsed by Blake, won. Since beginning her term in 2021, Jackson, like Sepulveda, supported recognition of Garifuna American Heritage Month in the New York State Assembly. She supported K117 "Memorializing Governor Andrew M. Cuomo to declare March 11, 2021, to April 12, 2021, as Garifuna American Heritage Month in the State of New York." The bill was introduced to the general assembly by Karines Reyes. The following year Reyes again introduced the bill to the new governor: K00646 "Memorializing Governor Kathy Hochul to declare March 11, 2022, to April 12, 2022, as Garifuna-American Heritage Month in the State of New York" (NYS Track bill; King 2022).

As previously mentioned, in most New York City elections the Democratic primary is the most competitive. For the most part, Latino and Black Americans are the front-runner candidates competing with each other. However, during the 2021 Democratic primary, out of the six candidates for the New York City Council 16th District there were two West Africans, Ahmadou T. Diallo and Abdourahamane Diallo (Skurnik 2017). There was also a candidate of Haitian descent, Yves Fillius. The Democratic primary winner was Althea Stevens, a Black New York native, receiving 90.8 percent of the vote, compared to 9.2 percent for her Republican rival. Althea Stevens replaced Vanessa Gibson, whose term ended and who was elected the Bronx borough president. Althea Stevens engaged the Garifuna community by hosting a "Ranked Choice Voting training" with local Garifuna community leaders. Garifuna Siria Alvarez, Stevens's deputy campaign manager, presided over the event (Election Results).[46]

Although the city council's 16th District has been held for several consecutive terms by African Americans, West Africans have in recent years competed for this position. The most recent and current wave of immigrants from West Africa is civically engaged in the Bronx. This situation presents opportunities for Garifuna organizations to forge future alliances with this group. In 2010 West Africans established the Bronx African Advisory Council, which is a group to advise the Bronx borough president on issues (e.g., crime, housing, discrimination in schools) of concern to their communities. For the 2013 city council elections representing the 16th District there were four West African candidates. Two candidates were Nigerian: Bola Omotosho, who served on the community board; and Abiodun Bello. Naaimat Muhammed, of Ghanaian parents, founded the 16th District African and Muslim Council, and was also a staffer for former city councilwoman Helen D. Foster. Ahmadou Diallo is from the country of Guinea (Wall 2013; Ademo 2011). As both groups continue their civic engagement, the prospects are high for a West African or a Garifuna elected official in the city. In addition, through collaborating to endorse a candidate, Puerto Rican political control in the Bronx can be challenged in obtaining more resources for their Black ethnic communities.

Alliances with the NAACP

Interestingly, since 2013 Garifuna organizations have increased their alignment with Black political candidates and collaborated with an African American organization. They adopted some approaches similar to those of other ethnic groups in New York City, such as Haitians, West Indians, and other Black ethnics (Wright Austin 2018; Kasinitz 1992). Since 2020 the International Garifuna Council (IGC), has been collaborating with the Bronx NAACP (National Association for the Advancement of Colored People) branch, engaging in voter education and registration. Although registered in 2020, the IGC had already been active a few years. Its leader, Belizean Garifuna Trevor Palacio, directs the organization from California with members in Garifuna communities in Central America as well as in U.S. cities. In New York City an IGC member introduced the Bronx NAACP president to the organization.[47] The IGC identifies itself as the "governing body for the Garífuna Nation." Palacio established his organization after encountering differences in seeking to work with the Garifuna Nation group. The IGC also seeks to address social, economic, and political well-being of the Garifuna in their entire communities. The IGC sustained an active social media presence during the COVID-19 pandemic that limited its on-site functions. Its activities are fundraising for development projects in Garifuna communities in Central America, hurricane relief support, raising awareness on issues like climate change impacts, promoting events, online programs discussing Garifuna issues and historical figures, and collaborating with organization leaders, including other ethnicities. As part of the IGC, Palacio established the Garinagu Ethnic Group Action Committee (GEGAC) focused on voter education and registration and lobbying for immigration legislation and against human rights violations. Included in GEGAC's political platform is raising awareness of Garifuna candidates and elections affecting them in their respective Central American states and in the United States. The IGC has also supported candidates for local office in New York City, including Garifuna Sonia Fernandez's unsuccessful 2017 candidacy for the city council. The Bronx NAACP president Biarni Burke served as one of Fernandez's advisers. Fernandez was nevertheless recognized by the Bronx NAACP for her community work at the organization's fundraiser attended by several Garifuna. Since then, Burke has collaborated with the ICG in voter education and registration panel discussions and presentations. During the 2020 and 2021 city elections, Burke was among the speakers scheduled to participate in Garifuna voter education, registration, and civic education community public meetings.

I first met Bronx NAACP president Burke during the inauguration ceremony of former State Assembly member Erik Stevenson. Burke told me that the NAACP is the largest and most recognized civil rights organization in the United States and invited me to attend the meetings. Through my studies I had knowledge of the organization's history of advocating for social, educational, economic, and political equity for all seeking to eradicate all forms of discrimination. Surprisingly, the Bronx NAACP headquarters was walking distance from my living quarters in the South Bronx. At the Bronx NAACP meetings I've attended, Mr. Burke presided and articulated his commitment to voter empowerment training and educating residents about the significance of participation. Other issues addressed at the meetings, in addition to low voter turnout in the Bronx, are crime and violence, unfair sentencing legislation, the contaminated environment, the need for health support services, housing, and socioeconomic inequalities. Garifuna leaders have attended the meetings and correspond with Burke. At the 2022 "Garifuna Community Development Campaign" in the Bronx, led by the IGC, Burke was among the listed guest speakers, public officials, and Garifuna activists. NAACP member and community leader Dion Powell represented Mr. Burke at the event. Powell, a 2020 candidate for the New York State Assembly 79th District in the Bronx, shared his connections with Garifuna leaders, who encouraged his desire to learn Spanish for greater community cohesion (Lewis and Williams 2022).[48] The IGC's association with the Bronx NAACP, as well as the Garifuna Coalition USA's with the Bronx Parkchester NAACP branch, presents potential for the ethnic group to increase its alliances with African American organizations. Several Garifuna leaders recognize the importance of forming alliances with African American organizations and politicians to ensure support of their community concerns. During conversations with several organization leaders, they expressed this importance especially with the recent increase in African American public officials in New York City elected to key positions (Green, Moloney, Giralt 2021; Balk, Sommerfeldt, Gartland 2022).

Conclusion

From the 1990s through the early decades of the 2000s, Garifuna have addressed their evolving social needs through their organizations, engaging in politics to address their issues. Among the community's needs their organizations have addressed are attending to their undocumented immigrant population, seeking meeting locations, advocating against police brutality and gun violence, establishing trades employment training, and creating activities for their youth. Garifuna identified with others in their community, collaborating to address many of these shared concerns, such as Garifuna leaders involved with Allianza America, the New York Hispanic Clergy association, and the Roman Catholic Church. In addition to collaborating with their community to support public officials, they have also lobbied for immigration reforms with Latino institutions. Garifuna organizations have collaborated to host town hall meetings with activities, inviting elected officials to attend and speak. Civically engaged in the new century, Garifuna organizations were able to gain financial support and legislation supporting their culture. During this period their groups allied with Black and Latino officials and organizations. Based on recent local election campaigns in New York City, their organizations' divided support for competing candidates shows that they are not a unified voting bloc. This reflects the fact that many of their organizations grew and became engaged politically. Garifuna organizations' political contacts on the local and national levels open opportunities to address issues in their home countries. The next chapter, focusing on Garifuna transnational connections with their homelands from the 1990s to the present, references this potential.

Chapter 7

Central America and St. Vincent from the 1990s to the Present

The post–Cold War rise in democracy in Central America facilitated cross-border exchanges between nations and ethnic groups. This was part of globalization's effects on transnationalism, defined as the linking of people across states through cultural, economic, and political ties. Garifuna connections with their homeland grew with the availability of the internet and the expansion of social media, facilitating exchanges among all their communities abroad. Brothers José and Tomás Ávila established an internet link for Garifuna in 1996; this expanded into the Garifuna World website in 1997, which provided audio links so that visitors could listen to Garifuna music (Ávila and Ávila 2017; England 2006). In 1999 Jorge "Garifuna" Cacho established Garinet, a comprehensive website encompassing news, entertainment, and live broadcasts from Honduran Garifuna communities. These early communication platforms were followed by web pages, blogs, Facebook, Google links, WhatsApp, Twitter, TikTok, and Instagram.[1] Another important information source was the *Being Garifuna* blog, started in 2012 by Teofilio Colon Jr. to document Garifuna cultural events and history (Pearson 2011).

In this chapter the book's argument is relevant particularly to Garifuna groups' role in facilitating efforts to address issues in their homeland. The chapter describes New York City Garifuna organizations' connections to their countries of origin and the outcomes of these contacts from the 1990s to the present. This experience is similar to that of other Black immigrant groups who also sustain ties with their countries of origin. A difference with the Garifuna is that their organizations in New York have consistently been Garifuna born in Central America. This circumstance contributes to the lack of conflict that otherwise could arise over deciding whether to focus on issues solely abroad or only in New York. In addition, New York City is considered by many Garifuna as an extension of their Central American communities through various transnational exchanges. A leader presented in this chapter who is involved both in New York City and in her homeland expresses her views on the causes of migration and demonstrates how Garifuna issues interconnect between both locations.

The chapter begins by highlighting international forums hosted by New York City Garifuna organizations and attended by delegates from their Central American communities. Forum discussions called for unity among the Garifuna, cultural preservation, and encouraging economic development in their Central American communities, including reparations. The next chapter segment turns to the new century with the application of some development investment measures, as new and long-standing Garifuna organizations with sustained ties to their homeland address issues there while simultaneously caring for their Bronx communities. What follows in the next chapter section are details about Garifuna land issues in Central America, as well as New York City forums held to address human rights and territorial challenges in Central America, including fatalities, repression, and threats Garifuna activists have experienced. The last segment features New York City Garifuna organizations' exchanges with their Carib descendant community in the island of St. Vincent, where ties have increased in this century.

1990s International Summit Meetings

A year after the 1990 Happy Land fire, the first in a series of Garifuna forums occurred. At the 1991 Garifuna summit meeting held at Medgar Evers College in Brooklyn, Garifuna from various U.S. cities, but primarily Los Angeles, gathered for the three-day event. Some of the objectives discussed were unifying Garifuna, addressing the needs of New York City Garifuna, supporting cultural preservation, encouraging economic development in Central American communities, lobbying the Honduran government to recognize Garifuna Day (April 12), and increasing Garifuna political representation. The summit's theme was *Uwala Busiganu, Garifuna Wagia* (Don't be ashamed, we are Garifuna). The keynote speaker was Dr. George Irish, who headed the Caribbean Research Center at Medgar Evers College and was also the founder and editor in chief of the scholarly journal *Wadabagei*.[2] Dr. Irish supported Garifuna community activities and participated in their 1997 bicentennial conference in Honduras. Tomás Alberto Ávila and José Francisco Ávila, organizers of the New York summit meeting, noted several outcomes, including HIV/AIDS workshops in the community, a Garifuna student club at City University of New York called Libana Baba (Father's Grandchildren), and Felix Miranda's radio program *Lumalali Garifuna* (Ávila and Ávila 2008; Garcia 2013).

The next summit, in 1992, was held in Los Angeles. It had the same goals as the first summit, and its theme was *Awaraüguni, Agibudaguni Liadun Aban* (Separation, Dispersion, Reunification). Garifuna and prominent leaders from Belize, Guatemala, and Honduras, as well as from St. Vincent and the Grenadines, attended the three-day meeting, as did many individuals who had participated in the first conference. At the 1992 summit, the idea of a bicentennial celebration to commemorate the Garifuna's arrival in Central America was first suggested. Both Hondurans Against AIDS and the Garifuna Council of New York emerged after this meeting (Ávila and Ávila 2008; Garcia 2013). The Garifuna Council of New York was led by Executive Director Felix Miranda and President Celso Castro, both of whom participated in the summits. In New York City, Miranda was involved with the Belizean group United Garifuna, Inc., and Castro had been part of Frente Unido Hondureño (FUH). The Garifuna Council of New York was established in January 1993 to improve Garifuna lives in New York, motivate youth involvement in the council's programs, establish branches in other states, and prepare the ethnic group for the twenty-first century. This group also responded to the summit's goal of unifying Garifuna, with a membership that included individuals from Belize, Guatemala, and Honduras (England 2006; Ávila and Ávila 2008).

In 1993 the Garifuna Council of New York drafted a document to be presented to the United Nations to petition the British government to pay reparations for the Garifuna's exile in 1797 from St. Vincent. The issue of reparations had been discussed at the 1992 summit in Los Angeles (England 2006; Ávila and Ávila 2008; King 2013). In November 1994 the Garifuna Council of New York held a forum in the city, continuing this dialogue with the community. This forum was smaller than the previous summits, but some of the same organizations attended the meeting. At the forum, Belizean Garifuna Dr. Theodore Aranda presented his discourse justifying reparations to the Garifuna as a response to Britain's illicit actions taken against Black Caribs on the island of St. Vincent (Aranda 1998). Claims by African Americans and, more recently, Caribbeans influenced many Garifuna groups to join the demand for reparations. In 1989, a year after Japanese Americans imprisoned during World War II were compensated, Michigan congressman John Conyers called for the U.S. government to study the impact of slavery on Blacks and make recommendations regarding reparations for their descendants. Black organizations took the lead in popularizing the reparations movement in the 1990s, noting that uncompensated Black labor had contributed to the United States' global economic leadership (Biondi 2003). Identifying the Garifuna as an African-descended population exploited by Europeans, Garifuna organizations began to make claims for reparations. Among the organizations present at the reparations forum were Unification of Garifuna Culture—*Unificación Cultural Garifuna* (UNCUGA), Libaya Baba Garifuna Students Association, United Garifuna Association, Association Garifuna Guatemalteca, Prometra Garifuna Society, and National Garifuna Council of Belize (Aranda 1998; Johnson 2007, 274). In the twenty-first century, through the Garifuna Coalition USA, reparations were pursued as Caribbean nations presented their claims to European nations. With all its great initiatives, the Garifuna Council of New York was short-lived. Such a fate was common for many Garifuna organizations in the city.

Other Transnational Connections and International Reunions

There was no follow-up to the 1992 Garifuna summit, but Garifuna leaders in Belize hosted a meeting in Dangriga in 1994. U.S. Garifuna and others throughout Central America were invited to attend, and participants from past summits were also present. One outcome of the meeting was the formation of the Central American Black Organization (CABO), or in Spanish, the Organización Negra Centroamericana (ONECA). CABO's goal was for Central American Blacks to unite and establish a platform to address their cultural, political, and economic concerns.[3] CABO members came from Belize, Costa Rica, Guatemala, Honduras, Nicaragua, and Panama (Garcia 2013). The number of international gatherings of Garifuna increased in both Central America and the United States. These transnational exchanges were part of the post–Cold War globalization era, which also included monetary transfer. The Garifuna became a significant part of the U.S. immigrant community, and they sent money home to family members, helping sustain their home countries' national economies (Endo et al. 2010). In addition to these monetary transfers, business, political, and religious transactions occurred across borders. For instance, Casa Gari, a Honduran-based Garifuna organization established in the 1990s, maintained ties with Garifuna in New York City. The group was awarded a grant by the Inter-American Development Bank to support its cassava production, business training, and a cooperative of Garifuna women engaged in producing the product. This Garifuna organization sought to capitalize on economic ties across borders by importing cassava bread (made from processed manioc) from Honduras to the United States (MacCulloch 2001).[4] Unfortunately, the project never materialized, ending the investment and time many had sown in this group.

Garifuna organizations in New York also supported the land rights movement in their home countries. For example, the Honduran group "Hope of Limon" (Lemenigui Limun) raised funds to reclaim usurped land in a part of the country known as Vallecito. It received support from Garifuna organizations in New York City, including the proceeds of a benefit concert (Garcia 2013; England 2006). After a long struggle that included threats and violence, Garifuna groups with the Black Fraternal Organization of Honduras (OFRANEH) were able to recuperate the land in Vallecito through legal victories. In Honduras, threats to Garifuna subsistence increased as the government pursued large-scale tourism as an alternative development for the government's own economic gains. In an attempt to address the 1990s economic crisis, laws were passed allowing foreign ownership of lands, circumventing constitutional provisions, and granting municipalities autonomy to coastal lands to allow Honduran or foreign purchasers to reap financial gains. Structural adjustment programs of the International Monetary Fund (IMF), recommending decentralization as part of development measures in Honduras, favored investors' initiatives to purchase land in the coastal region for development projects.[5] Further pressures Honduran Garifuna faced were agricultural laws stating that after a period of three years of uninterrupted squatting on land, any citizen above the age of sixteen has the right to claim it as their property (Brondo 2017; Loperena 2010). In the following century, the adverse effects of government legislation resulted in more Garifuna mobilizing with support of organizations in New York City to defend their land rights and denounce repression.

Nevertheless, international gatherings were prevalent during this period. Garifuna evangelical Christians of various denominations held annual conventions, starting in 1990 with meetings in Belize, Honduras, and Guatemala. Evangelical Garifuna in New York and other U.S. cities were actively engaged in these meetings and made the trip to Central America each year.[6] In the conventions, panel discussions on social, cultural, and health issues were also part of the program. Another international exchange centered on the 1997 bicentennial celebration of the Garifuna's arrival in Central America. It was a multifaceted event held in La Ceiba, Honduras, and encompassed cultural, political, and educational forums attended by Garifuna from the United States, Belize, Guatemala, and Nicaragua and representatives from the Caribbean islands. Prominent dignitaries, scholars, and government officials spoke at the event. One result of this initiative was greater awareness of the Garifuna's existence and contributions, resulting in new legislation in Honduras associated with the group. As mentioned in the previous chapter, the Garifuna Coalition USA emerged after the bicentennial celebration. Honduran Garifuna José F. Ávila, who organized both U.S. summit meetings, was involved in organizing the celebration, along with his brother Tomás A. Ávila. José, an accountant, was introduced to the New York City Garifuna community through his contact with Prometra Garifuna Society leader Leslie Avila Lacayo. Many of the proposals discussed in the forums regarding economic development and cultural preservation were implemented in the next century.

The New Century: Development Measures, New Organization Ties to Homelands

Amid the challenges Garifuna communities faced in the new century, one positive event early in the first decade resonated in the Garifuna community. In 2001 UNESCO acknowledged Garifuna language, music, and dance as an Intangible Cultural Heritage of Humanity, attesting to the importance of promoting and preserving Garifuna culture (M. Cayetano and R. Cayetano 2005). This effort was spearheaded by the Belizean organization National Garifuna Council (NGC). It was a fulfillment of past forums' discussions calling for preservation of the Garifuna culture. Years after, follow-up meetings were held for its implementation, with representation of Garifuna organizations from various regions (J. Ávila 2021). Also, in this century international forums continued, and investment began in Garifuna tourism, led by their investment club founded in 2001 in New York City. Garifuna organizations continued being involved in the Bronx as well as in their homelands. In addition, a transnational Garifuna organization initiated action to address concerns in their homeland. As they resisted usurpation of their lands in Central America, Garifuna faced increased repression and human rights violations. Different strategies surfaced among Garifuna in handling land issues. A plan to have Garifuna use their financial transfers in recovering lost land was discussed. Some measures were applied and others were not.

Remittance, Tourism Investment, International Meeting

A topic I discussed with Garifuna leader José Ávila during our first meeting was remittance and its effects on Garifuna communities. Our discussion centered on findings of a study of remittance and Garifuna communities. The study comprised his contacts with the Inter-American Development Bank and noted scholar, Manuel Orozco, who worked on remittances. Sending money to their home country (transfer of payments, remittances) is widespread among Hondurans, as well as with other Central American immigrants. In Honduras, remittances fulfill an important component of the country's gross national product (GNP). The 2019 total value of revenue from remittances was 22 percent of Honduras's gross domestic product (GDP) (Bustamante 2020). And it was even higher in 2021 with 25.29 percent, thus far the highest level reached (Honduras Remittance 2023). The country is heavily dependent on remittances as part of its GDP, which contributes to the reasons the Honduran government embraces immigration diplomacy. This measure the government uses to shore up the Honduran economy. Studies have shown that Garifuna participate substantially in sending remittances to their communities, which lack adequate infrastructure and have many other needs. Family remittances help support small businesses, education, building or renovating houses, and assisting with basic needs. Remittances for community needs, such as for churches, electricity, and water systems, are also common (Endo et al. 2010). Unfortunately, the downsides of remittance are that Garifuna have grown dependent on it and that permanent migration contributes to broken kinship networks, causing loss of cultural knowledge (a traditional role of women). In addition, there is a shift away from agriculture and toward relying on monetary transfers, while at the same time Garifuna seek opportunities to migrate abroad (Mark Anderson 2009, 206). Based on study results showing substantial Garifuna remittance revenue, José Ávila envisioned a plan to shift finances from "consumption to productive use" that would facilitate applying capital to recuperate Garifuna lands lost through legal procedures. Although it was a great plan, it did not materialize.

Being part of the Garifuna Coalition USA allowed Ávila to apply his investment initiatives. Ávila embraces the opportunities of free enterprise to benefit the Garifuna. This he has promoted in his New Horizon Investment Club, investing in real estate, stocks, and also tourism in Honduran Garifuna communities, discussed later. In addition, he believes in working with public officials, private business, and international institutions to uplift the Garifuna community in the United States and Central America. Ávila's views contrast with those of some Garifuna leaders and analysts of international institutions' negative effects on community development (Brondo 2017; Loperena 2010; J. Ávila 2021). Although faced with strong sentiments against him by some Garifuna, he continues his mission initiating various community projects.

In 2005 Ávila and the Garifuna Coalition USA led a retreat advocating unity among all Garifuna, including those in Central America. Garifuna leaders' desire for unity had been an ongoing challenge, and the concept of a "Garifuna Nation" was a popular discussion topic. At the coalition's July 2005 retreat in the Pocono Mountains of Pennsylvania, economic development in Garifuna communities was another objective—specifically, capitalizing on the tourism potential in Honduras. In addition to the various New York City organizations, Honduran Garifuna presidential candidate Bernard Martinez, a representative of the current Honduran president, and the mayors of Puerto Cortés and Limon participated in the conference (Ávila and Ávila 2008; J. Ávila 2006).[7] Primarily Honduran Garifuna organizations participated in the Poconos retreat (see the list in appendix B)—a reflection of the Garifuna Coalition USA's majority-Honduran leadership.

When Honduran president Ricardo Maduro (2002–6) visited the United States in 2005, the Garifuna Coalition USA, upon invitation, sent Tomás Ávila to represent it at a meeting in Miami, Florida. The Ávila brothers sought to establish ties with the Honduran government to facilitate their development initiatives for the Garifuna community there. Through José Ávila's involvement with the New Horizon Investment Club and the Garifuna Coalition USA, he created a tourism initiative. New Horizon invested in the initiative on behalf of two Honduran Garifuna communities. The Garifuna investors became 7 percent shareholders of the Honduran Tela Bay Tourism Development. They had a five-year period (2006–11) to purchase stock, according to the contract. As president of the investment club, Ávila acted as the financial representative of the Garifuna communities of Tornabé and Miami, initiating negotiations with private and state entities in Honduras. The two communities in the Tela Bay region had long protested large-scale development. A political rally was also held in 2004 in Tornabé opposing the sale of land. Several New York City Garifuna organizations also opposed the sale of their lands in Honduras and financially aided the rally. The Hondurans Against AIDS organization led in raising funds ($1,000.00) to pay for buses to transport people to Tornabé to participate in the demonstrations (Carrillo 2004). Nevertheless, the tourism project initiatives continued and the resort opened a decade later.[8]

Ávila also established a partnership with the National Garifuna Tourism Chamber to centralize Garifuna businesses so that they could capitalize on tourism investments in the region with microbusinesses (Ávila and Ávila 2008; Endo et al. 2010). Several Garifuna opposed this initiative, which many perceived as giving in to government demands, and some Garifuna groups completely resisted the government's tourism initiatives. During discussions of the tourism project in Honduras, Ávila addressed critics' questioning whether Garifuna (U.S. and Honduras) had the financial means to partner in this business. He stated:

> The Garifuna community is prepared to assume the challenge and has the financial ability to fulfill the commitment, since according to the Study Remittances and Development: Lessons of the Honduran Garifuna Transnational Community, the Garifunas residing abroad sent a record 270 million dollars to their native country last year and we recognize our role as key actors who can affect, with the remittances that we send, the economic and social life of our communities and it is our intention to promote the productive use of remittances for saving and investment. Furthermore, the Garifunas plan to get in contact with multilateral development organizations, such as the Inter-American Development Bank (IABD) and the World Bank, to explore the possibility of obtaining financing to assure the participation [of] the members of the Garifuna communities of Honduras. (Ávila and Ávila 2008, 124)

Ávila's view supporting economic growth measures for the Garifuna community willing to collaborate with international institutions, the Honduran government, and business reflects the diverse opinions in the ethnic group's vision of development. His views align more with the Organization for Community Development (ODECO), which collaborated with him in Garifuna international forums. Both support Garifuna economic gains from tourism project initiatives and working with the Honduran government. ODECO, compared to OFRANEH, supports different strategies addressing Garifuna claims for economic, social, and political justice. ODECO tends to view tourism development measures initiated by the Honduran government on Garifuna territories as inevitable, and the strategy is to work with the state's tourism initiative to guarantee that Garifuna as partners receive a fair share in the development project. In contrast, OFRANEH supports complete autonomy for Garifuna territory, opposing neoliberal economic development plans (Brondo 2017; Anderson 2009; Garcia 2013). At the next retreat in April 2007 in La Ceiba, Honduras, the same initiative supporting economic development through tourism was discussed, in addition to advocating for Garifuna unity (Ávila and Ávila 2008).

Continued Homeland Connections

Garifuna continued to engage with their Central American communities directly as well as indirectly as they addressed issues in their U.S. communities. Before she started Garifuna Community Services in 2016, I met Gregoria Flores and learned of her experiences in Honduras and the challenges confronting the Garifuna. Previously Flores was the general coordinator of OFRANEH. In May 2005, she was shot and wounded in Honduras while collecting data to present to the Inter-American Court of Human Rights. She discussed the Honduran government's role in human rights abuses that Garifuna experienced in defending their lands. She explained that this, along with threats to her life, contributed to her migration as a political exile to the United States, where she continues her work. Her political activism transferred also to supporting Garifuna migrants in New York City. Flores provided historical analysis of Garifuna migration to the United States. She describes this phenomenon as being a result of the Honduran government's granting foreign enterprises authority to use the Garifuna northern coastal territory as part of their business ventures. She states that U.S. policy makers working on immigration reform should take into consideration the migration of Hondurans to the United States as a result of U.S. industries exploiting Honduran coastal lands since the early 1900s. Flores explains that this trend by the Honduran government in seeking to reap economic benefits from exploiting the northern coastlands continues with new projects involving foreign enterprises and further threatens the Garifuna group's existence. Her views of Garifuna development align with OFRANEH's stance questioning rather than supporting foreign investment in their land.[9]

Flores is active in community affairs in New York City, attending a variety of events as a representative of her organization. At a meeting at Hostos Community College in the Bronx that focused on domestic violence survival, local officials were present along with representatives of nonprofit organizations working on human trafficking and violence associated with migration. Local officials Vanessa Gibson, Rafael Salamanca Jr., and Nathalia Fernandez all were familiar with the Garifuna, having attended past Garifuna events. Flores, representing her organization, was present together with a Garifuna migrant, and they both spoke. In her presentation

Flores sought to connect conditions in the countries of origin to the cause of migration to the United States:

> There is a separation, it is about untying, it is about disconnecting the violations suffered by the person from the political and social condition of the country. And it must be understandable for all those who are navigating this system that if the state-government of each one of the countries does not establish mechanisms to guarantee the human rights of individuals, to guarantee the human rights of people within the countries, these people will, regardless of whether it is a case of domestic violence or a case of violence and persecution by gangs, if there are no mechanisms on the part of the state to resolve these cases and that . . . has a direct link with the asylum application, these women may be indigenous women and we can link it directly to the issue of race. Because this woman, in addition to being a woman, also belongs to a social group, in a way that is differentiated by her race. And governments do not really have an effective policy for the guarantee and defense of the process. (Iborra Mallent 2019, 153)

Flores was expressing her concerns that structural and political issues in the country of origin are not considered in the application process for U.S. asylum. She emphasized that human rights violations are not taken into consideration, opposing actions taken against racial minorities and indigenous populations in countries of departure such as Honduras. Indirectly, Flores was also referring to the Honduran government, as she pointed to the Garifuna woman accompanying her seeking asylum. Flores stressed that until the countries of origin address issues of violence, persecution, and crime, migration to the United States will be constant. Iborra Mallent (2021) looked into this situation, interviewing Garifuna leaders in New York City. He links migration to usurpation of Garifuna lands, based on discussions with Gregoria Flores and OFRANEH leader Carla Garcia in New York City. He explains Garifuna's attempts to use this claim to help recently arrived migrants obtain political asylum to remain in the United States. When unable to obtain political asylum, migrants present alternative claims such as domestic and sexual abuse.

A study by Garifuna journalist Kenny F. Castillo (2019a) offers a more comprehensive view of Garifuna migration. The journalist also documents repression and violence that Garifuna experience defending their land rights. Like Iborra Mallent's, his study focuses on the 2013–14 Garifuna migration wave. He provides reasons for Garifuna migrating to the United

States primarily because of lack of opportunities due to racial discrimination and employment. Castillo's analysis aligns with my observations made on annual visits to Garifuna communities in the Port of Cortes, Tela Bay, Trujillo area, and the Colón province region from which many have recently departed for the United States. Speaking to Garifuna leaders and residents there and also in New York City, I learned that most Garifuna migrate to seek employment opportunities to improve their living standards. A small number of Garifuna do qualify for political asylum because of their activism or related cases and have been granted such a stay. Although Garifuna Community Services is a more domestically centered organization, its leader, Flores, continues to be engaged in Garifuna land rights. She maintains ongoing communications with OFRANEH leaders and supports their functions, such as community forums in New York. The significance here is that the Garifuna leader conveys Garifuna migration as a domestic issue, also connected to challenges in her homeland, as well as to foreign industries exploiting Honduran coastlands. Flores encourages deported Garifuna to become involved in their communities' resistance to usurpation of their lands upon return to their homelands.

Another Garifuna organization in New York with sustained ties to Central America is SHANY. The leader of the group, Garifuna Cresencio Bulnes, has long maintained direct contact with his Honduran homeland, aiding humanitarian relief efforts and sending medical supplies and other goods, listed in the previous chapter. He also is politically engaged in Honduras. This he accomplishes while at the same time SHANY provides services to the community in New York City. Since the early 2000s, Bulnes has been involved in attempting to form a political platform to address Garifuna needs in New York City as well as Honduras. He is active in his internet radio program, providing updates on Honduran politics and interviewing activists, local public officials, and organization leaders in both Honduras and New York. In 2014, when OFRANEH sought to establish its office in New York, SHANY allowed the use of its facility. Cresencio's organization also has served as a location where nationals can process their Honduran passports. SHANY was also one of the many Garifuna organizations fundraising to support the African Heritage Month celebration in Honduras. The organization supported the 2011 "Drum March" gathering in the capital, Tegucigalpa. Performances by Garifuna music artists and folkloric dance groups and other activities celebrated the culture.

Like Bulnes, Mirtha Colón, founder of the Casa Yurumein/Hondurans Against AIDS organization, attends to Garifuna community issues in the Bronx as well as in Central America. Her organization is affiliated with several other groups, including ODECO, based in La Ceiba, Honduras, in addition to the Central American Black Organization (CABO), both mentioned in the previous chapter. She has been part of CABO since it started in the past century, addressing political, social, and economic concerns of Blacks in Central America. Colón also has supported land rights activism and humanitarian relief efforts in Honduran Garifuna communities, hosting fundraisers in New York. In Honduras she sustains contacts with Garifuna leaders throughout the country. Since 2021 her group has supported youth development projects in Garifuna communities such as teaching them to cultivate small crops (Aparicio 2021). Overall, Flores, Ávila, Bulnes, and Colón continue their connections to their home countries, simultaneously managing issues in their New York City communities. Other Garifuna organizations that address issues in both locations are presented later in the chapter.

The Garifuna Nation, Transnational Organization

In the same year as the 2014 migration wave, Garifuna Nation, a transnational Garifuna organization, started in New York. (There had been past discussions about creating such a group during the bicentennial committee's 1998 retreat, and Garifuna Nation had been considered as a name for the Garifuna Coalition USA.) The organization held its first forum in the Bronx at Casa Yurumein's meeting location. Its goals were to unite the ethnic group as a nation and to support the economic, social, and political autonomy of all Garifuna communities (Vad 2020). Two young Garifuna activists, Pablo Blanco and Hector Zapata, in the past had also articulated the importance of the ethnic group uniting as one nation.[10] In addition to Central American and U.S. Garifuna who attended the first Garifuna Nation event in the Bronx, Garifuna descendants from St. Vincent were present, including Dr. Cadrin Gill, Trish St. Hill, and Senator Jomo Sanga Thomas. On May 30, 2014, Sanga Thomas introduced a bill in the senate of St. Vincent and the Grenadines that would bring legal action against the French and British governments for the injustices committed against the Garifuna and slaves on the island (W. Ramos 2014, 2015).

Garifuna Nation is involved in several transnational issues affecting the Garifuna. For instance, after armed authorities attempted to forcefully evict Garifuna from their Honduran community of Barra Vieja to expand the Tela Bay beach resort tourism project, the organization responded. In October 2014 one of the organization's leaders, Wellington Ramos, submitted a letter of complaint to the assistant secretary of state for Western Hemispheric affairs. The organization has also submitted letters and filed complaints about the ongoing human rights violations in Honduras to the United Nations, Organization of American States, Caribbean Community (CARICOM) intergovernmental organization, governments of Honduras and the United States, members of the U.S. Congress, Human Rights Watch, Amnesty International, and other pertinent institutions. One positive result came in May 2014 when U.S. Representative Janice Schakowsky from Illinois's 9th Congressional District introduced a resolution highlighting the many human rights and land abuses being committed by the Honduran government against the ethnic population.[11] Garifuna Nation and other organizations also protested the imprisonment of Honduran Garifuna activist Omar Suazo. Ramos submitted letters to Honduran officials, and other organizations held fundraisers and town hall meetings on behalf of the activist (Miller 2019).[12] Since its establishment I have attended Garifuna Nation meetings in New York as well as their Honduran gathering in Tornabé, in the Tela Bay region of Honduras. In Tornabé representatives from various Garifuna communities were present; aspiring and former political candidates, Garifuna education leaders, and university professors were among the attendees. Discussion focused on the need for self-sustainability, land rights issues, the need to sustain cultural (Garifuna) education, and increased Garifuna unity to establish a nation. Although the Garifuna Nation is registered in New York, its executive body and members are in different Garifuna communities in the United States and Central America. All throughout the COVID-19 pandemic, events and meetings were conducted online.

Land Issues in Central America

Other events during this period featured land rights issues occurring in Garifuna's Central American homelands. Garifuna organizations in New York attempted to address concerns. Honduran Garifuna experienced greater challenges than their counterparts in Belize. The post-coup period Garifuna and Indigenous territorial, environmental, and human rights violations increased in Honduras. Narcotics traffickers and gangs operated in remote areas and cities. Miskito and peasant communities also faced intensified threats by hired assassins, soldiers, businessmen, drug traffickers, and police officers regarding their land status. OFRANEH was also part of the resistance movement denouncing the coup, as opposed to the other Garifuna organization, ODECO, negotiating with the new government and lobbying for antidiscrimination and development initiatives. Titles to

Garifuna lands were secured by ODECO prior to the coup, but the process was flawed by restrictions. Challenges to Garifuna leaders increased after the coup. Participating in a peaceful protest in the outskirts of the city of Tela on March 28, 2011, OFRANEH's president, Miriam Miranda, was shot at with a tear gas cannister and was arrested and charged with sedition. During this period the tourist project in the Tela Bay region, funded by the Inter-American Development Bank and opposed by Garifuna organizations, was completed, followed by an airport nearby in May 2015 (Proceso Digital 2015). The Honduran Congress also approved the construction of special zones, or charter cities, in July 2013, granting transnational companies full autonomy separate from the country's laws. Legislation was presented on the pretext of opening employment opportunities. In addition, the Honduran Congress approved laws with stipulations for the state authority and control of minerals and metals in its entire national territory and maritime zone. Mining laws supporting construction of hydroelectric dam projects and exploration of hydrocarbons were approved. Another threat in the coastal region faced by the Garifuna and Misquito dwellers in the region was the government proposal to industrialize the fishing industries (Loperena 2016; Anderson 2009; Almendarez 2020).

New York City Forums Addressing Territorial and Human Rights

Several public forums in New York City focused on Garifuna territorial challenges, showing the Garifuna community's ongoing transnational activism and concerns. Garifuna New York City resident Carla Garcia, the international coordinator of the Honduran-based group OFRANEH, maintains contact with local human rights organizations and universities participating in forums involving Garifuna land and human rights violations. On October 26, 2017, a two-hour symposium titled "Canadian Imperialism in Latin America: Land Grabbing of Garifuna Communities" was held at the CUNY Graduate Center with more than two hundred people in attendance, including representatives of Garifuna organizations. The panel focused on the relationship between emergent imperialism in Canada and the dispossession and resettlement of the Garifuna in Honduras. OFRANEH leader Miriam Miranda was one of the panelists, and Professor Todd Gordon shared details from his coauthored book *Blood of Extraction: Canadian Imperialism in Latin America*. One of the chapters, "Authoritarian Capitalism: The New Normal in Honduras," focuses on Garifuna communities' current territorial challenges.[13] Gordon and Webber (2016) highlight the Honduras post-coup period and the Canadian government's relations ensuring its business interests. A Canadian tourism project is highlighted in the Trujillo Bay region. Facilitated by the Honduran government, the Canadian private business was granted illegal occupation of several Garifuna territories. Garifuna leaders with ties to community activists in this Honduran location, facing death threats and falsely imprisoned, were present at this forum. OFRANEH leaders also provided updates on this situation and court proceedings challenging the local government in this case, as well as accounts of other Honduran Garifuna communities experiencing challenges.

A similar event was held on July 12, 2017, at New York University (NYU). The organization Grassroots International hosted "An Evening with Miriam Miranda," sponsored by the NYU Center of Latin American and Caribbean Studies and cosponsored by several other organizations. Environmental, Garifuna, and Native American activists were present among the college students who were the majority of the audience. Present was the daughter of Berta Caceres, the indigenous Honduran environmentalist who was killed in 2016 while resisting a government-sponsored hydroelectric dam project in her community. The discussion centered on recent Honduran government legislation negatively impacting the Garifuna, the indigenous, and the poor. The history of Garifuna mobilization efforts and U.S. government influences in Honduras was also discussed.[14] Miranda stated that Honduras was second in the export of African palm globally, behind Colombia. African palm is cultivated extensively across the Caribbean coast and also illegally in Garifuna communities by outsiders. The activists stated that the Honduran Congress in 2012 supported a special zone charter cities *"Ciudad Modelos"* initiative, which to her was the second coup. Other concerns she raised were the country's status as a criminally organized narco-state and the fact that 60 percent of drugs pass through Honduras.

At a September 2019 meeting at Casa Yurumein in the Bronx, Garifuna Omar Suazo and Belinda David, alongside other Honduran leaders, explained the challenges they faced in their individual communities.[15] Suazo had been the president of the Garifuna village township association of Sambo Creek in La Ceiba, 85 miles from San Pedro Sula. For years, they had successfully resisted the building of a dam in the Sambo Creek River, a project in which the Japanese International Cooperative Agency was involved. At a public gathering in his hometown, Suazo was attacked by several men, thrown to the ground, and knifed in the back. Gunshots came from somewhere outside, injuring one individual and killing another.

As a result, Suazo was arrested in May 2017 and charged with murder. Suazo explained that he was accustomed to death threats, and he believed he had been set up because of his community activism. He expressed his gratitude to everyone who had rallied behind him to secure his release in 2018 (Miller 2019).

The Garifuna Coalition USA provided a gesture of support in another Garifuna land rights issue. Ávila sent a letter in August 2019 to the Honduran minister of human rights expressing the coalition's solidarity with OFRANEH and demanding that the government comply with the December 18, 2015, verdict of the Inter-American Court of Human Rights.[16] OFRANEH had filed grievances in 2006 on behalf of two Garifuna communities, after exhausting its legal remedies through the Honduran court system and the special prosecutor for ethnic groups. Part of the verdict declared that the Honduran government was to provide demarcation of land originally granted to the communities of Punta Piedra and Triunfo de la Cruz and ensure that the Garifuna had free access to their land, which had been hindered by mining regulations. In addition, the resolution called for the government to investigate the murders of Garifuna activists. The response deadline of December 2017 passed, but the Garifuna community continues to wait for a response to this and many other grievances related to territorial challenges in their coastal communities. Garifuna Nation also supported this action, and one of its leaders, Ruben Reyes, traveled to San Jose, Costa Rica, to be present when the verdict was handed down (Almendarez 2020).

2019 Challenges

The year 2019 was challenging. There were several deaths and the repression of Garifuna due to criminal acts and others associated with activists organizing and resisting seizure of their lands by outsiders. In the northeast Garifuna community of Masca, 25 miles from San Pedro Sula, several Garifuna community leaders' lives have been threatened and some were murdered. On September 8, 2019, an unidentified assailant arrived at the restaurant of Mirna Suazo Martinez and shot and killed her, driving away on his motorcycle. Mirna was president of the community board in the region, which had repeatedly for a long time rejected the construction of a hydroelectric power plant in the Masca river. Oscar Francisco Guerrero was also shot to death the following month on October 18, 2019. He had been assigned as part of Mirna's security team because of the death threats she constantly received. On December 28, 2019, Karla Ignacia Piota Martinez, Mirna's sister, was also shot, receiving seven gunshot wounds and two weeks later dying. Ignacia was seventy years of age and president of the Masca community board of trustees. These occurrences continue from the past, as on October 14, 2017, Garifuna community leader/businessman Silvinio Zapata Martinez was killed, shot five times by unknown individuals while closing his restaurant business, also in Masca. Zapata contributed in leading the community's successful resistance to the building of the hydroelectric dam in the Masca river, which was supported by the United Nations Carbon Fund. Community protests and demonstrations by OFRANEH resulted in pausing development efforts. In another incident earlier the same year, on January 24, 2019, Garifuna leader Celso Guillen was detained by authorities although he had been cleared of charges brought by a Canadian landowner in his community. Guillen, an activist from the Garifuna community Funda (Guadalupe), in the municipality of Trujillo, 140 miles from San Pedro Sula, was arrested and mistreated by police in October 2017. A lawsuit and order of capture was filed by a Canadian businessman against Guillen for trespassing on land they purchased originally belonging to the activist. Canadian businessman Randy Jorgensen obtained about 1,500 acres of Garifuna land, constructing tourism and a real estate project in this Trujillo Bay region of the Garifuna territory. OFRANEH was successful in contacting the United Nations as well as the Honduran government Special Prosecutor of Ethnic Groups, absolving Guillen and freeing him from arrest (IACHR 2019; HRD; WHRD; Castillo 2019b).

Defending Territorial Rights in Belize and Honduras

Land issues in Belize have also been addressed at Garifuna organizations' New York meetings. The newly formed political party Belize People's Front (BPF), the United Garifuna Association (UGA), and Believers Mennonite Garifuna Ministries held a meeting on April 7, 2019, at the community center of the First Mennonite Church in Brooklyn. The discussion focused on whether the International Court of Justice should address border conflicts between Belize and Guatemala. The Garifuna organizations discussed the possibility of Belizean communities being taken over by Guatemala, threatening their subsistence. There has been a significant influx of non-Belizeans, Maya, and Mestizo in Garifuna villages in southern Belize. This, in addition to the discovery of oil and other natural resources in the south, poses a threat to the Garifuna, as the Belizean government is in discussions to grant foreign companies concessions to extract these resources from the region. Although Blacks in Belize have economic and political power, challenges persist for the Garifuna, as the Black Creole elite are in control. Garifuna continue to experience racism, inequality, and discrimination. For the most part, they reside in the southern districts (Toledo, Stann Creek), which have the lowest indices of health, economics, and education, except for Garifuna residing in Belize City. They seek to overcome issues such as high unemployment, lack of access to capital, inadequate housing, and an inability to reestablish sustainable farming and fishing industries. In addition, they are subjected to pollution and environmental challenges due to coastal sea changes. The Belizean-based National Garifuna Council (NGC) represents the Garifuna with branches in their local communities. In New York, UGA leader Wellington Ramos follows the activities of the NGC and keeps Garifuna informed through meetings or online postings and writing articles for local Caribbean newspapers (W. Ramos 2018).[17]

Ramos, who is also a member of Garifuna Nation, addressed a recent incident that occurred in a Honduran Garifuna community. On July 15, 2020, a group of armed, masked paramilitary men abducted five Garifuna men from the village of Triunfo de la Cruz. One of the kidnapped men was the president of the village council, and he had recently been involved in securing the community's territorial claims at the Inter-American Court of Human Rights. On behalf of Garifuna Nation, Ramos sent a letter informing the prime minister of St. Vincent and the Grenadines about this situation. During his tenure as prime minister, Gonsalves has supported the Garifuna reconnecting with their ancestral homeland of St. Vincent and has led the case for reparations from Britain. The prime minister immediately sent a letter to Honduran president Juan Orlando Hernandez, calling the incident a matter of international human rights and saying that he planned to express his concerns to UN secretary-general Antonio Guterres. As chair of CARICOM, Gonsalves called for member states' support, and his representatives reached out to the Organization of African Unity (OAU), which took an interest in the matter.[18] Other organizations in both the United States and Central America rallied in support, contacting various international agencies. Members of the U.S. Congress sent a letter to the State Department, informing it of the ongoing persecution of Garifuna land activists. The five men are still missing, with no clue as to their whereabouts (Lakhani 2020).[19]

Historically, Garifuna organizations in New York have supported the defense of their homelands for many reasons. Injustice and human rights violations are important motives; however, another reason is that the survival of their culture is connected to their land. Encroachment on Garifuna territories threatens their spiritual traditions because *dugu* ceremonies can be performed only in their homelands. Garifuna spiritual leaders and the Buyei Council in New York have made progress in recent years to ensure the preservation of their traditions. The organization Brotherhood of Truth (Ibirinaun Garifuna Lanigu Inarunei) in New York contributed to the recently established temple in a location known as "Quehueche Siete Altares" in Livingston, Guatemala.[20] In addition, spiritual pilgrimages, such as families traveling back to their homelands for *dugu* ceremonies, increased in the twenty-first century (Johnson 2007). In general, spiritual connection to the land motivates Garifuna New Yorkers' continued involvement with and defense of their homelands.

Connections with St. Vincent and the Grenadines: Garifuna Carib Descendants

Garifuna organizations' connection to their homeland extends beyond Central America. It also includes St. Vincent and the Grenadines islands. Exchanges between the Garifuna (in both New York and Central America) and St. Vincent Garifuna Carib descendants increased during this century.[21] Vincentians in New York also started their own group in the city. Representatives of the organization, Garifuna Indigenous People of St. Vincent and the Grenadines, Inc. (GIPSVG), established in 2015, attended the annual Garifuna American Legislative Day in Albany for the first time in 2018. Garifuna Carib descendants from St. Vincent living in New York make up the members of this group. GIPSVG was established to address the needs of their Garifuna communities in St. Vincent. Their goals encompass revitalization, preservation, and maintenance of the culture. An additional goal is support of small development projects of Garifuna communities on the island (King 2018, 2019). During the April 2021 La Soufrière volcanic eruption, the EGCC consulted with the GIPSVG to coordinate support in the aftermath. The volcano is in proximity to the Garifuna Carib community, and many evacuated their homes, moving to other regions in the island. Many were in dire need of financial assistance for their subsistence. International agencies and neighboring countries pledged support, assisting many residents displaced by the volcano eruption.

In St. Vincent, Garifuna descendants recognized as Carib communities are dispersed throughout the island. On the north windward side of the island some of the settlements are Orange Hill, Overland and Magnum,

London, Sandy Bay and Waterloo. The villages of Greiggs, Fancy, Owia, Rose Hall, and Rose Bank sustain more of the Carib culture. Communities range in size, Sandy Bay having the largest population. Their ethnic and racial population also varies, with Caribs living alongside a mixed population of African Caribbeans. Improvements continue in their communities, overcoming challenges such as lack of proper infrastructure, poor health facilities, and high unemployment. Marginalization due to their cultural differences was also more prevalent in the past. However, the resurgence of the culture has offset Carib negative stereotypes. In addition, the promotion of the Carib cultural heritage by the Garifuna descendants abroad (Central America, United States) and their visits to the island strengthen their identity (Twinn 2006).

New York City Garifuna Organization Outreach and Exchanges

Correspondence between New York City Garifuna community leaders and St. Vincent Garifuna descendants in the city began in the latter part of the last century. The earliest New York City Garifuna group to visit St. Vincent collectively were members of the EGCC with the Garifuna for Christ Ministries committee group. In 1996 several pastors and members from other churches participated in a ten-day gospel concert and crusade on the island of St. Vincent. While there, they visited Garifuna communities. Afterward, Garifuna ministers from St. Vincent also visited the Bronx Evangelical Garifuna church. Some of the Garifuna church leaders who traveled to St. Vincent for this 1996 trip were Celso Jaime, Galileo Bernardez, Andrew Nunez, Simon Diego, Reverend Parker, and Edward Diego, who established the Garifuna for Christ group.[22] The trip served to connect Central American Garifuna with their St. Vincent counterparts.

In 2009 the Garifuna Coalition USA organized the Garifuna Reunion in St. Vincent and the Grenadines. During this visit a delegation of the Garifuna Coalition USA met with dignitaries, attended ceremonies, and visited the prime minister. The purpose was to enhance U.S. Garifuna connections with St. Vincent and the Grenadines and develop economic, social, and political exchanges. Another follow-up reunion in St. Vincent and the Grenadines took place in 2019, ten years later. Members of various Garifuna organizations in New York participated in this trip, reinforcing ties with the government and the Garifuna Carib community in the island. The New York City–based Garifuna Coalition USA, Garifuna Indigenous People of St. Vincent and the Grenadines (GIPSVG), The Council of St.

Vincent, and Grenadines Organizations USA (COSAGO) were among the members of the planning committee working with the Minister of Tourism, Sports and Culture of St. Vincent and the Grenadines on the 2019 reunion (J. Ávila 2009, 2017a; IWN, 2019).

Since the 2009 visit to St. Vincent and the Grenadines, New York City Garifuna leaders' connection with St. Vincent and the Grenadines continued, with the organization Yurumei Garifuna Cultural Retrieval (YuGaCuRe) striving to reestablish the culture on the island.

YuGaCuRe began hosting summer programs in St. Vincent in 2011. The organization was started in New York by St. Vincent Garifuna descendant Trish St. Hill and Belizean Garifuna musician James Lovell. At the well-attended summer workshops led by Lovell, children and adults learn aspects of the Garifuna language, dance, and music (King 2018b; Ajani 2011; Clarke 2013; Minsky 2015b). It is believed the increased awareness and exchanges of Garifuna in New York with St. Vincent and the Grenadines descendants in the city contributed to the development of the St. Vincent–based Garifuna organization in the city. A result is also St. Vincent Carib descendants' increased participation at Central American Garifuna functions in New York. This was apparent at the 2014 Garifuna Nation meeting in the Bronx with St. Vincent Garifuna attending, as well as in other activities.

Garifuna Nation officer Wellington Ramos also contributed to connecting Garifuna in New York City with their St. Vincent and the Grenadines counterparts. In the summer of 2015, Ramos and a fellow member of the United Garifuna Association visited St. Vincent and the Grenadines to meet with public officials. Arnhim Eustance, leader of the opposition party New Democratic Party (NDA), invited Ramos and UGA member Joseph Guerrero to the island, where they held rallies in the Garifuna communities and meetings with officials and organization leaders (IWN 2015; W. Ramos 2015). One of the discussions centered on granting Garifuna in the diaspora honorary citizenship in St. Vincent and the Grenadines.

Another issue Ramos pursues is opposing the sale of Balliceaux, one of the islands of St. Vincent. The government of St. Vincent and the Grenadines plans to sell the island to entrepreneurs. Ramos, a guest columnist on *Caribbean News Now* online, explained the significance of Balliceaux island to all Garifuna. He presented the history of Garifuna Carib descendants who were captured and surrendered while resisting the British and were taken as prisoners to Balliceaux island, where they continued to be tortured. Many died, and those who survived were sent to Central America, the ancestors of present-day Garifuna. In modern times, during visits to St. Vincent, Garifuna from the diaspora visit Balliceaux island, paying homage where many of their ancestors suffered, dying without proper burials. It has become a special pilgrimage location for Garifuna connecting with their ancestors. Ramos criticized the selling of the island, proposing it to become a national memorial museum. He expressed the government could generate revenue from the island serving as a tourist museum site. Simultaneously, it can also serve as a point of cultural, spiritual connections with Garifuna in the diaspora during their visits (W. Ramos 2008, 2017; Lewis 2008).

Ramos stays informed about issues on the island specifically related to the Garifuna community. He frequently articulates the need for New York Garifuna organizations' participation in St. Vincent and the Grenadines government's petitions for reparations. The country's prime minister, Ralph Everard Gonsalves, gained international prominence when he raised the issue of British reparations in the Caribbean. At the 2018 Sparer Symposium at the University of Pennsylvania Law School, sponsored by the National African American Reparations Commission (NAARC), José F. Ávila represented the Garifuna Coalition USA on the panel "The Caribbean Claim for Reparation." Since 2011, the coalition had supported Gonsalves on the issue of reparations. This led to Ávila's participation in the first regional reparations conference held in 2013 in St. Vincent and the Grenadines. In his speech, Ávila expressed that he was looking forward to working with the Caribbean Community (CARICOM) Reparations Commission, along with Garifuna representatives in their diaspora (King 2013).[23]

The convergence of the re-initiation of reparations dialogue, Garifuna organizations' contact with St. Vincent Garifuna, and St. Vincent organizations in New York City that identify as Garifuna increasing alliances with their Garifuna counterparts all occurred early in this century (J. Ávila 2011; King 2013). The participation of New York City–based Central American Garifuna groups in functions with St. Vincent and the Grenadines Garifuna organizations increases the ethnic group coalition. Having a larger population group will further hold politicians' attention in implementing Garifuna organizations' requests. This unity also facilitates Garifuna lobbying of public officials to address territorial issues in Garifuna homelands, as well as economic and political marginalization they experience. Garifuna leaders attribute these concerns to the effects of the colonial period. In St. Vincent and the Grenadines prior to Garifuna relocation to Central America, they sustained an independent, flourishing economy trading with Europeans. Once in Central America, Garifuna constantly attempted to rebuild their economic system, but they continued to experience challenges to their subsistence.

Conclusion

Traditionally, Garifuna always sustain connections with their families in Central America. However, early Garifuna organizations' international forums planned their outreach to their homelands to address specific issues, implemented in the new century. Technology facilitated an increase in cultural, political, and economic exchanges between New York City and their homelands. Garifuna organizations led in their transnational connections, advocating for land and human rights, economic development, and cultural support. Being organized, Garifuna were able to inform the general public of challenges in their homeland and contact local officials, dignitaries, and international agencies to solicit support for their causes. Garifuna organizations engaged in their New York City communities as well as in their homeland without conflicts. Perhaps in the future, with their increased civic engagement and a newer generation involved in organizing, conflict between being involved in their homelands and concentrating on their interests in New York City may surface. Overall, land means more than a physical space for the Garifuna. Whether in their Central America communities or in the island of St. Vincent, there is a cultural and spiritual connection to the land. Though Garifuna reside in separate distant locations, their spiritual ties to their homelands remain through their songs and visits during which they hold ceremonies honoring their ancestors.

CONCLUSION

AS GARIFUNA ORGANIZATIONS planned for the 2020 census, opinions differed on how it should be carried out to ensure inclusion of the ethnic group. Discussions were held about entering "Garifuna" in the space designated "Other" in the ethnicity and race section of the census form. On the Bronx cable program *Centro America Show*, community organizer Mirtha Colón supported Garifuna participation in the census but expressed concerns about the Garifuna being undercounted. She stated that many Garifuna marry outside the group, and others identify with different ethnic minorities.[1] Colón's points are noteworthy. To understand the Garifuna community in its entirety, its demographic diversity must be considered. It is commonly recognized that as immigrant generations advance, they integrate and assimilate into society. Many Garifuna have assimilated and embraced U.S. cultural norms to such an extent that they have become indistinguishable from the Americans in their communities. Others have integrated and adapted to their communities while maintaining their Garifuna identity. Another feature of Garifuna demographic diversity is that there are four generations of them in New York City, in addition to new waves of immigrants arriving in the city. Moreover, with their different nationalities, some speak primarily Spanish, others speak only English, and not everyone is able to communicate in the Garifuna language. In addition, some have limited or no knowledge of their culture. For example, there are many first-, second-, third-, and fourth-generation Garifuna immigrants who have never been to Central America. Because of having English versus Spanish surnames and being of mixed race or ethnicity, Garifuna may assimilate with different populations. But despite its demographic diversity, for the most part, the Garifuna community in New York City is recognized by its Spanish-speaking population and its Central American–born community leaders.

Assimilating through Popular Culture, Sports, and Entertainment

Generations of Garifuna have assimilated into their communities at various levels, but this is more common among recent generations. Traditionally, Garifuna reside in Black and Latino communities, so many assimilate as African American, blending in with Black youth playing basketball and football and embracing the rap and hip-hop culture. The chances of achieving fame and fortune in the sports and music industries are slim, but several Garifuna have established successful careers. Henry "Hen-Gee" Garcia and his brother DJ Evil E, sons of Honduran Garifuna parents, grew up in Brooklyn and became prominent in the hip-hop industry. They moved to California and were part of the early 1980s rap and break-dancing movie craze and contributed to the growth of West Coast hip-hop.[2] Garcia has worked with many other prominent artists, including Ice-T, Tupac, and Snoop Dogg.

A more recent artist is Juan Oswaldo Cayetano Jr., known as King Tiger. He was born in Harlem to Garifuna parents from Honduras and Guatemala and was raised in the Bronx.[3] Another hip-hop artist of Garifuna descent is Odis Oliver Flores, known as O.T. Genasis. His parents are from Belize, and he grew up in Long Beach, California. He initially signed with G-Unit Records in 2011 and later signed with Busta Rhymes's Conglomerate Records. He has performed with famous artists such as Snoop Dogg, Chris Brown, and Lil Wayne.[4] Record producer Imsomie Mahogany Leeper, born in Boston and raised in the Bronx, is another Garifuna associated with hip-hop and R&B. He has produced albums for Dr. Dre, Jay-Z, Big Pun, and Mariah Carey and has worked with various labels, including Island Def Jam, Ruff Ryders Entertainment, Universal, Loud, and G-Unit. At the 2017 GALENT music awards, he received a lifetime achievement award (J. Ávila 2017c).[5]

Another Honduran Garifuna, Wilson Morales, is also part of the African American entertainment industry, working in television and film. Morales is an entertainment journalist who highlights Black talent both behind the scenes and in the front of the camera. For twenty years he was the editor of

Blackfilm.com and served as copresident of the Black Film Critics Circle. Morales continues to be an advocate for the voices of African Americans and their stories through his website blackfilmandtv.com. He promotes films, theater productions, and television projects emphasizing African American stories and talent (Davis 2020).

Several Garifuna athletes have reached high levels in sports. Rakeem Nuñez-Roches, who was born and raised in the Garifuna town of Dangriga, Belize, has been playing football in the NFL, signing with the Kansas City Chiefs in 2015; from 2018 to 2022 he played with the Tampa Bay Buccaneers, and in 2023 signed with the New York Giants. When he was eight years old, Nuñez-Roches and his mother immigrated to the United States, and they spent time in the South and on the West Coast. In high school he earned a football scholarship to Southern Mississippi University, where he began his athletic career (Stroud 2020; Chiefs 2017).

Another Garifuna in the NFL was former Miami Dolphins head coach Brian Flores. Flores was born in Brooklyn to Garifuna parents from Honduras. Like many early Garifuna settlers, his father was a seaman. Flores started playing football at age twelve and continued to play at Brooklyn Poly Prep High School and Boston College. An injury prevented him from playing in the NFL, but he began his coaching career in 2004 with the New England Patriots; he was hired by Miami in 2019 (Deen 2019). An earlier Garifuna NFL coach was Clayton Lopez, born in Los Angeles. He was a defensive back at the University of Nevada (1991–94) and started his coaching career in 1999 with the Seattle Seahawks. Lopez also coached for the St. Louis Rams, Detroit Lions, and Oakland Raiders (Pro Football 2021).

Kache Palacio, another Garifuna athlete, had a short NFL career with the Los Angeles Rams (2016) and Seattle Seahawks (2017). He later competed in mixed martial arts. Palacio, whose family is of Belizean Garifuna descent, was born outside of Los Angeles and was a standout linebacker at Washington State University (Moore 2021).[6]

Several Garifuna basketball players have achieved various degrees of success. Kenton Paulino had a successful college basketball career as a point guard with the University of Texas Longhorns (2002–6). He played for the Austin Toros (the G League team of the NBA's San Antonio Spurs) in 2007–8. He has distinguished himself in a series of college basketball coaching positions including his alma mater, Fresno State, Tulsa, UTEP, Oral Roberts, and Wichita State.[7] Similar to Paulino, Milton Palacio was born in the United States to Belizean Garifuna parents; he was raised in Los Angeles. Palacio played basketball at Junipero Serra High School in Gardena, California, and at both Midland College and Colorado State

University. He spent seven years (1999–2006) in the NBA playing point guard or shooting guard for the Vancouver Grizzlies, Boston Celtics, Phoenix Suns, Cleveland Cavaliers, Toronto Raptors, and Utah Jazz (Garinet 2003; Washburn 2020).[8] Several Garifuna men and women had successful collegiate basketball careers in the NCAA: the Texas Longhorns' Kyra Lambert, North Florida Ospreys' Nubia Benedith, Syracuse University's Amaya Finklea-Güity, and Iowa Hawkeyes' Joe Toussaint (Armando 2020).[9]

The high-profile Garifuna in sports and entertainment are representative of a broader segment of this ethnic group. These Garifuna who have reached the pinnacle of their careers share the same values and aspirations as many African American youths in U.S. cities. Another way Garifuna integrate with African Americans is by joining Black fraternal organizations. Many Garifuna study in colleges and universities and join African American associations. Substantial numbers of Garifuna participate in African American fraternities and sororities such as Alpha Phi Alpha, Phi Beta Sigma, Kappa Alpha Psi, Omega Psi Phi, Alpha Kappa Alpha, Zeta Phi Beta, and Delta Sigma Theta, among others (Perry 1999). Future studies of the Garifuna population will contribute to an understanding of the Garifuna community as it continues to grow.

Challenges to Comprehensive Community Development

Some Garifuna organizations and leaders have come to understand that economic empowerment is the key to the community's political growth. Up to this point, Garifuna's political gains have largely been limited to individual and cultural recognition, funding for certain projects, and invitations to annual events such as Abrazo Garifuna and Garifuna American Legislative Day. Attempts have also been made to develop the community economically. In the early 2000s, Lanichuga Garifuna Restaurant was one of the first businesses to open, followed by Garifuna Star Restaurant, Garifuna Kitchen of NY, and My Garifuna Cuisine.[10] Unfortunately, each of these businesses closed shortly after opening, which some attribute to a lack of promotion or little support from the Garifuna community. If the general public wants to enjoy authentic Garifuna cuisine, the only options are vendors at city parks or during festivals, fundraisers, and other events. Garifuna food is also available at some citywide events provided by Garifuna Isha G. Sumner's Weiga (translated "Let's Eat") catering business (Culinary Backstreets 2019).[11]

Another Garifuna entrepreneurial activity that has achieved modest gains is transporting goods to Central America. Several Garifuna independent shipping companies, both registered and unregistered, operate in the community. Some of the registered Garifuna cargo businesses are the Honduras Shipping Cargo and Freight Company/Garifuna Shipping, Labuga Puerto Barrios Shipping Cargo, Inc., and Victoria Honduras Cargo (J. Ávila 2017b). Some have a visible presence, as their vans travel through the Bronx displaying their contact information. Refrigerators, buses, cars, and clothing are some of the items transported in large shipping containers to Central America.

Other promising business and economic ventures have faltered, however. These include the New Horizon Investment Club, which invested in tourism in a Honduran Garifuna community, and the Garifuna Coalition USA Bronx Immigrant Entrepreneurship Initiative, which supported Garifuna's small business. Although the entrepreneurship initiative no longer exists, some of the small businesses continue to operate. Other than these businesses, the only indication of a Garifuna community presence in the Mott Haven section of the Bronx are two large signs outside a building that read "Evangelical Garifuna Church" and "Garifuna Community Center." The signs display the colors of the Garifuna flag—white, black, and yellow—signaling a Garifuna presence in the borough. Evidence of the ethnic group's presence may be visible in some sections of the Bronx when visiting certain parks, shopping for groceries, or traveling by public transportation. The Garifuna language may be spoken by individuals conversing with each other or speaking on their cell phones.

Some may ask why Garifuna community development has been so slow compared with that of other immigrant populations in the city. According to my analysis and understanding, it is due to their unique experiences. A major difference between the Garifuna and other groups such as West Africans and Dominicans is that these other immigrants come from countries where they are not in the minority. West African restaurants, mosques, churches, butcher shops, and markets in the Morrisania and Melrose sections of the Bronx indicate that this group is integrating into the Bronx economy and benefiting both themselves and the general community (Ademo 2011; Roberts 2014). The Garifuna are a minority in their Central American countries, where they experience social, economic, and political marginalization. Unlike the Garifuna, other Black ethnic immigrant populations have a high number of educated, financially stable individuals with the ability to immediately establish businesses in New York City. As a minority population in their home countries, most Garifuna immigrants are low-skilled working-class people; there is no wealthy class of Garifuna to invest in their adopted country. Many Garifuna professionals who do migrate are unable to transfer their occupations to the United States. Although there are many U.S.-born Garifuna professionals, for the most part, they are not directly involved in the leadership of prominent Garifuna organizations. Eventually, once they are completely incorporated into the community, this segment of the Garifuna population can potentially contribute to their own economic and political development.

Additionally, I believe the effects of colonialism contribute to the social norms that impede the Garifuna's comprehensive community development. I reached this conclusion based on their past experiences on the island of St. Vincent. During the colonial period on St. Vincent, Garifuna society organized separately and united under a chief only during conflict (C. Taylor 2012). Europeans struggled to dominate them due to their decentralized governance structure. Today, most Garifuna organizations have a decentralized leadership structure, hindering their ability to sustain a strong, long-lasting collaborative working group. The longevity of the organization is dependent on one individual leading the group. In addition, their history of decentralized leadership contributes to the Garifuna tradition of being independent minded. Several other social norms evident among the Garifuna come into play. For example, disagreement within the group may be considered offensive or disrespectful, leading some individuals to remain silent or leave and form other groups. Additionally, organizations' lack of transparency in the allocation of funds has been a problem, which tends to hamper trust. Some have noticed a growing individualism among the Garifuna—a change from their past collectivity—which also impedes community growth. However, this may simply be an indication of general society becoming more individualistic, reinforced by communication media and the excessive use of technological devices hindering personal interaction.

For the most part, the New York City Garifuna community tends to be led by individuals born in Central America who are saturated with positive cultural knowledge. However, continuing the traditional way of doing things means that new generations with innovative ideas may be ignored. Nevertheless, youths continue to engage, as do adults supporting Garifuna organizations and events held in the city. One advantage of having Honduran, Belizean, and Guatemalan Garifuna residents is the potential to increase their interaction, collaboration, and unity. Honduran Garifuna are still the majority, with an estimated twenty-two hometown associations for their forty-eight Central American communities (Endo et al. 2010). However, the range of different nationalities also makes it more difficult to stay united for comprehensive community development. In general, unity tends to occur only in emergency circumstances. This was evident after the Happy Land nightclub fire, when many groups came together and formed a coalition, only to later disperse into separate organizations.

One challenge that is becoming less problematic is Garifuna racial identity and solidarity with their neighbors. It can be challenging for Garifuna identity to coexist with racial identity. Common among most incoming Black ethnic groups is an emphasis on ethnic rather than racial identity to avoid discrimination. For them, ethnic identity is more highly valued than a shared African racial heritage with Black Americans. In addition, Black ethnic immigrants may avoid associating with African Americans; some may embrace the negative media portrayal of African Americans and conclude that assimilating with Black Americans will not advance their social status (Greer 2013). The theory of "elevated minority" imposed on Black ethnic immigrants by society favors them as different from and better than Black Americans (Greer 2013). This is apparent among some incoming Garifuna immigrants. Moreover, within the Garifuna community, debates linger among community leaders regarding their status as African descendants or Garifuna. Many like to emphasize that their ancestors were not slaves to differentiate themselves from other Blacks, preferring to use the term Garifuna without negating any description associated with Africa. Yet history shows that the Garifuna population expanded on St. Vincent as they mixed with escaped slaves from neighboring Caribbean islands (D. Taylor 1951; Gullick 1976). Nevertheless, like Haitians and West Indians, many of the new generations of Garifuna identify with African Americans, embracing the mainstream culture and minimizing their own. However, newly arrived Garifuna in New York City may perceive little in common with their local racial counterparts because they lack personal experience in understanding African American culture and political conditions. Some Garifuna leaders born in Central America continue to hold the erroneous view of their ethnic group's elevated status compared to others, although this appears to be changing with their civic engagement. Over time and with subsequent generations of Black ethnic immigrants, this perception of an "elevated minority" status changes, facilitating greater integration with Black Americans. Like other Black ethnic groups, Garifuna recognize that shared racial challenges can facilitate the formation of alliances to address community concerns and improve their economic and social status.

Urban Challenges

As part of the urban New York City community, Garifuna experience the same challenges as their Black and Latino neighbors residing in economically and socially marginalized regions. The Bronx, where the Garifuna are concentrated, is considered one of the poorest places in the nation, lagging on many indices. Garbage incinerators and vehicle exhaust from the highways surrounding the borough contribute to residents' health challenges, including the historically high incidence of asthma in the South Bronx (Dow 2020). Of the estimated more than two hundred Garifuna who died during the COVID-19 pandemic, many had preexisting health conditions, including asthma (Sequeira 2021).[12] Other challenges facing the Garifuna are juvenile delinquency, gang violence, incarceration, teenage pregnancy, immigration issues, police brutality, assault, and poor housing. While some events make the local news, others are not considered worthy of media coverage and are discussed only within the community. In May 2007, when an unarmed Honduran Garifuna man was shot and killed by police officers in the Bronx, the story was on the front page of the *New York Amsterdam News*, with a picture of the family supported by community activists (Moorer 2007; Boyd 2007). Central Americans crossing the border from Mexico, including many Garifuna women and children (some fleeing violence), were featured several times in the local Latino newspaper *El Diario*. Falsely told that they would be granted entry and residency, many Central Americans made their way to the U.S. border. Some children, unaccompanied by their parents, ended up in detention centers in the city (Cortes de Solano 2015).

Increased violence and delinquency among youth are additional concerns. In 2019 Garifuna were involved in several unfortunate incidents. In June a twenty-four-year-old man was killed by another Garifuna at St. Mary's Park in the Bronx, a popular summertime hangout for members of the ethnic group. Apparently, the incident was gang related, and I learned that many Garifuna youth are part of the gang culture (Moynihan 2019). In October 2019 violence erupted between a young Garifuna couple, and one partner stabbed the other in the homeless shelter where they resided (Burke, Tracy, and Rayman 2019). Another incident in October involved the stabbing of a Garifuna man at a Bronx bodega he frequently visited. The owner's son apparently had differences with the Garifuna man he had stabbed. The Garifuna community came together to protest at the Bronx courthouse, demanding justice; they later marched on the main avenue, hoisting Central American and Garifuna flags to demonstrate solidarity

(Burke, Parascandola, and Annese 2019). In December a Garifuna girl who had been having problems with her mother falsely claimed she had been kidnapped. The story made the newspapers when an Amber Alert was issued in the city. These recent events show that the Garifuna are not immune to the problems of urban residents (Sandoval 2019; Newsbreak 2020).

Rising Above the Challenges

Despite being a small, scarcely known ethnic group, the Garifuna have played significant roles in American society. Many have achieved high ranks in the military, such as Tuskegee Airman Wilfredo Stokes Brown Baltazzar, a Guatemalan and second lieutenant in the U.S. Air Force; U.S. Navy logistic chief Jairo Guity; and U.S. Coast Guard master chief petty officer George Lopez.[13] In the sciences, the Garifuna are represented by Honduran Garifuna Rony F. Arauz, a postdoctoral fellow at the National Cancer Institute studying lung cancer. He completed graduate work in environmental health sciences at the University of Michigan–Ann Arbor and earned a PhD at the University of Minnesota.[14] His brother Nixon Ricardo Arauz is a public health researcher at Virginia Commonwealth University School of Medicine and has worked as a fellow for the Centers for Disease Control and Prevention (CDC). He obtained master's and bachelor's degrees from Columbia and Cornell Universities and is in the process of completing his doctorate (T. Colon 2010c; VCU 2021).[15] Like the Arauz brothers, Belizean Garifuna Dean M. Martinez immigrated to New York when he was young. A U.S. Army veteran and aerospace engineer who graduated from Tuskegee University, Martinez helped design rocket motors for the U.S. space shuttle program. He has managed both private and government projects related to alternative energy and infrastructure, such as water and wastewater solutions. Martinez has also been involved with local government in Utah and has worked with the governor's office of economic development (Oneil 2004; Carlislie 2020).

Many Garifuna women high achievers also contribute to society. Dr. Nadia Lopez, born and raised in Brooklyn, New York, to Guatemalan and Honduran parents, is a recognized outstanding educator. She opened a school in an economically marginalized and high-crime area in Brooklyn and successfully served as a principal for ten years. Dr. Lopez was invited to meet former president Barack Obama in the White House, received accolades for her "Ted Talk on the Education Revolution," and also served as a guest lecturer at Harvard University's Graduate School for Education. There she taught students on the subject matter of "Transformative Justice,

Education, and the School-to-Prison Pipeline" (Lopez; Hunter 2015). Another U.S.-born Garifuna woman achieving accolades is Genesis Ramos, of Honduran heritage. Ramos, at twenty-nine, became one of the youngest people and the first woman of color elected to the Orange County Legislature in New York State. Ramos, a Democrat, overcame the challenges of racism and sexism in narrowly defeating a Republican challenger, winning District 6, divided between the city and town of Newburgh. She also was the first in her family to graduate from college and earn a master's degree (Bellamy 2021).

Several Garifuna have been associated with high-profile public officials. Honduran Garifuna Marvin B. Figueroa studied Latin American studies and political science at Vanderbilt University and education policy and management at Harvard University's Graduate School of Education, where he earned a master's degree. For six years he worked for Senator Mark Warner of Virginia, and he was the political director of Hillary Clinton's 2016 presidential campaign in that state. He also served as the legislative director for Virginia governor Ralph S. Northam. More recently, he has been with the U.S. Department of Health and Human Services (HHS), serving as director of the Office of Intergovernmental Affairs (IEA) (King 2022a; Avendaño 2016).[16] Honduran Garifuna Julio Guity-Guevara graduated from American University's Master of Law program and was a deputy director in Washington, D.C., mayor Muriel Bowser's Office on Latino Affairs. He also served as a consultant for the Organization of American States and the World Bank (*Jamaica Observer* 2018).[17] Belizean Garifuna Thomas M. Zuniga, who died in 2012, was head of the Housing Finance Agency during Marion Barry's tenure as mayor of Washington, D.C. He also served with the Department of Housing and Urban Development (1998–2000) during the Clinton administration (Schudel 2012).

In 2020 a group of Garifuna professionals born in the United States established La Fuerza Garifuna, Inc., to empower the Garifuna diaspora through community and civic engagement, education, networking, and mentorship.[18] Its founders are Selacy Chimilio, a psychologist and educator who works for the New York State Department of Education; Sergio Gregorio, a lawyer with more than twenty years' experience who is licensed to practice in New York and Washington, D.C.; Lindsay Gregorio, a civil engineer with more than twenty-five years' experience as a project manager on large construction projects as well as the Obama Presidential Center; Stevaughn Bush, a lawyer and CEO and founder of the Fannie Lou Network, an advocacy group supporting retirement security; and Daisy Guzman, whose doctoral research at the University of Texas–Austin focuses on Black diaspora transnationalism, gender, and Guatemalan Garifuna migrants during the civil war.[19] This new organization created by these professional Garifuna shows their desire to give back to their community by sharing their skills and experience.

In closing, Garifuna were among the early Black immigrant groups with several ethnic-based organizations in New York City. Their organizations are central to their community development and growth. Similar to other Black ethnics, Garifuna possess a unique culture encompassing their language, spiritual practices, music, and culinary traditions. Since their presence in New York City in the postwar period, Garifuna organized by associating with different ethnic groups in their community. Their early voluntary religious associations, social and community support organizations, and soccer clubs where some ways Garifuna established the foundations for political participation. Scholars emphasize sports clubs, Catholic associations, and community support groups among organizations recognized bringing individuals together resulting in prerequisites for civic engagement and increased participation (Putnam 2004; Coleman 1988). Garifuna organizations' progression over the years reflect this trend.

Garifuna as well as other minority groups benefit from African American–led initiatives and legislation from the struggle for civil rights. Changes in U.S. immigration policy; affirmative action; and education, housing, and employment programs are some gains Garifuna as well as other minority groups benefited from during the era of social struggle. Past and present Garifuna have identified and associate with Black Americans. As with other Black immigrants, Garifuna also unite with African Americans, in spite of their cultural differences to address inequalities and racism experienced. Also, contrary to previous studies Garifuna organizations in New York are civically engaged in the city, simultaneously addressing concerns in their Central American communities (Jones-Correa 1998). Natural disaster relief, land rights activism, cultural/religious ceremonies, economic investments (remittance), and electoral politics are different methods by which Garifuna have continued transnational ties to their homelands. As a minority population in New York City, Garifuna collaboration with other minority groups (African Americans/Latinos) is central to their ability to present their political concerns. Some issues where they coalesce participating politically with other minority populations include immigration, better health services, and prevention of youth delinquency. Forming alliances with political factions is reminiscent of what Garifuna descendants did on St. Vincent, and during their early years after arrival on the Central American mainland. Such Garifuna ancestors did for their subsistence in the past, and now their descendants in New York also form alliances to obtain community resources. Political participation manifests itself in various forms. Although traditionally scholars cite voting as the most common conventional form of political participation, other forms exist, including contacting elected officials, participating in informal community activity, contributing money to political candidates, and taking part in protests, marches, and demonstrations (Vargas-Ramos 2003; Wong 2003). Protests and demonstrations tend to be the principal option for minorities who are isolated from the political system and provide an alternative form of political participation that also influences government action directly as well as indirectly (Cobb and Elder 1971; Marable 1996; Wong 2003). The recent widespread Latino protest concerning the U.S. immigration debate over Temporary Protection Status, deportation, and border enforcement measures exemplifies such participation in politics through protest and demonstration. Garifuna organizations and members of their communities continue to be involved in these and other issues central to their communities as they participate politically.

Appendixes

Appendix A

U.S. Garifuna Merchant Marine Seamen Crew Ship List, 1920s–50s

List of 100+ Garifuna Seamen

The earliest assignment date given for each seaman in the Passenger and Crew Ship list was selected. Some may have sailed earlier dates. Records were not accessed for tanker ships. Periods 1918–1950s.

1918–1930s

Felix Arzu
Arrival Date: September 13, 1923
Port of Departure: La Ceiba, Honduras
Ship Name: *Tegucigalpa*
Race: Black

Juan Blanco
Arrival Date: January 3, 1926
Port of Arrival: New York, NY
Port of Departure: Limon, Honduras
Ship Name: *Ulua*

Peter Ellis
Arrival Date: April 9, 1924
Port of Arrival: United States

Port of Departure: Puerto Castilla, Honduras
Ship Name: *Saramacca*

Francisco Flores
Arrival Date: June 24, 1929
Port of Arrival: United States
Port of Departure: Tela, Honduras
Ship Name: *Abangarez*

Antonio Gomez
Arrival Date: August 3, 1939
Port of Arrival: New York, NY
Port of Departure: Puerto Cortés and Tela, Honduras; Puerto Barrios, Guatemala
Ship Name: *Metapan*

Andres Martinez
Arrival Date: August 23, 1929
Port of Arrival: New York, NY
Port of Departure Tela, Honduras
Ship Name: *Iriona*

Inez P. Martinez
Arrival Date: August 17, 1931
Port of Arrival: United States
Port of Departure: Belize
Ship Name: *Turrialba*

Timothy Martinez
Arrival Date: September 22, 1931
Port of Arrival: New York, NY
Port of Departure: Puerto Castilla, Honduras
Ship Name: *Toltec*

Anselmo Nunez
Arrival Date: August 18, 1932
Port of Arrival: New York, NY
Port of Departure: Cortés, Honduras
Ship Name: *Musa*

Gregory Nunez
Arrival Date: September 9, 1926
Port of Arrival: New York, NY

Port of Departure: Puerto Cortés, Honduras
Ship Name: *Choluteca*

Antonio L. Ogaldez
Arrival Date: September 28, 1918
Port of Arrival: United States
Port of Departure: Puerto Barrios, Guatemala
Ship Name: *Bowden*

Clyde Vincente
Arrival Date: July 27, 1926
Port of Arrival: New Orleans, LA
Port of Departure: Puerto Castilla, Honduras
Ship Name: *Coppename*

Andrew Zuniga
Arrival Date: March 5, 1924
Port of Arrival: New York, NY
Ship Name: *Zacapa*
Place of Origin: British Honduras

1940s

Victor Arriola
Arrival Date: October 2, 1944
Port of Arrival: New York, NY
Port of Departure: Cienfuegos, Cuba
Ship Name: *El Oceano*

Apolonio Arzu
Arrival Date: October, 6 1947
Port of Arrival: New York, NY
Port of Departure: Puerto Cortes, Honduras
Ship Name: *Platano*

Celestino Arzu
Arrival Date: April 14, 1949
Port of Arrival: New York, NY
Port of Departure: Puerto Barrios, Guatemala
Ship Name: *Maravi*

Crispin Arzu
Arrival Date: October, 5 1942
Port of Departure: Belize, Belize
Ship Name: *Yarmouth*

Domingo Arzu
Arrival Date: January, 5 1944
Port of Arrival: New York, NY
Port of Departure: Liverpool, England
Ship Name: *Mauretania*

Francisco Arzu
Arrival Date: March 5, 1942
Port of Arrival: United States
Port of Departure: Puerto Cortés, Honduras
Ship Name: *Castilla*
Birth Date: about 1920
Race: Black

Francisco Arzu
Arrival Date: May 27, 1944
Port of Arrival: New York, NY
Port of Departure: New York, NY
Ship Name: *William McKinley*

Francisco Arzu
Arrival Date: May 5, 1945
Port of Arrival: New York City, NY
Ship Name: *George Matthews*
Last Permanent Address: Honduras

Julian Arzu
Arrival Date: June 9, 1942
Port of Arrival: United States
Port of Departure: Tela, Honduras
Ship Name: *Tanamo*

Marcelo Arzu
Arrival Date: December 14, 1947
Port of Arrival: New York, NY
Ship Name: *Iriona*
Birth Date: about 1925

Rufino C. Arzu
Arrival Date: May 24, 1946
Port of Arrival: New York, NY
Port of Departure: Baltimore, MD
Ship Name: *Chapel Hill Victory*

Tomas Arzu
Arrival Date: December 14, 1947
Port of Arrival: New York, NY
Port of Departure: Tela, Honduras
Ship Name: *Iriona*

Ventura O. Arzu
Arrival Date: July 8, 1948
Port of Arrival: New York, NY
Port of Departure: Port Armuelles, Panama
Ship Name: *Parismina*

Vicente Arzu
Arrival Date: January 5, 1944
Port of Arrival: New York, NY
Port of Departure: Liverpool, England
Ship Name: *Mauretania*

Zacarias Arzu
Arrival Date: October 17, 1943
Port of Arrival: United States
Port of Departure: Puerto Cortés, Honduras
Ship Name: *Howard*

Mateo Avila
Arrival Date: April 14, 1949
Port of Arrival: New York, NY
Port of Departure: Puerto Barrios, Guatemala
Ship Name: *Maravi*

Victor R. Avila
Arrival Date: January 13, 1945
Port of Arrival: New York, NY
Port of Departure: New York, NY
Ship Name: *John Mitchell*
Place of Origin: Honduras

Vincente Avila
Arrival Date: January 13, 1947
Port of Arrival: New York, NY
Port of Departure: New York, NY
Ship Name: *America*

Melecio Avila Bernardes
Arrival Date: April 20, 1949
Port of Arrival: New York, NY
Port of Departure: Puerto Barrios, Guatemala
Ship Name: *Darien*

Francisco Batiz
Arrival Date: October 17, 1944
Port of Arrival: New York, NY
Port of Departure: Oran, Algeria
Ship Name: *Darien*

Domingo Benedict
Arrival Date: April 14, 1949
Port of Arrival: New York, NY
Port of Departure: Puerto Barrios, Guatemala
Ship Name: *Maravi*

Pablo Blanco
Arrival Date: January 17, 1949
Port of Arrival: New York, NY
Port of Departure: Puerto Cortés, Honduras
Ship Name: *Mabay*

Jose E. Cacho
Port of Arrival: New York, NY
Port of Departure: Bizerte, Tunisia
Ship Name: *Thomas Todd*

Robustiano Castro
Arrival Date: September 24, 1945
Port of Arrival: New York, NY
Port of Departure: Antwerp, Belgium
Ship Name: *Darien*

Simeon R. Castro
Arrival Date: June 16, 1944
Port of Arrival: Mobile, AL

Ship Name: *Juniata*
Gender: Male

Julio Clotter
Arrival Date: October 17, 1944
Port of Arrival: New York, NY
Port of Departure: Oran, Algeria
Ship Name: *Darien*

Pedro Clotter
Arrival Date: April 14, 1949
Port of Arrival: New York, NY
Port of Departure: Puerto Barrios, Guatemala
Ship Name: *Maravi*

Antonio E. Colon
Arrival Date: November 28, 1948
Port of Arrival: New York, NY
Port of Departure: Puerto Cortés, Honduras
Ship Name: *Maya*

Francisco Cordova
Arrival Date: July 1942
Port of Arrival: United States
Port of Departure: Puerto Cortés, Honduras
Ship Name: *Chirripo*

Franciso Cordova
Arrival Date: November 23, 1942
Port of Arrival: New York, NY
Port of Departure: Havana, Cuba
Ship Name: *Chirripo*

Fulgencio F. Cordova
Arrival Date: February 11, 1944
Port of Arrival: New York, NY
Port of Departure: Tela, Honduras
Ship Name: *Maya*

Alfonso Ellis
Arrival Date: December 18, 1940
Port of Arrival: Boston, MA
Port of Departure: Puerto Cortés, Honduras
Ship: *Amacitia*

Pedro F. Fernandez
Arrival Date: December 25, 1943
Port of Arrival: New York, NY
Port of Departure: Bizerte, Tunisia
Ship Name: *Toltec*

Ernesto Flores
Arrival Date: November 19, 1941
Port of Arrival: New York, NY
Port of Departure: Puerto Barrios, Guatemala
Ship Name: *Musa*

Genaro Flores
Arrival Date: September 25, 1943
Port of Arrival: United States
Port of Departure: Puerto Cortés, Honduras
Ship Name: *La Playa*

Felix Gonzalez
Arrival Date: May 28, 1948
Port of Arrival: New York, NY
Port of Departure: Genoa, Italy
Ship Name: *T. J. Stevenson*

Gilberto Guity
Arrival Date: July 1942
Port of Arrival: United States
Port of Departure: Puerto Cortés, Honduras
Ship Name: *Chirripo*

Nicolas Guity
Arrival Date: October 17, 1944
Port of Arrival: New York, NY
Port of Departure: Oran, Algeria
Ship Name: *Darien*

Robustiano Guity
Arrival Date: February 1, 1942
Port of Arrival: New York, NY
Port of Departure: Havana, Cuba
Ship Name: *Sagua*

Manuel Herrera
Arrival Date: September 19, 1947
Port of Arrival: New York, NY
Port of Departure: New York, NY
Ship Name: *Hawkins Fudske*
Birth Date: about 1917

Catarino Hill Reyes
Arrival Date: November 21, 1953
Port of Arrival: New York, NY
Port of Departure: Baltimore, MD
Ship Name: *Choloma*

Frederico Johnson
Arrival Date: April 14, 1949
Port of Arrival: New York, NY
Port of Departure: Puerto Barrios, Guatemala
Ship Name: *Maravi*

Tomas N. Johnson
Arrival Date: September 9, 1948
Port of Arrival: New York, NY
Port of Departure: Puerto Cortés, Honduras
Ship Name: *San Jose*
Birth Date: about 1899

Benito F. Lambert
Arrival Date: February 7, 1948
Port of Arrival: New York, NY
Port of Departure: Southampton, England
Ship Name: *America*

Macario Lambert
Arrival Date: February 14, 1944
Port of Arrival: United States
Port of Departure: Tela, Honduras
Ship Name: *Chirripo*

Maximo Lambert
Arrival Date: July 31, 1941
Port of Arrival: New York, NY

Ports of Departure: Havana, Cuba; Puerto Cortés, Honduras; and Puerto Barrios, Guatemala
Ship Name: *Musa*

Silverio Lambert
Arrival Date: August 8, 1940
Port of Arrival: New York, NY
Port of Departure: Kingston, Jamaica; Cristóbal, Canal Zone, Panama; and Puerto Cortés, Honduras
Ship Name: *Musa*

Emeterio M. Martinez
Arrival Date: December 18, 1943
Port of Arrival: United States
Port of Departure: Cortés, Honduras
Ship Name: *Chirripo*

Isabel Martinez
Arrival Date: August 1, 1944
Port of Arrival: New Orleans, LA
Port of Departure: La Ceiba, Honduras
Ship Name: *Yoro*

Juan Martinez
Arrival Date: December 10, 1946
Port of Arrival: New York, NY
Port of Departure: Curaçao, Dutch West Indies
Ship Name: *Francis R. Hart*

Julian Martinez
Arrival Date: January 8, 1942
Port of Arrival: New York, NY
Port of Departure: Puerto Cortés, Honduras
Ship Name: *Platano*

Luis Martinez
Arrival Date: August 15, 1949
Port of Arrival: New York, NY
Port of Departure: Puerto Cortés, Honduras
Ship Name: *Everagra*

Teofilo Martinez
Arrival Date: August 23, 1949
Port of Arrival: New York, NY

Port of Departure: Tela, via Puerto Cortés, Honduras
Ship Name: *Darien*

Urbano M. Martinez
Arrival Date: August 21, 1946
Port of Arrival: New York, NY
Port of Departure: Cristóbal, Canal Zone, Panama
Ship Name: *Levers Bend*

Zoilo Martinez
Arrival Date: December 18, 1943
Port of Arrival: United States
Port of Departure: Cortés, Honduras
Ship Name: *Chirripo*

Calixto Moreira
Arrival Date: April 4, 1947
Port of Arrival: New York, NY
Port of Departure: New York, NY
Ship Name: *Willard Hall*
Place of Origin: Honduras

Calixto Moreira
Arrival Date: July 16, 1948
Port of Arrival: New York, NY
Port of Departure: New York, NY
Ship Name: *Washington*

Roberto C. Morales
Arrival Date: October 2, 1943
Port of Arrival: United States
Port of Departure: Tela, Honduras
Ship Name: *Yoro*
Race: Black

Andres Nunez
Arrival Date: July 9, 1941
Port of Arrival: New York, NY
Port of Departure: Puerto Cortés, Honduras, via Puerto Barrios, Guatemala
Ship Name: *Platano*

Cayetano Nunez
Arrival Date: January 5, 1946
Port of Arrival: New York, NY
Port of Departure: Le Havre, France
Ship Name: *George Leonard*

Joaquin Nunez
Arrival Date: April 4, 1944
Port of Arrival: New York, NY
Ship Name: *Aztec*
Place of Origin: Honduras

Vincente Nunez
Arrival Date: 22 Mar 1945
Port of Arrival: New York, NY
Port of Departure: Southampton, England
Ship Name: *John Ericsson*
Birth Date: about 1920

Pedro Nunez Martinez
Arrival Date: September 18, 1944
Port of Arrival: New York, NY
Port of Departure: Bariita [*sic*; Bari, Italy]
Ship Name: *Zacapa*

Nicasio Reyes
Arrival Date: May 28, 1946
Port of Arrival: New York, NY
Port of Departure: Cette, France
Ship Name: *William L Yancey*

Thomas Rocha
Arrival Date: June 18, 1944
Port of Arrival: United States
Port of Departure: Tela, Honduras
Ship Name: *Chirripo*

Policarpo Sambula
Arrival Date: August 28, 1944
Port of Arrival: New York, NY
Port of Departure: Oran, Algeria
Ship Name: *Toltec*

Abelino Santos
Arrival Date: December 17, 1945
Port of Arrival: Baltimore, MD
Port of Departure: New York, NY
Ship Name: *American Builder*
Place of Origin: Honduras

Julio Sanchez
Arrival Date: May 20, 1948
Port of Arrival: New York, NY
Port of Departure: Antwerp, Belgium
Ship Name: *Marine Tiger*

Catarino Sanchez Blanco
Arrival Date: May 21, 1947
Port of Arrival: New York, NY
Port of Departure: Havana, Cuba
Ship Name: *Phoebe Knot*

Lorenzo Tifre
Arrival Date: November 23, 1942
Port of Arrival: New York, NY
Port of Departure: Havana, Cuba
Ship Name: *Chirripo*

Patrocinio A. Velasquez
Arrival Date: January 5, 1944
Port of Arrival: New York, NY
Port of Departure: Liverpool, England
Ship Name: *Mauretania*
Birth Date: about 1904

1950s

Pedro Alvarez Norales
Arrival Date: November 21, 1953
Port of Arrival: New York, NY
Port of Departure: Barranquilla, Colombia
Ship Name: *Choloma*
Birth Date: March 2, 1914

Francisco Arzu
Arrival Date: September 19, 1951
Port of Arrival: New York, NY
Port of Departure: Puerto Cortés, Honduras
Ship Name: *Musa*

Ines Arzu
Arrival Date: April 26, 1950
Port of Arrival: New York, NY
Port of Departure: Puerto Cortés, Honduras
Ship Name: *Junior*

Vincente M. Arzu
Arrival Date: August 18, 1952
Port of Arrival: New York, NY
Port of Departure: Santa Marta, Colombia
Ship Name: *Veragua*

Prisciliano Avila
Arrival Date: September 9, 1952
Port of Arrival: New York, NY
Port of Departure: Libertador
Ship Name: *Copan*

Pedro P. Ballesteros
Arrival Date: October 26, 1954
Port of Arrival: New York, NY
Port of Departure: Guayaquil, Ecuador
Ship Name: *Maya*

Abraham Bermudes
Arrival Date: November 21, 1953
Port of Arrival: New York, NY
Port of Departure: Baltimore, MD
Ship Name: *Choloma*

Bonifacio Bernardez
Arrival Date: September 2, 1952
Port of Arrival: New York, NY
Port of Departure: Armuelles, Panama
Ship Name: *Choluteca*

Victor L. Blanco
Arrival Date: May 3, 1952
Port of Arrival: New York, NY
Port of Departure: New York, NY
Ship Name: *Independence*

Pablo S. Cacho Sambula
Arrival Date: November 21, 1953
Port of Arrival: New York, NY
Port of Departure: Baltimore, MD
Ship Name: *Choloma*

Ambrosio Castro
Arrival Date: May 30, 1956
Port of Arrival: New York, NY
Port of Departure: La Ceiba, Honduras
Ship Name: *Contessa*
Place of Origin: Honduras

Efrain Castro
Arrival Date: January 19, 1954
Port of Arrival: New York, NY
Port of Departure: Panama Canal and Puerte Armuelles, Panama
Ship Name: *Choluteca*

Perfecto Castro
Arrival Date: August 6, 1955
Port of Arrival: Baltimore, MD
Port of Departure: Puerto Ordaz, Venezuela
Ship Name: *Ore Transport*

Simeon Castro Rivas
Arrival Date: August 11, 1953
Arrival Port: New York, NY, to New Orleans, LA
Departure Port: La Ceiba, Honduras
Ship Name: *Contessa*
Ethnicity/Nationality: Honduran

Jorge Clotter
Arrival Date: September 13, 1954
Port of Arrival: New York, NY

Port of Departure: Puerto Cortes, Honduras
Ship Name: *Aztec*

Leo M. Ellis
Arrival Date: July 31, 1953
Port of Arrival: New York, NY
Port of Departure: Hamburg, Germany
Ship Name: American importer
Birth Date: September 12, 1918

Juan J. Gomez
Arrival Date: October 26, 1954
Port of Arrival: New York, NY
Port of Departure: Guayaquil, Ecuador
Ship Name: *Maya*

Marcos Gomez
Arrival Date: December 11, 1952
Port of Arrival: New York, NY
Port of Departure: Caibarien, Cuba
Ship Name: *Manaqui*

Laureano J. Guity Lalin
Arrival Date: November 21, 1953
Port of Arrival: New York, NY
Port of Departure: Baltimore, MD
Ship Name: *Choloma*

Catarino Hill Reyes
Arrival Date: November 21, 1953
Port of Arrival: New York, NY
Port of Departure: Baltimore, MD
Ship Name: *Choloma*

Moises Johnson
Arrival Date: January 12, 1954
Port of Arrival: New York, NY
Port of Departure: Bocas Del Toro, Panama, and Tela, Honduras
Ship Name: *Maya*

Francisco Lambert
Arrival Date: June 14, 1954
Port of Arrival: New York, NY

APPENDIX A: U.S. GARIFUNA MERCHANT MARINE SEAMEN · 209

Port of Departure: La Ceiba, Honduras
Ship Name: *Eros*

Froilan Lambert
Arrival Date: July 27, 1953
Port of Arrival: New York, NY
Port of Departure: Puerto Cortés, Honduras
Ship Name: *Veragua*

Herminio Lambert
Arrival Date: November 17, 1954
Port of Arrival: New York, NY
Port of Departure: Puerto Cortés, Honduras
Ship Name: *Choloma*
Birth Date: April 25, 1934

Justo Lambert
Arrival Date: December 14, 1954
Port of Arrival: Baltimore, MD
Port of Departure: Guayaquil, Ecuador
Ship Name: *Platano*

Luis Lambert
Arrival Date: October 26, 1954
Port of Arrival: New York, NY
Port of Departure: Guayaquil, Ecuador
Ship Name: *Maya*

Mateo A. Martinez
Arrival Date: December 13, 1951
Port of Arrival: New York, NY
Port of Departure: Santa Marta, Colombia
Ship Name: *La Playa*

Juan Martinez Chamorro
Arrival Date: June 28, 1951
Port of Arrival: New York, NY
Port of Departure: Puerto Cortés, Honduras; California
Ship Name: *Aztec*

Ambrosio Martinez Herrerra
Arrival Date: June 28, 1951
Port of Arrival: New York, NY

Port of Departure: Puerto Cortés, Honduras; California
Ship Name: *Aztec*

Ismael Nunez
Arrival Date: July 2, 1953
Port of Arrival: New York, NY
Port of Departure: La Ceiba, Honduras
Ship Name: *Eros*

Cornelius Nunez Cacho
Arrival Date: January 5, 1953
Port of Arrival: New York, NY
Port of Departure: Santa Marta, Colombia
Ship Name: *Talamanca*

Julian B. Reyes
Arrival Date: August 13, 1951
Port of Arrival: New York, NY
Port of Departure: Antwerp, Belgium
Ship Name: *Redstone*

Ponciano Rocha Lacayo
Arrival Date: February 18, 1953
Port of Arrival: New York, NY
Port of Departure: Puerto Cortés, Honduras
Ship Name: *Cibao*

Cesar Santos Johnson
Arrival Date: November 21, 1953
Port of Arrival: New York, NY
Port of Departure: Baltimore, MD
Ship Name: *Choloma*

Domingo Zuniga
Arrival Date: September 2, 1952
Port of Arrival: New York, NY
Port of Departure: Armuelles, Panama
Ship Name: *Choluteca*

Sources

New York State Passenger and Crew Lists, 1917–1967 [database on-line]. Ancestry.com.
Selected Passenger and Crew Lists and Manifests. 2008. The National Archives at Washington, D.C. Ancestry.com.

Appendix B

Honduran Garifuna Organizations Participating at the Garifuna Nation Pocono Retreat, 2005

Association of Black Women from the city of La Ceiba—Asociación de Mujeres Negras de Honduras
Ebeners Developers
Funds for the Martinez Family—FODEMA, Fondo de la Familia Martinez
Garifuna Women Marching—Mujeres Garifuna en Marcha (MUGAMA)
Government of Ricardo Madura Joest—Honduran president representative
Honduras Consulate office of New York
Horizon Real Estate Partners, LLC
Innovation Party of Unity–Social Democrat—Partido Innovación y Unidad–Social Demócrata, PINU-SD
Inter-American Foundation, independent entity of the U.S. government
Limon Ladies Organization in New York—Organización de Damas Limoneñas en New York
Milenio Real Estate Group, LLC, Rhode Island
Municipality of La Ceiba, Honduras, mayor's office
Municipality of Limon, Honduras, mayor's office
Municipality of Puerto Cortes, Honduras, mayor's office
National Project of Ecosystems in Honduras—Proyecto Nacional Ecosistemas de Honduras
New Horizon Investment Club

Only for Women—Solo para Mujeres, La Ceiba, Honduras
Organization for the Development of Aguan—Organización Pro Desarollo de Aguan (OPDA)
The Solís Mejia Family Foundation
Travesia Organization New Wave—Organización Travesía Nueva Ola

Source

Ávila, José Francisco, and Tomás Alberto Ávila. 2008. *Mundo Garifuna*, 159–60. Providence, RI: Milenio.

Appendix C

U.S. Immigration Data from Belize, Guatemala, Honduras, 1930–2017

The numbers below show immigrants from selected Central American countries who came to the United States each decade between 1930 and 2010, and the total number obtaining permanent legal status from 2011 to 2017. Most Garifuna in New York City migrate from the three Central American countries listed and are part of this authorized immigrant population. However, Garifuna are also part of the undocumented immigrant population. The Pew Research Center data presents that between 1990 and 2007 the undocumented U.S. Latino immigrant population increased (Lopez, Bialik, and Radford 2018). Changes to U.S. immigration restriction laws occurred in 1996, 2002, and 2006 as a result of increased undocumented immigration and U.S. terrorism concerns (Cohn 2015).

Immigration Data

	1930–39	1940–49	1950–59	1960–69	1970–79	1980–89	1990–99	2000–2009	2010	2011	2012	2013	2014	2015	2016	2017
BZ																
	193	433	1,133	4,185	6,747	14,964	12,600	9,682	997	905	875	969	823	804	878	754
GUA																
	423	1,303	4,197	14,357	23,837	58,547	126,043	156,992	10,263	10,795	9,857	9,829	9,871	11,466	12,548	12,792
HON																
	679	1,874	5,320	15,078	15,651	39,071	72,880	63,513	6,381	6,053	6,773	8,795	8,025	9,071	12,996	11,147

Sources

Cohn, D'Vera. 2015. "How U.S. Immigration Laws and Rules Have Changed through History." *Pew Research Center*, September 30, 2015. http://pewresearch.org.

Lopez, Gustavo, Kristen Bialik, and Jynnah Radford. 2018. "Key Findings about U.S. Immigrants." *Pew Research Center*, November 30, 2018. http://pewresearch.org.

United States Department of Homeland Security. 2011. Table of Persons Obtaining Lawful Permanent Resident Status by Region and Selected Country of Last Residence. Fiscal Years 1820–2017 (reviewed). *Yearbook of Immigration Statistics*, 2011. Washington, D.C: U.S. Department of Homeland Security, Office of Immigration Statistics…

Appendix D

Bronx Community Board Appointees, 2019–20

Many of the individuals listed also belong to various Garifuna organizations, women's groups, and soccer, musical, and cultural clubs.

Garifuna Coalition USA Inc.

New York Garifuna Civic Participation Political Positions

Rosemary Ordoñez-Jenkins—Vice Chair Executive Board of the Bronx Democratic Party, 87th Assembly District Judicial Delegate.

Gustavo Santos—2018 New York Union Proud Trustee Candidate, delegated to the Convention for 15 years and a shop steward for 20 years. He is a member of Political Action Committee (PAC) and has been for the past 16 years and was a vice chair of the Region 8 PAC. (NYUP 2018)

Appointed Positions, 2019–20

José Francisco Ávila	New York City Nightlife Advisory Board
Cecil K. Brooks	Bronx Community Board 1
Evelyn Arauz-Chamorro	Bronx Community Board 2
Barbara Lopez	Bronx Community Board 2
Xiomara Arriola	Bronx Community Board 3
Pablo Blanco	Bronx Community Board 5

Nelson Chimilio	Bronx Community Board 6
Carmen Miranda	Bronx Community Board 7
Cruz Garcia	Bronx Community Board 9
Felipa Manaiza	Bronx Community Board 9
Vilma Zuniga	Bronx Community Board 8

NYC Office of the Mayor; NYC Mayor's Community Affairs Unit

Staff Members

Mirtha C. Sabio	General Counsel at Office of Bronx Borough President
Marcia Gomez	Board of Elections in the City of New York
Daysi Nuñez	Board of Elections in the City of New York
Karen Cacho-White	Community Liaison at Office of City Council Member Fernando Cabrera
Jeffrey Velasquez	District Director at Office of City Council Member Vanessa Gibson
Maritza Wiggins	Community Liaison at Office of City Council Member Rafael Salamanca Jr.

Updated January 26, 2020.
(J. Ávila 2021)

Sources

Ávila, José Francisco. 2021. *Pan-Garifuna Afro-Latino, Power of Pride: My Quest for Racial, Ancestral, Ethnic and Cultural Identity*. Bronx, NY: Garifuna Afro-Latino Entertainment.

NYC Mayor's Community Affairs Unit. Find your Community Board. https://www.nyc.gov/site/cau/community-boards/bronx-boards.page.

NYC Office of the Mayor. The Official Website of the City of New York, Office of the Mayor. https://www.nyc.gov/office-of-the-mayor/.

NY Union Proud (NYUP). 2018. "Gustavo Santo—2018 New York Union Proud Trustee Candidate." NYUP. http://nyup2018.org/gustavo-santos

Appendix E

Founding Members of the Garifuna Coalition USA

Belizean Garifuna

Felix Miranda (Garifuna Council of New York)

Guatemalan Garifuna

Victor Bermudez (Organización Garifuna de Guatemala)

Honduran Garifuna

Antonieta Maximo (FEDHONY)
Dionisia Amaya (MUGAMA)
Rejil Solis and Juan Laboriel (Bicentennial Committee members)
Mirtha Colón (Hondurans Against AIDS)
Celeo Álvarez Casildo (Bicentennial Committee and ODECO)
José Francisco Ávila (Garifuna World)
Tomás Alberto Ávila (Garifuna World)
Lydia Sacasa Hill (Garifuna House)
Luz Solis (Hamalali Wayunagu Dance Co.)
Jorge Centeno (Unificación Cultural Garifuna)
Roseanne Tifre (Garifuna House)
Abelina Rochez (Club Femenino Santa Fe)

Celso Castro (Castro Family Foundation)
Pablo Gómez (Honduran Parade Committee, Inc.)

Source

Ávila, José Francisco. 2021. *Pan-Garifuna Afro-Latino Power of Pride: My Quest for Racial, Ancestral, Ethnic and Cultural Identity.* Bronx, NY: Garifuna Afro-Latino Entertainment.

NY Union Proud (NYUP). 2018. "Gustavo Santos—2018 New York Union Proud Trustee Candidate." NYUP. http://nyup2018.org/gustavo-santos

ACKNOWLEDGMENTS

First thanks to the Creator Most High Almighty for guiding me every step in this project. I also acknowledge the entire Garifuna community for their contributions, and my family's and friends' support, including those who knowingly or unknowingly played a role in this research. Thank you, Mom! Others I recognize as contributing to this study are scholars and journalists who document the Garifuna, Fordham University Press staff, Cabrini University colleagues and friend, and classmates and professors at Ohio University and West Virginia University. Moreover, I feel obliged to mention names of individuals who recently passed, such as my centenarian grandmother, Ms. Kate, who reflected moral values and grace in her lifetime that I adopt. And New Hope COGIC Elder Mason Johnson, who was another centenarian who inspired me to continue seeking greater spiritual heights. Lastly, my respects to Professor Zelbert L. Moore of SUNY New Paltz, who inspired me to research and study the African diaspora, mentoring and motivating me to expand my academic horizons.

NOTES

Introduction

1. Some studies use *Garifuna* as the singular form and *Garinagu* as the plural form when describing this ethnic population.

2. The Garifuna population is estimated at 100,000 to 200,000. Other New York City Black ethnic groups are West Indians (from English Caribbean island nations, excluding groups of Hispanic origin), estimated at more than 490,000; Haitians, 156,000 to 400,000; Panamanians, 25,000 to 40,000 (75 percent Afro-Panamanian); and Africans, 100,000 (70,000 in the Bronx). Dominicans, for the most part, are not considered an organized, established Black group because few embrace their African identity; they total an estimated 369,000. This group has the highest number of local elected officials (News Americas 2017; Roberts 2006, 2014; All Peoples 2012).

3. Tuttle (2012) counted 331 publications about the Garifuna in disciplines such as anthropology, dance and arts, ethnohistory, education, tourism, spirituality, and health and medicine.

4. Years later, another period of increased migration occurred, primarily of Honduran Garifuna, but it was not large enough to be considered a wave. Initiation of Temporary Protection Status (TPS) as part of the Immigration Act of 1990 allowed individuals with alien status to extend their U.S. residence because of armed conflicts or environmental disasters in their countries of origin. After Hurricane Mitch devastated Honduras and Nicaragua in 1998, the U.S. government extended this temporary period of residence for individuals from these regions. The purpose was to assist in the economic restoration of these countries by allowing migrants from Honduras and Nicaragua to contribute financially to their home countries. The effects of the 1998 hurricane reportedly set the Honduran economy back several years, exacerbating the country's long-established lag in development. Hondurans in the United States, including Garifuna organizations and embassy officials, have successfully lobbied the U.S. government to extend the TPS provision a total of seven times. However, it ended in 2017–18

during President Donald Trump's administration and is in review due to legal challenges (England 2006; USCIS 2007; Molina 2007; NYC Mayor 2022).

5. Conversation with Honduran Garifuna leaders: in New York City (2017) with Gregoria Flores, and in Honduras (2021) with Humberto Castillo.

6. Other Guatemalan Garifuna settlements in the periphery located along the Atlantic coast are Agua Sagarei, Flowas, Funa-tagu, Quehueche, and Milinda. In Puerto Barrios, the Garifuna population is concentrated, for the most part, in the neighborhoods of Barrio El Rastro, Barrio El Estrecho, and Las Colinas (Ellington 1998, 26).

7. Putnam emphasizes two profound aspects of social capital: bounding and bridging. Bounding involves maintaining social capital within an exclusive, more class-oriented group. Bridging social capital encompasses individuals from various social strata and enhances social exchanges in the community. Bounding, deemed the dark side of social capital, is harmful to the democratic process and excludes the community at large; the author blames a generational change for the decline in civic engagement.

8. Many Dominicans prefer not to identify as Black or Mulatto because of traditional negative racial stereotypes and this group's being the most impoverished in their country (Reynoso 2003).

9. Alejandro Portes and Min Zhou (2018) are credited with proposing the theory of segmented assimilation.

10. The term *community development* is used in this study to indicate the process in which members of a community collaborate with one another to address their needs or issues important to them. This also encompasses reaching out to local agencies. Community growth refers to the increase of Garifuna exchanging both within their group and with non-Garifuna for their social and political advancement. This occurred simultaneously with an increase in Garifuna population and organizations.

11. In New York City, Garifuna are concentrated in the boroughs of Manhattan, Brooklyn, and the Bronx. The Bronx has the largest percentage, with Honduran Garifuna accounting for the largest number. The Belizean Garifuna, in contrast, reside mostly in Brooklyn, in African American and West Indian communities that share the English language and the Caribbean culture, which includes reggae, Rastafarian traditions, and an annual West Indian Day parade (which Guatemalan and Honduran Garifuna also support) (England 2006).

12. The Honduran Garifuna community of Sambo Creek, located close (18.9 km) to the city of La Ceiba, is a popular tourist destination. The Palma Beach Resort is nearby. The Tela Bay area has several resorts, including the Ensenada Beach Resort and Convention Center and the Indura Beach and Golf Resort. A newly constructed airport is also in the vicinity. About 163 km east of Tela is the city of Trujillo. Private vacation homes owned by foreigners are located in the Garifuna communities of Rio Negro and Guadalupe. The Njoi Trujillo resorts are located outside the city of Trujillo in Garifuna communities.

13. Honduran Garifuna in the United States are among the leaders in sending money home to family members and making substantial contributions to the Honduran economy (Endo et al. 2010, 50).

Chapter 1. Origins, Surviving, Ensuring Subsistence, and Culture

1. Later, between 1832 and 1860, they settled in Nicaragua's Atlantic coastal region.

Chapter 2. Livelihood on the Caribbean Coast

1. Stann Creek changed its name to Dangriga in 1975; Punta Gorda is also known as Peini in Garífuna.
2. Victor Virgilio López Garcia, personal communication, August 8, 2018, Tornabé, Honduras.
3. Garcia, August 8, 2018.
4. Another Honduran president of Garifuna descent, Carlos Flores Facussé (1998–2002), also implemented policies that negatively impacted the ethnic group (Suazo 2012; Centeno García 2001). Honduran Garifuna Gilberto Cacho, who had a radio program in La Ceiba titled "El Aporte de los Negros a la Democracia," shared that Oscar Armando Flores was his friend and was a Garifuna Mulatto.
5. Santos Centeno García, personal communication, May 3, 2016, La Ceiba, Honduras.
6. Centeno García, May 3, 2016.
7. Wellington Ramos, personal communication, January 2, 2019, Bronx, NY.
8. Conversations with Victor Avila Roches in Bronx, NY; Alejandro Lambert, personal communication, August 4, 2017, Puerto Cortés, Honduras.
9. Conversations with Victor Avila Roches in Bronx, New York; Rufino Arzu, personal communication, September 3, 2017, Long Island, NY.
10. Delegates at the convention: Alonzo Velasquez—Dangriga, Alcadio Marin—Seine Beight, Peter Avila—Punta Gorda, Simeon M. Sampson—Dangriga, Reginal Arana—Barranco, Salvatore B. Daniels—Punta Gorda, Eugenio Cayetano—Barranco, and Nicodemus Castillo—Punta Gorda. It is known that Cristales y Río Negro is one of the earliest Honduran Garifuna organizations, established 1912 and recognized November 23, 1951 by the government (Centeno García 1997; Ávila and Ávila 2008).
11. Roy Cayetano, lecture in Trujillo, Honduras, 2015 Second Regional Garifuna Central American Convention—*Il Encuentro Regional Garífuna Centroamericano*.
12. Another precedent of the National Garifuna Council was the Waribagabaga International Dance Group created by Phyllis Cayetano to rescue and sustain Garifuna traditional dances.
13. Catalina Avila Clotter, personal communication, August 8, 2015, Puerto Cortés, Honduras.
14. Julio Clotter, personal communication, August 3, 1995, Puerto Cortés, Honduras; Noe Caballero, personal communication, October 22, 2019; Priciliano R. Avila, personal communication, March 5, 2019, Puerto Cortés, Honduras; Margarito Alvarez, personal communication, November 4, 2019. Francisco Arzu (Don Paulito) was also a merchant marine seaman and supporter of the Carib American Association. He acknowledged Timothy Martinez in a 1987 event in Travesía, Honduras, following Martinez's death. Francisco Arzu appears in the picture collections of Carib American Association files of Timothy Martinez. Arzu was also one of the early seamen who left Honduras as early as the 1940s included in the seamen list in appendix A.
15. Sigatoka has various names. It is also known as black Sigatoka disease and Black Leaf Streak Disease (BLSD). It is a leaf spot disease caused by a fungus visible in a banana leaf. The banana tree gradually loses its leaf surface as the pathogen reduces its photosynthetic ability (Yonow et al. 2019).
16. Angel Martinez, conversation with Juan Martinez's brother, 2018, Middletown, NY; Margarito Alvarez, personal communication, November 4, 2019.

Chapter 3. Early U.S. Garifuna Communities

1. Melvinia Martinez Lambert (daughter-in-law of Victor Avila), personal communication, January 20, 2020, Bronx, NY. Timothy Martinez's picture lists Victor Avila as one of the founding members of the Carib American Association.

2. "Liston Ogaldez" in *Selected Passenger and Crew Lists and Manifests*. New York State Department of State, Division of Corporations: *Carib American Association, Inc.*, June 25, 1946.

3. Melvinia Martinez Lambert (wife of Juan Martinez and daughter-in-law of Victor Avila), personal communication, January 19, 2020, Bronx, NY; Rufino Arzu, personal communication, September 3, 2017, Long Island, NY.

4. The association is registered under the title Carib American Association without a hyphen. However, all the tickets, programs, newspaper articles, etc., pictured in figures 3, 5, and 6a, b, and c use a hyphen in the title: Carib-American Association.

5. Angel Martinez, personal communication, March 3, 2019, Puerto Cortés, Honduras.

6. New York State Department of State, Division of Corporations: *Carib American Association, Inc.*, June 25, 1946.

7. Thomas Vincent Ramos (September 17, 1888–November 13, 1955) died at the age of sixty-eight.

8. Mary Pitillo, personal communication, February 2, 2020, Queens, NY; Angel Martinez, personal communication, March 3, 2019, Puerto Cortés, Honduras; Rufino Arzu, personal communication, September 3, 2017, Long Island, NY.

9. Angel Martinez, personal communication, March 3, 2019, Puerto Cortés, Honduras.

10. Timothy Martinez married an Afro–Puerto Rican; Julio Clotter had a child in Houston, TX; Juan Martinez had a child in New Orleans, LA; Victor Avila's first marriage was to an African American in South Carolina. Source: conversations with their families. Personal communication with Alejandro Lambert and Melvinia Martinez Lambert (wife of Juan Martinez and daughter-in-law of Victor R. Avila), January 19, 2020.

11. After the transnational population left the Central American coast, many English Blacks in positions of power discriminated against the Garifuna.

12. Ethnic solidarity refers to Garifuna in New York City born in either Honduras, Guatemala, or Belize coming together regardless of differences in language or nationality.

13. Margaret Thompson, personal communication, February 20, 2020; Angel Martinez, personal communication, March 3, 2019, Puerto Cortés, Honduras.

14. I was fortunate to speak with Julio Clotter before his abrupt passing in the Caribbean Sea in his own boat. Julio Clotter, personal communication, August 3, 1995, Puerto Cortés, Honduras.

15. Angel Martinez, personal communication, March 3, 2019, Puerto Cortés, Honduras; Alejandro Lambert, personal communication, August 4, 2017, Puerto Cortés, Honduras; Marcello Arzu, personal communication, February 5, 2020.

16. Merchant Mariners of World War II Act-S. 1272—10th Congress.

17. Angel Martinez, personal communication, March 3, 2019, Puerto Cortés, Honduras; Alejandro Lambert, personal communication, August 4, 2017, Puerto Cortés, Honduras; Marcello Arzu, personal communication, February 5, 2020.

18. Margarito Alvarez Martinez, personal communication, November 4, 2019; Melvinia Martinez Lambert, personal communication, February 17, 2019, Bronx, NY.

19. Melvinia Martinez Lambert, personal communication, February 17, 2019, Bronx, NY.

20. Margarito Alvarez Martinez, personal communication, November 4, 2019; Melvinia Martinez Lambert, personal communication, February 17, 2019, Bronx, NY.

21. Alejandro Lambert, personal communication, August 4, 2017, Puerto Cortés, Honduras.

22. *The Black Caribs of Honduras* was produced by Doris Stone and recorded by Peter Kite Smith in 1952 for Folkways Records, located in New York City. The label recorded folk music from around the world. Another early artist, Mr. Pollo Martinez and Brothers, recorded several albums, including *Caribbean Country Songs from Spanish and British Honduras*, and *Country Songs from Spanish Honduras*, produced in Brooklyn, NY.

23. Alejandro Lambert, personal communication, August 4, 2017, Puerto Cortés, Honduras.

24. Alejandro Lambert, personal communication, August 4, 2017; Margarito Alvarez Martinez, personal communication, November 4, 2019; Melvinia Martinez Lambert, personal communication, February 17, 2019, Bronx, NY.

25. Names of the seamen listed in Timothy H. Martinez's letter: Pablo F. Blanco (Aguan), president; Gerardo Guerrero (Masca), vice president, Honduras; Pedro F. Fernandez, chaplain; Cayetano Nuñez, treasurer; Perfecto Castro (Limon), recording secretary; Lino Reyes, sergeant-at-arms; and Timoteo H. Martinez (Masca), business manager. The earliest arrivals by passenger ship were Pedro F. Fernandez, December 1943; Cayetano Nuñez, February 1945; Pablo F. Blanco, January 1949; Perfecto Castro, August 1955; Gerardo Guerrero, April 1956; and Lino Reyes, June 1961.

26. Abelardo Flores was president of the Club San Antonio Progressivo, and Jimmy Cordova was vice president (August 6, 2020 personal communication with Jimmy Cordova).

27. Jimmy Cordova, personal communication, October 1, 2020.

28. Aida Lambert (sitting in middle) identified during my meeting with her and daughter Sonia Lambert, April 25, 2021. During my meeting with René Mena, he identified Juan Marin in the photo.

29. New York State Department of State, Division of Corporations: Honduras Football & Social Club, Inc., June 11, 1965; René Mena, personal communication, September 2, 2006, Bronx, NY.

30. René Mena, personal communication, September 2, 2006, Bronx, NY.

31. Personal communications: Catalina Avila, Marcello Arzu, Paul Arzu, Alejandro Lambert.

32. Alejandro Lambert, personal communication, August 4, 2017, Puerto Cortés, Honduras; Rufino Arzu Rufino, personal communication, September 3, 2017, Long Island, NY.

33. René Mena, personal communication, September 2, 2006, Bronx, NY.

34. Ivan Warner, son of immigrants from the Caribbean island of St. Kitts, was elected in 1958 from Morrisania, following Walter H. Gladwin.

Chapter 4. Identity and Cultural Growth: *Garifunadao*

1. Although most Garifuna are soccer fans, I noticed that baseball was popular in one Nicaraguan community when I saw a sizable baseball stadium in Orinoco village during my visit there.

2. Herman Badillo appears in a photo with Garifuna in the 1960s—Timothy Martinez photo files.

3. Another sign that there were fewer employment opportunities in maritime work was the sale of one of the NMU's main buildings in New York City in 1987. In 1988 the NMU attempted to merge with the Marine Engineers Beneficial Association, but it was not until 2001 that it actually merged with the Seafarers International Union.

4. U.S. Merchant Marine Document Z417-54-8385 D1—Aruba trip; 417 54 8385 D1—Lisbon, Portugal (documents obtained from Melvinia Martinez Lambert, wife of Juan Martinez).

5. Melvinia Martinez Lambert (wife of Juan Martinez), personal communication, January 19, 2020, Bronx, NY.

6. Marcello Arzu and Victor Avila were among the men Juan Martinez helped obtain asbestos exposure compensation. Source: personal communication with Marcello Arzu, February 20, 2020.

7. Lorenzo Tifre, Julian Reyes, Prisciliano Avila: names recorded in Selected Passenger and Crew Lists and Manifests, The National Archives at Washington, D.C., accessed on Ancestry.com.

8. SS *Texaco Oklahoma* Collection 2005, p. 4; "Catarino Blanco," in Selected Passenger and Crew Lists and Manifests.

9. Terms used to describe the Garifuna in the past were "Morenos" (Spanish translation of dark skin), also "Caribes," "Caribes Morenos," and dark-skin French, "Morenos Franceses." Years later "Garifuna" became the common term used to describe the ethnic group.

10. The Garifuna Settlement Day Group started in the 1960s in Los Angeles. Another organization, the Carib Settlement Day Association, started in 1972; in 1974 it changed its name to the Belizean Settlement Day Association (BSDA).

11. Jimmy Cordova, personal communication, August 11, 2020.

12. Other Garifuna bands included Estrella Ubou, Nulfo y su Orquesta, Figaga (Houston, TX), and Marcony Star.

13. In 1980 Los Sicodelicos changed its name to Constellacion Latino. Celso Centeno, personal communication, January 15, 2018; Gilberto Cacho, conversation, June 5, 2017, Bronx, NY; Juan A. Martinez, personal communication, January 20, 2017; Margarito Alvarez, personal communication, June 10, 2017; Galileo Bernardez. conversation, May 13, 2017, Bronx, NY.

14. Conversation with Pantaleon Lambert Hill, 2018, Bronx, NY. Pantaleon Lambert Hill mentioned who was in the band's photograph in figure 8. Although not mentioned by Pantaleon, Margarito Alvarez Martinez shared with me that he was also part of the Satelites band.

15. In a conversation with Jimmy Cordova (March 3, 2021), he mentioned that Batis created the music in Honduras and taped it with a boom box; once in the U.S., he converted it to a vinyl album. Album title: *Batiz, Presenta Los Travadores Del Caribe en Ritmo Garifuna* (album hit: "Wata Foncha"). Honduran Garifuna Eduardo Ballesteros is also one of the early Garifuna music writers.

16. Conversations with Gilberto Cacho; Jimmy Cordova, March 3, 2021. They said that Batis's nightclubs attracted many Puerto Rican patrons, as Latino bands were also invited to perform there.

17. René J. Mena, interview, September 2, 2006, Bronx, NY.

18. Melvinia Martinez Lambert, personal communication, March 30, 2018, Bronx, NY. There were several popular nightclubs patronized by the Garifuna. Garifuna leader German Cayetano mentioned a place named "Rondevu," circa 1960s. He also mentioned that the Honduran Ladino nightclub Lempira was popular and that Jorge Gamboa's social club was popular in the 1970s–80s. Cayetano also mentioned Lampara and Cangrejeros. Paul Arzu mentioned La Barra, in the Bronx. John Mariano also had a nightclub in Brooklyn, in addition to Fermin Clotter in the 1980s. Garifuna Social Club, Inc., DOS ID 571396, registered in New York State by Jorge Gamboa, July 21, 1979.

19. Aida Lambert, personal communication, April 25, 2021; Aida mentioned that before Club Cangrejeros, a Garifuna from Bluefields named Mr. Lopez had a popular social club in the same area in Harlem.

20. The Sociedad Honduras New York, Inc., was registered August 1, 1958, in New York City. Others she invited were Pablo Gomez, Crecencio Bulnes, and Neto Arzu (Guatemalan Garifuna). Aida Lambert. Interview meeting, April 25, 2021.

21. Moises Colon, conversation, March 2019, at Garifuna Believers Mennonite Church, Brooklyn, NY.

22. Garifuna Social Club Inc., DOS ID 571396, was registered in New York State by Jorge Gamboa, July 21, 1979. Garifuna leader German Cayetano explained that it was one of the many hangout and dance locations of many Garifuna.

23. Other members/affiliates were Arsenio Ramos, Amado Lambert, Amado Martinez, Magna Colon, Janet Guity Sabio, Amilcar Sabio, Simeon Lambert, Carmen Martinez, Rigo Lambert, Aida Lambert, Celea Johnson, Tina Lambert, Antonieta Maximo, Erico Castro, and Fernando Castro. The December 1971 *Reflejos* publication provides a list of forty-three members. Sources: Efraim Castro, personal communication, December 17, 2020; Sandra Colon, personal communication, August 24, 2020; Celso Castro, personal communication, May 25, 2020.

24. A segment of film of the September 1971 West Indian Day parade with FUH concession stand is in Timothy Martinez Movie Reel 35–42; Efraim Castro, personal communication, December 17, 2020; *Reflejos: Organo de Divulgacion F.U.H.*, December 1971, New York, NY.

25. Efraim Castro, personal communication, December 17, 2020; Celso Castro, personal communication, May 25, 2020.

26. Cesar Johnson, Florentine Johnson, and Freddie Johnson (merchant marine sailors and friends of Juan Martinez). Florentine Johnson was a captain in the Honduran army and served in the special National Guard unit for President Ramon Villeda Morales. Source: Paul Arzu, personal communication, August 20, 2020.

27. Sandra Colon, personal communication, August 24, 2020.

28. In a past conversation (September 2000–May 2001) I had with Fernando Castro, he told me that, as a student at City College of New York, he was involved with the Young Lords. Aida Lambert is a founding member of the annual New York Hispanic Day Parade, held in October on Fifth Avenue, that emerged in the mid-1980s; personal communication with Sandra Colon, August 4, 2020.

29. Raphael Castro mentioned that José F. Ávila and his father, Francisco "Tito" Ávila Mena, visited the FUH from Boston. According to Castro, "Tito" Ávila Mena had immigrated from Honduras in 1968 and was organizing the Garifuna in Boston. Raphael Castro, personal communication, August 27, 2020.

30. Grupo Solidaridad por el Pueblo de Honduras changed to Centro Información de Honduras—Information Center of Honduras; see Doris Garcia, "Place, Race and the Politics of Identity in the Geography of Garinagu Baundada" (PhD diss., Louisiana State University and Agricultural & Mechanical College, 2014); personal communication with Paul Arzu, Sandra Colon, Celso Castro.

31. Marcos Gomez and Pablo Blanco were with the Carib American Association; Amado Lambert, Efraim Castro, Antonieta Blanco (Maximo), Erico Castro, Lucia Arzu, Lidia Hill, Pantaleon Hill, Dionisia Amaya, and Santos Batiz were among the individuals listed as COPROD members.

32. There are approximately forty-eight Garifuna communities in Honduras, each with a village township association known as a patronato.

33. "New York accounts for 22 informal HTA [hometown associations] and 4 registered HTA like Organización de Damas Limoneras [sic], Travesia Nueva Ola, Jóvenes de Funda, and Pro Desarollo de Aguan. Others are Bajamar, Las Aquellas, and Unión Corozaleña" (Endo et al. 2010).

34. Alejandro Lambert, conversation, August 4, 2017, Puerto Cortés, Honduras.

35. Sonia Lambert, who was present during this period, noticed a Garifuna township association starting this trend of excluding others from attending its functions; meeting, April 25, 2021, New York, NY.

36. Corozal Hometown Association (ASUNCOR) was founded in 1969 by Natividad Mena; source: Garifuna Heritage Foundation, www.garifunaheritagefoundation.org.

37. Celso Castro, conversation, April 18, 2021. According to Celso Castro, an early group from the community of Limon was Solteros Limonenos, which became Comité Pro Desarollo de Limon (CPDL). At first, CPDL's successor was named Frente Juventud Limoneña, but this was changed to "Frente Social Limoneno, Inc." (the New York State Division of Corporations database uses full caps for names and omits diacritics) when it was incorporated on October 28, 1977. DOS ID 453188.

38. Celso Castro mentioned that Honduran Garifuna Dr. Jorge Bernardez, also involved in the community, assisted in distributing the newsletter.

39. Ismael Melendez and Edelmira Melendez, conversation, July 12, 2016, Bronx, NY.

40. The album *Carnaval del Caribe*, produced by Luciano M. Valencia, represents the only album from the Honduran coast. Garifuna Records Presents—"Reggae Nuwanee No. 1"—featured Eugenio Bonillo, Fidelis Garcia, Maria Elliot, and Virgin Enriquez, accompanied by the Ritmo Caribe Combo; album produced by Belizean Garifuna.

41. Belizean and Guatemalan Garifuna also supported development in their communities through their organizations.

42. Rosita Alvarez, conversation in St. Vincent and Grenadines during the Garifuna Vincy Homecoming, August 2020.

43. Wellington Ramos, conversation, January 2019; Ismael Melendez and Edelmira Melendez, conversation, July 12, 2016.

44. Asamblea Catolica 2010, *Garifuna*, DVD video.

45. Iriondo Josu, personal communication, October 21, 2006, Bronx, NY.

46. Paul Arzu, personal communication, August 20, 2020; Wellington Ramos, personal communication, January 2019; Moises Colon, conversation April 3, 2022, Brooklyn, NY.

47. Interestingly, Mena was in several Mexican films when he lived in the country. He gave me the names of the films, and my friend in Guanajuato, Mexico, provided a complete list.

48. In the late 1990s Garifuna artists and their bands, such as Belizean Andy Palacio and the Garifuna Collective and Honduran Aurelio Martinez and the Garifuna Soul, popularized the parranda genre, gaining international acclaim with their records.

49. Noe Francisco Caballero shared that Rodolfo "Popo" Martinez, Julio Lopez, and Roy Martinez were members of the Honduran Sea Boys band and helped the group gain popularity. A modern dance version of their song "Garifuna Wagia," the ethnic group's national anthem, gained mass appeal.

50. Mujeres Garinagu en Marcha Pro-Educación, Inc. (MUGAMA), incorporated November 8, 1990—New York State Department of State, Division of Corporations, DOS ID 1487692.

51. Leslie Avila Lacayo originally founded the Comité Pro Mejoramiento de Travesía (PROMETRA) in 1986 in the Bronx to teach Garifuna youth about the culture and involve them in Catholic Church activities in the city.

52. Nancie Gonzalez lists the organization as United Garifuna Cultural Association of Greater New York and states that the group was primarily Belizean Garifuna. According to Mary Petillo, Gonzalez visited her and her husband, Robert Petillo, at their home in New York while completing her book project.

53. It was registered in New York State as the Evangelical Garifuna Church, Inc., in July 1992. New York State Department of State, Division of Corporations: Evangelical Garifuna Church, Inc., July 1992.

54. In Brooklyn, both Andrew Nunez and German Cayetano assisted the church. It was eventually renamed Believers Mennonite Garifuna Ministries, with Nunez as the minister.

55. Andrew Nunez, conversation, October 1, 2016, Bronx, NY; Celso Jaime, personal communication, November 2016.

Chapter 5. Music, Dance, and Sports from the 1990s to the Present

1. Honduran Garifuna Mariano Gutierrez was also actively engaged in the Garifuna leagues that played in Linden Park around this time. Miguel Guity, an active member of the soccer league, led his teams in tournaments at Van Cortlandt Park in the Bronx and Fort Washington Park in Manhattan during the 1980s and 1990s. Conversation with German Cayetano, August 2019, Bronx, NY. Franco Mena, president of the Trujillo Sporting Club, a New York soccer team, also known in the community, trained youths in the Bronx, including at Crotona Park.

2. Eventually, many Ladino punta bands developed in Honduras as the musical genre became recognized as representative of the country.

3. Local media exposure of the ethnic group helped Garifuna organizers gain access to locations they could rent for events.

4. BronxNet program aired October 2020—Garifuna Census 2020—Quisia Gonzalez, Lesly, Ovelio Lopez–Guests. In an interview, Murphy Valentine expressed that after the Happy Land Social Club nightclub fire incident, Garifuna gained new contacts as city and private agencies extended their support for the community. City residents learned about the ethnic group that many had not known about. Garifuna had the opportunity to become part of the local Bronx cable programs offered through the BronxNet network.

5. "Theatre International, Inc. presents Hamalali Wayunagu featuring Isery Imenigi, June 26, 1994. Director and Choreographer Luz F. Solis, Executive Director Rey Allen" (program).

6. Garifuna Expo '99, May 1999 at the Richard Green Middle School in the Bronx. I attended this event in 1999. In the program distributed the event is listed as "Garifuna Expo 99."

7. "Garifuna Settlement Day Cultural Mass. Celebrant Father Lawrence Nicasio, Father ED Mason, Deacon Victor Elijio. Sunday November 10, 2013. Our Lady of Mercy Church. Brooklyn, New York" (program).

8. Garifuna Settlement Day Cultural Mass program.

9. "Garifuna Settlement Day Committee of the Bronx, Tribute to Thomas Vincent Ramos. Intermediate School 139 Bronx, Brook Ave. Garifuna Settlement Day Committee of the Bronx. November 1996" (program).

10. GAHFU, "Garifuna American Heritage Foundation United Inc. 3rd Annual Garifuna Community Forum, New York 2007. 'Sailing towards a New Horizon.' Charles R. Drew Educational Center Auditorium, Bronx, NY. April 14, 2007" (program).

11. I attended the program and gathered information. The forum's theme was "Sailing towards a New Horizon."

12. 2015 GALENT Musical Tribute to Aurelio Martinez. GALENT hosts the annual Garifuna Music Awards, recognizing artists in different categories of music. In 2017 GALENT recognized Mahogany Beatz, a hip-hop artist of Garifuna descent, with a lifetime achievement award.

13. In 2017 the Hamalali Wayunagu became Wabafu; Solis worked with Murphy Valentine at BronxNet cable television, cohosting the *Central America Show*; source: "Bronx Music Heritage—Presents Bronx Living Legend Luz Soliz March 23, 2019 Hostos Community College Repertory Theatre" (program).

14. Dancing to drumbeat patterns is also a feature of Afro–Puerto Rican "bomba and plena" music. Call and response, a chorus, and rhythmic dancing alongside synchronized drumbeats reflect the Puerto Rican Black slave heritage. Garifuna in the Bronx partner with the Puerto Rican tradition of Christmas caroling, featuring bomba and plena music and Garifuna parranda folk music presentations (Martinez 2016).

15. Maximo Martinez attended Crisanto Melendez's visit to the Bronx, Casa Yurumein, January 9, 2015; The Chief Joseph Chatoyer Folkloric Ballet of New York performs at various public and civic events in the city, including hosting its own theatrical musical play at the Symphony Space on Broadway; it also has performed at annual Garifuna events in Belize and St. Vincent. Budari and the Bodoma Garifuna Cultural Band also perform at city-sponsored events and universities, as well as at events hosted by Garifuna organizations (Gonzalez-Ramirez 2017). The dancers in the company, for the most part, consist of young Garifuna men and women from Honduras, Guatemala, and Belize.

16. Conversation with German Cayetano, September 2018.

17. Conversation with Lando Suazo, December 2017.

18. Pablo Gomez, interview, October 12, 2018, Bronx, NY.

19. José F. Ávila also registered the International Honduran and Central American Day Parade, Inc., on June 18, 1997, in New York State. Pablo Gomez, interview, October 12, 2018, Bronx, NY.

20. José F. Ávila, personal communication, July 29, 2021; January 7, 2022.

Chapter 6. Social Issues in New York City from the 1990s to the Present

1. Bronx minority borough presidents include Herman Badillo (1966–70), Fernando Ferrer (1987–2001), Adolfo Carrion (2002–9), Rubén Díaz Jr. (2009–21), and Vanessa Gibson (2022–present).

2. During this period, the Bronx was undergoing renovation. Community development organizations such as the People's Development Corporation (PDC), Mid Bronx Desperados (MBD) Community Housing Corp., South East Bronx Community Organization, and Banana Kelly Community Improvement Association, Inc., were actively engaged in rehabilitating abandoned buildings and supporting new developments.

3. FEDHONY obtained an estimated $150,000 from the fine paid by the club owner.

4. FEDHONY dissolved because of disagreements among Garifuna leaders; the center never materialized, and the money remained unaccounted for.

5. ODECO, founded in 1992 and recognized in 1994, grew from members of OFRANEH (Brondo 2006; Mark Anderson 2009).

6. Since the peak period of the COVID-19 pandemic ended in 2021, Casa Yurumein/Hondurans Against AIDS has held their meetings at a temporary location in the Bronx.

7. New York State Department of State, Division of Corporations: Sociedad Hondureña Activa de New York (SHANY) Corp., June 8, 1994.

8. Wilberto Oliva, personal communication, October 2015, Bronx, NY.

9. The conch shell used in Garifuna music is called *wadabágei*.

10. Recent churches have been established in San Antonio, TX; Tampa, FL; and Baltimore, MD; conversation with Andrew Nunez, October 2015, Bronx, NY; Evangelical Garifuna Council of Churches 20th Anniversary, October 23, 24, 2015 (program).

11. The Garifuna Coalition also sought to support youth development. It started the Lirahüñü Chatoyer Garifuna Youth Leadership Development Program. Its goals were to "assist, support and nurture Garifuna youth, by providing educational opportunities, guidance and validation all within the context of reinforcing pride in the student's cultural background and his/her self-esteem" (J. Ávila 2021, 290). An essay contest encouraged Garifuna students to describe what it means to be Garifuna American.

12. In 2005 the administrators of the coalition were president Rejil Solis, vice president Marcia Gomez, secretary Hazel Perez, treasurer José F. Ávila, and fiscal officer Emelinda Blanco.

13. Casa Gari was one of the first transnational entrepreneurial endeavors. In 2001 it received a grant from the Inter-American Development Bank to develop its cassava business. Ávila sought to pick up business with O'Big Mama and Wagabari Cassava through the New Horizon Investment Club.

14. José F. Ávila, personal communication, October 2006, Bronx, NY.

15. Honduran Garifuna are dispersed, living in either predominantly Latino or African American communities in the New Orleans metropolitan area. However, most Garifuna live in the Latino area served by Oportunidades NOLA, Reach NOLA, and Common Ground Health Clinic. Their common Spanish language supports their employment, social services, and other needs. Connections with Latinos also helped Garifuna obtain permission to use their facilities to hold their activities as their community grew.

16. In 2006 I spoke with Mirtha Colón at St. Margaret Episcopal Church in the Bronx, who told me that Casa Yurumein was at St. Augustine Church in 2009; in 2012 it moved to its new location on Prospect Avenue.

17. On February 6, 2008, the Garifuna Coalition received a $42,500 grant to establish an advocacy center to provide social services and advocate for community members.

18. There was also discussion of naming the street Garifuna Village Boulevard.

19. Bertram Llewellyn Baker (January 10, 1898–March 8, 1985) was a member of the New York State Assembly from 1948 to 1970, representing central Brooklyn, NY. Walter H. Gladwin (1902–1988), the first Black elected governmental official in the Bronx, was born in Berbice, Guyana. Gladwin was elected to the New York State Assembly in 1952.

20. Mirtha Colón, president of Hondurans Against AIDS, attended the inauguration of Asemblyman Eric Stevenson at Jane Adams High School in the Bronx. The Chief Joseph Chatoyer Garifuna Folkloric Ballet performed.

21. Bronx Garifuna from the 79th District have associated with Black representatives Michael Benjamin (2003–10), Eric Stevenson (2011–14), and Michael Blake (2017–21). Chantel Jackson (2021–present) thus far is not as engaged as her predecessors attending Garifuna

activities. Other public officials attending Garifuna events include Joel Rivera, Pedro Espada, Guillermo Linares, Luis Sepulveda, Marc Crespo, and Vanessa Gibson.

22. State senator Rubén Díaz Sr. introduced a resolution in the New York State Senate, memorializing Governor Andrew Cuomo to declare March 11–April 12, 2011, as Garifuna-American Heritage Month in New York State.

23. Maximo Martinez attended the Garifuna American Legislative Day event, May 25, 2018, Albany, NY.

24. The Senate of the State of Texas, Senate Proclamation No. 1294, In recognition of the Greater Houston Garifuna American Partnership celebrating the 208th anniversary of Garifuna settlement in the Americas 2010, November 19 to December 19. Source: "Garifunas in the Gulf Coast to Celebrate Historic Settlement Day Recognitions," Keimon Houston, email correspondence.

25. "City of Los Angeles State of California Resolution. Garifuna Heritage Month. Council of the City of Los Angeles commends the Garifuna American community and declares November 12–December 12 as Garifuna Heritage Month in the city of Los Angeles. Resolution adopted November 14, 2014; "Your Guide to the 2014 National Garifuna Settlement, Education and Awareness Month"; "Massachusetts Governor asks citizens to Observe November 12 to December 12 in Honor of Garifuna Settlement. Patrick, Deval. L. Commonwealth of Massachusetts A Proclamation his excellency Governor Deval L. Patrick. November 12, 2011 through December 12, 2011 Garifuna Settlement Education and Awareness Month"; "Quinn, Pat. Governor of the State of Illinois. Proclaim November 2011 as Garifuna-American Heritage Month in Illinois. To encourage all citizens to learn about the contributions of Garifuna-Americans to the state and nation. Issued November 1, 2011. Filed by the Secretary of State November 14, 2011. Article 2011–391." Keimon Houston, email correspondence, accessed October 25, 2014.

26. Several years later, on April 14, 2017, the New Orleans City Council recognized Honduran Garifuna Bernard Guerrero with a proclamation citing his fifty years of leadership and service to the Garifuna community. Guerrero was part of the New Dawn Iseri Idwanini organization in Limon, Honduras, and since migrating to New Orleans, he has actively sought to organize the Garifuna in the city. In 2012 the Las Vegas City Council renamed a local park Kianga Isoke Palacio Park, honoring the work of the late Belizean Garifuna community organizer who died in 2009. Palacio cofounded Sisters in Society Taking Action, a rites-of-passage and mentoring program for young girls established out of the West Las Vegas Arts Center. "Your Guide to the 2014 National Garifuna Settlement, Education and Awareness Month," Keimon Houston, email correspondence, accessed October 25, 2014.

27. Maria Elena Maximo was convicted of defrauding immigrants. Maximo was arrested in 2006 facing accusations of overcharging undocumented immigrants for services such as work permits and green cards. More than one thousand fraudulent applications were found by state and federal prosecutors. Maximo pleaded guilty to two counts of mail fraud and faced a maximum sentence of twenty years in prison for each count.

28. Maximo Martinez attended Abrazos Garifuna March 21, 2013, in the Bronx, NY.

29. The Reverend Wilberto Oliva was recognized by Congressman Charles B. Rangel in 1990 with an achievement award; Brooklyn borough president Howard Golden awarded the reverend a citation on June 30, 1989. Oliva ministered and taught at the Christian Bible Institute in the city for several years. Wilberto Oliva, personal communication, October 2015, Brooklyn, NY.

30. Sonia Fernandez, personal communication, November 2017, Bronx, NY; Edson Arzu, personal communication, November 2017.

31. In 2012 the Garifuna Coalition cohosted a showing of the film *Garifuna in Peril* at the New York African Diaspora Festival at Teachers College, Columbia University. Edson Arzu, conversation, November 2017.

32. The August 2014 immigration forum I attended was held at the Bronx Spanish Evangelical Church auditorium. Discussed at the meeting were children who had made the journey by themselves, many of whom were placed with non-Garifuna families. There were several young mothers at the forum who had made the journey with their children. One of the mothers stood up and spoke about the hardships she endured on the journey and the mistreatment by immigration agents once she arrived. She said the immigration officials' tone of voice and attitude made her feel inhuman.

33. Remembering New York City's Garifuna 2010–2019 Decade—Galent 12/16/2019—Two Education Bills Proposed 3972 January and 4925 March (Bill No. A09791).

34. Prior legislative attempts to amend the state education law to include Garifuna people in history were April 5, 2016, with Senator Rubén Díaz Sr. introducing Senate Legislative Bill No. S07175, and April 8, 2016, with Assemblyman Luis R. Sepulveda introducing Bill No. A09791 to the assembly (Ávila 2021).

35. Another Honduran Garifuna woman was a candidate for a local political office, but outside of the Bronx. Salka Valerio, whose parents were born in Honduras, was running for a seat on the Binghamton City Council. All the candidates represented the Democratic Party. On election day, Valerio's name did not appear on the ballot (Albany Center; Dean 2019).

36. Also in 2017, councilmember Rafael Salamanca Jr. was the primary sponsor of resolution 1358–2017 recognizing April 12 as Garifuna Heritage Day in New York City (Ávila 2021).

37. Garifuna Heritage 2019. Office of Council member Vanessa L. Gibson. "Garifuna Heritage Celebration. April 11, 2019. Bronx Museum of Arts" (program).

38. Event Maximo Martinez attended at Lincoln Hospital Auditorium, Bronx, NY; "Encuentro Garifuna y Centro Americano 2018," Garifuna and Central American Town Hall, April 21, 2018. NYC Mayor's Office of Immigrant Affairs.

39. Event Maximo Martinez attended at Police Athletic League Auditorium, Longwood Ave., Bronx, NY. I also participated in the early meetings to organize the Garifuna 2020 census in the Bronx.

40. Garifuna Coalition USA resumed leadership of the annual Garifuna-American Legislative Day in Albany held Tuesday, May 15, 2023 (King 2023b).

41. Jamalali Uagucha was politically engaged early. Maria Maximo was on the Bronx Community Board 6, and the organization's cofounder Francisco Ruiz Rivas established a political platform titled Plataforma política garífuna USA (Zambito 2006).

42. H.R. 1945 (116th): Berta Caceres Human Rights in Honduras Act; previously introduced—Jun 14, 2016; Mar 2, 2017; Mar 28, 2019.

43. Another public official who traveled several times to Honduras and understands the challenges of Garifuna: former Sacramento, California, councilman (2012–20) Allen Warren. He is friends with Luther Harry Castillo, Garifuna physician and activist who fled to Sacramento following death threats and imprisonment after the coup. The hospital Castillo founded in a remote Garifuna community was also forced to close following the coup. Dr. Castillo was politically active defending the ethnic group's rights and denouncing the forced removal of the president (Crockett 2018; Mark Anderson 2012). Allen Warren and Danny Glover have

frequently visited and participated in Garifuna panels discussing community concerns. Actor and comedian Cedric the Entertainer has also accompanied them on a trip.

44. "Conversando con Arnold Ciego—Accion Civica Garifuna," Facebook, June 14, 2021 (Ciego 2021).

45. March 19, 2022, International Garifuna Council (IGC) event held in the Bronx, NY.

46. "Ranked Choice Voting Training w/Garifuna Community"—YouTube.

47. Garifuna community activist and minister German Cayetano, IGC member, is involved with the NAACP and introduced Garifuna leaders with ICG to the African American civil society organization.

48. Maximo Martinez attended the IGC event March 19, 2022, in the Bronx, NY.

Chapter 7. Central America and St. Vincent from the 1990s to the Present

1. I often saw Jorge "Garifuna" Cacho with other Garifuna, including Jerry Castro, outside All Saints Lutheran Parish in the Bronx, two blocks from my residence at the Forest Houses public housing project. All Saints Lutheran Parish opened its doors to support primarily Garifuna youth activities. It also had a quarterly magazine, *Alternative Visions*, featuring Garifuna news updates; some of the youths were involved in publishing the magazine. *Alternative Visions: The Quarterly Magazine of the South Bronx Photographic Center—All Saints Lutheran Parish*, Winter 1997, no. 10.

2. The *wadabágei* is a conch shell the Garifuna use in their music; historically, it was used to summon a community gathering.

3. According to Felix Miranda, CABO's initial goal when it was established in Belize was to unify all Garifuna; however, that was revised when it incorporated all Blacks from the region. Conversation with Felix Miranda in Hopkins, Belize, June 2015.

4. Quisia Gonzalez, a trained physician and activist of Garifuna descent, described her involvement with the group as "fiscal." Her September 1998 trip to Honduras to monitor the group's economic progress was disappointing, given its downward trend. Her assessment was correct, and unfortunately, the project never materialized. According to Gonzalez, many people lost their money, including executive director Jose Angel Manaiza, Otilia Gomez de Limon, Domingo Martinez and her husband Negil Nunez, and Nahum Gonzalez (her late brother).

5. In 1990, Decree Law 90/90 was passed by the Honduran Congress to circumvent constitutional provisions, which were a barrier to the state plans for tourism development. The 134-90 Law of Municipalities was presented by the National Congress in 1990, and this became effective in January 1991, granting municipal autonomy to coastal regions. The Honduran government passed the Law for Modernization and Development of the Agricultural Sector that came under Decree 31-92. The result of this legislation legalized privatizing lands for investment that favored foreign financiers.

6. Galileo Bernardez, who used to be part of the Evangelical Council of Churches, contributed to the annual conventions. Wilberto Oliva was one of the earliest supporters. Conversation with Galileo Bernardez, October 2016.

7. HAMPAC supported Honduran Garifuna presidential candidate Bernard Valerio Martinez during his visit to New York City on November 10, 2005, introducing him to local legislators, such as the Bronx borough president, and union leaders.

8. Los Micos Project became the Indura Beach & Golf Resort.

9. Personal communication with Gregoria Flores, February 9, 2007, Bronx, NY. Other personal communication meeting discussions, April 20, 2017 and September 20, 2017.

10. Pablo Blanco and Hector Zapata founded Elite Carib International, which manages primarily Garifuna musicians and introduces the culture and musical heritage of the African diaspora to the world (Wall 2013).

11. Wellington Ramos, Garifuna Nation, Joint Letter to the State Department Urging Action to Protect Human Rights in Honduras, October 3, 2014.

12. Omar Suazo's wife, Sendy Vaughn Suazo, a scholar and university administrator in Boston, contacted members of the Congressional Black Caucus, who supported her cause (Facebook video conference 2020). According to Wellington Ramos, Garifuna Nation also supported Omar Suazo.

13. CUNY Graduate Center, "Imperialism and Latin America: Land Grabbing of Garifuna Communities," October 26, 2017, Center for the Humanities. Maximo Martinez attended.

14. NYU Arts and Sciences, "An Evening with Bertha Zuniga Caceres and Miriam Miranda," Center for Latin American and Caribbean Studies, July 12, 2017. Maximo Martinez attended; I also attended OFRANEH Community Meeting *Convocatoria* July 9, 2022, in the Bronx, led by Miriam Miranda, Carla Garcia, and Ronny Castillo. Follow-up and new community challenges were presented.

15. Garifuna Belinda David, from Guadalupe, shared her experiences and warned of dangers including false charges by Canadian land usurpers, imprisonment, and death threats. I attended the forum held on September 30, 2019, at Casa Yurumein in the Bronx.

16. A Letter to Honduras's Minister of Human Rights by José Francisco Ávila López—Garifuna Coalition USA, August 29, 2019, email correspondence.

17. The ICJ Issue, 2019 Meeting, Belize People's Front (BPF), United Garifuna Association, Inc., and Believers Mennonite Garifuna Ministries meeting on the IDJ Isssue, April 7, 2019, Brooklyn, NY.

18. Prime Minister Gonsalves said he would raise the matter at the UN, where the country is a nonpermanent member of the Security Council. As chairman of CARICOM, Gonsalves also raised the issue there, calling for member nations to join him in demanding that the Honduran president take immediate action. Letter from Ralph Gonsalves to Garifuna Nation.

19. Wellington Ramos, "Gonsalves Writes to UN, Honduras President Garifuna Abuse," Garifuna Nation, August 9, 2020, email correspondence.

20. Sanctuary Garifuna of Guatemala USA, Inc., registered in New York State August 19, 2011; Julio Arzu, "Politicas de uso y mantenimiento del templo. Hermandad Garifuna de la Verdad" (copy courtesy of Julio Arzu).

21. Members of the GIPSVG also participated in the annual mini marathon of EGCC in March 2019.

22. Conversation with Edward Diego, September 2013.

23. "Reparations Now—The Caribbean Claim for Reparations—2018 Sparer Symposium at Penn Law School"—YouTube, January 29, 2018.

Conclusion

1. Gil 2019: BronxNet *Honduras Centro America Show* 2019, hosted by Katy Gil, with Mirtha Colón among the guests.

2. "Hen-Gee & Evil E: Biography," Last.fm, edited February 6, 2010, https://www.last.fm/music/Hen-Gee+&+Evil-E/+wiki.

3. King Tiger's recordings include the studio singles "Started Off" (2014) and "Taking You Home" (2015), the studio album *Tatankhamun* EP (2015), *Tha 999 Album* (2016), and mix-tape

editions "Streetz & Romance" (2013). Source: "King Tiger (rapper)," Fandom, Gyaanipedia Wiki, www.gyaanipedia.fandom.com.

4. O.T. Genasis's albums include *Black Belt* (2013), *Catastrophic 2* (2014), *Rhythm & Bricks* (2015), and *Coke N Butter* (2016). Sources: O.T. Genasis biography, All Music, www.allmusic.com; "O.T. Genasis," Wikipedia, www.en.wikipedia.org.

5. "Mahogany Music, Profile," *Global14* (blog), www.global14.com.

6. Wikipedia; Facebook, February 20, 2021, Kulcha Buck E Ciego.

7. "Men's Basketball: Kenton Paulino," Wichita State University website, accessed July 3, 2023, https://goshockers.com/sports/mens-basketball/roster/coaches/kenton-paulino/1129.

8. "Milt Palacio," Wikipedia, www.wikipedia.com

9. University of Texas Longhorns Women's Basketball, 2020–21 Women's Basketball Roster: Kyra Lambert, Duke University (2015–19), Texas Longhorns (2020–21) (Grad student), https://texassports.com/sports/womens-basketball/roster; University of Iowa Men's Basketball, 2020–21 Men's Basketball Roster: (2019–21) Sophomore Joe Toussaint, https://hawkeyesports.com/sports/mbball/roster/season/2020-21/player/joe-toussaint/; North Florida Ospreys Women's Basketball, 2020–21 Women's Basketball Roster: (2020–21) Freshman Nubia Benedith, https://unfospreys.com/sports/womens-basketball/roster/nubia-benedith/9958; Syracuse Women's Basketball, 2020–21 Women's Basketball Roster: (2017–21) Senior Amaya Finklea-Güity, https://cuse.com/sports/womens-basketball/roster/amaya-finklea-guity/19509; other source: José Francisco Ávila. Among the more than 460,000 NCAA student-athletes are trailblazing young athletes of Garifuna descent, such as Nubia Benedith—North Florida Ospreys, Guard; Freshman Joe Toussaint—Iowa Hawkeyes, Sophomore, Guard #1; Amaya Finklea-Güity—Syracuse University, Center, Senior #22. Facebook post, March 2, 2021, accessed March 5, 2021.

10. New York State Department of State, Division of Corporations: Lanichuga Garifuna Restaurant, Inc., October 18, 2004, Bronx, NY; Garifuna Star Restaurant, Corp., November 6, 2006, Bronx, NY; Garifuna Kitchen of NY, Corp., August 14, 2009, Bronx, NY; My Garifuna Cuisine, LLC, March 23, 2016, Bronx, NY. J. Ávila, "30 Years of Garifuna Advocacy & The 20th Anniversary in NYC," January 2017. Email correspondence.

11. New York State Department of State, Division of Corporations: Weiga Let's Eat LLC, April 23, 2019.

12. José F. Ávila, "Covid-19 Impact on NYC's Garifuna Community," Garifuna Coalition, April 25, 2020. Email correspondence.

13. Edson Arzu, "Garifuna Veterans of America," Find Local, www.findlocal.com.

14. National Cancer Institute, Center for Cancer Research, Rony F. Arauz, Profile.

15. Nixon Arauz, "The Last Thing That People Lose Is Their Dignity," VO1SS, September 14, 2019.

16. Linkedin, Marvin B. Figueroa, Deputy Secretary of Health and Human Resources for the Commonwealth of Virginia, Office of Governor Ralph S. Northam.

17. GovSalaries, Julio Guity Guevara, Deputy Director, Ofc On Latino Affairs 2018, Profile, GovSalaries.com.

18. La Fuerza Garifuna, Inc., Facebook page, accessed March 5, 2021.

19. "Conversando Con Arnold Ciego," Facebook post, February 27, 2020; La Fuerza Garifuna, Inc., Facebook page, accessed March 5, 2021.

REFERENCES

651 Arts. 2007. "Infectious Blend of African and Latin Acoustic Roots." 651 Arts (website), "Caribbean Life—Aurelio Martinez," Music Section, May 9 (accessed January 4, 2018). www.651arts.org.

Abramson, Mitch. 2015. "Local Bronx Boxer Eddie Gomez Plays Tour Guide for Floyd Mayweather during Recent Trip to NYC." *New York Daily News*, July 8.

Ademo, Mohammed. 2011. "African Immigrants Add Their Own Flavor to the South Bronx." *Bronxink*, December 13. http://bronxink.org.

Agudelo, Carlos. 2012. "The Afro-Guatemalan Political Mobilization: Between Identity Construction Processes, Global Influences, and Institutionalization." In *Black Social Movements in Latin America: From Monocultural Mestizaje to Multiculturalism*, edited by Jean Muteba Rahier. New York: Palgrave Macmillan.

———. 2017. "Afrocaribeños en el 'corazón del mundo Maya': Los garífuna de Guatemala entre marginalidad e inclusión." V Congreso Asociación Latinoamericano de Antropología—XVI Congreso de Antropología en Colombia. Bogota, June 6–9.

Ajani Publishing. 2011. "Vincentians get Taste of Garifuna Culture." *Caribbean Life*, October 4. Retrieved from www.caribbeanlifenews.com.

Albany Center Gallery. n.d. "Salka Valerio." In "Artist Talk: Nina Berman." Albany Center Gallery (website). Accessed March 26, 2022. https://albanycentergallery.org/events/artist-talk-nina-berman.

Alfano, Peter. 1979. "Glover Dies after Bout; Disease Found." *New York Daily News*, February 1.

Allen, Dashiell. 2021. "A New Temporary Protected Status for Central America." NACLA (website), November 4. https://nacla.org/new-temporary-protected-status-central-america-garifuna.

———. 2023. "Casa Yurumein, 'The Garífuna People's House,' Reopens in the South Bronx." *Mott Haven Herald*, February 28, 2023. https://motthavenherald.com/2023/02/28/casa-yurumein-the-garifuna-peoples-house-reopens-in-the-south-bronx/.

Allianza Americas. 2019. "Garifuna Youth Call on Legislators to Change in US Foreign Policy to Central America." Allianza Americas (website), April 10. https://www.alianzaamericas.org/blog/garifuna-youth-call-on-legislators-to-change-in-us-foreign-policy-to-central-america/?lang=en.

All Peoples Initiative. 2008. "Panamanians in the New York Metro Area." *Unreached New York* (blog). Accessed September 22, 2018. Retrieved from https://unreachednewyork.com/wp-content/uploads/2012/11/Panamanian-Profile-Final.pdf.

Almendarez, Juan. 2020. "El Exterminio del Nuevo Amanecer." *Reflexiones Juan Almendarez* (blog), January 10. http://juanalmendarez.blogspot.com/2020/01/el-exterminio-del-nuevo-amanecer.html.

Alternative Vision. 1997. *Alternative Vision: Quarterly Magazine of the South Bronx Photographic Center—All Saints Lutheran Parish*, no. 10 (Winter 1997).

Alvarez, Siria. 2021. "Ranked Choice Voting Training w/ Garifuna Community." Belinda Crisantos-Lewis—*Hablando Con Belili*, May 27. Accessed March 22, 2022. https://www.youtube.com/watch?v=gu9mFokl7vA&t=185s.

Anderson, Mark. 2009. *Black and Indigenous: Garifuna Activism and Consumer Culture in Honduras*. Minneapolis: University of Minnesota Press.

———. 2012. "Garifuna Activism and the Corporatist Honduran State since the 2009 Coup." In *Black Social Movements in Latin America: From Monocultural Mestizaje to Multiculturalism*, edited by Jean Muteba Rahier. New York: Palgrave Macmillan.

Anderson, Monica. 2017. "African Immigrant Population in U.S. Steadily Climbs." Pew Research Center (website), February 14. https://www.pewresearch.org/short-reads/2017/02/14/african-immigrant-population-in-u-s-steadily-climbs/.

Angotti, Tom. 2008. *New York for Sale: Community Planning Confronts Global Real Estate*. Cambridge: Massachusetts Institute of Technology Press.

Aparicio, Marta S., ed. 2014. "Ceremonia de Graduación y Reconocimientos de la Escuela Shany Corp–NY." *La Voz de Honduras*, May 27. https://www.facebook.com/LaVozDeHonduras.

———, ed. 2015. "Actos de Graduación Escuela de Mantenimiento SHANY." *La Voz de Honduras*, March 1. www.facebook.com/LaVozDeHonduras.

———, ed. 2016. "En un acto organizado por SHANY." *La Voz de Honduras*, April 2. https://www.facebook.com/LaVozDeHonduras.

———, ed. 2021. "Mirtha Colón, más de 50 años de lucha por los garífunas desde EEUU." *La Voz de Honduras*, April 2. https://lavozdehondurasnews.com/web/mirtha-colon-mas-de-50-anos-de-lucha-por-los-garifunas-desde-eeuu/.

Aranda, Theodore. 1998. "The Question of Reparation and the Origins of the WGO: The Texas Garifuna-Belizeans Community." Garinet, March 2. Accessed April 12, 2018. www.garinet.com.

Armando, José. 2020. "La Legión Hondureña del Baloncesto Universitario en Estados Unidos." *Deporte Total USA* (blog), November 23. https://deportetotalusa.com/blog/la-legion-hondurena-del-baloncesto-universitario-en-estados-unidos/.

Arrivillaga Cortés, Alfonso. 2005. "Marcos Sanchez Diaz: From Hero to Hiuraha—Two Hundred Years of Garifuna Settlement in Central America." In *The Garífuna: A Nation across Borders*, edited by Joseph O. Palacio. Benque Viejo del Carmen, Belize: Cubola.

———. 2009. *La población garífuna migrante*. Guatemala. Comisión Presidencial contra la Discriminación y el Racismo. Guatemala: CODISRA.

———. 2017. "*Warigóun águyu*, de vuelta a casa . . . Una historia caminante: de la dispersión a la diáspora garífuna." *Ciencias Sociales y Humanidades* 4 (1). https://1library.co/document/qm33jj9y-warigoun-caminante-dispersion-garifuna-warigoun-dispersion-garifuna-population.html.

Ashford, Grace. 2022. "Noncitizens' Right to Vote Becomes Law in New York City." *New York Times*, January 9. https://www.nytimes.com/2022/01/09/nyregion/noncitizens-nyc-voting-rights.html.

Associated Press. 2017. "El hondureño que fundó liga de fútbol para jóvenes migrantes en Nueva York." *La Prensa*, August 10. Retrieved from www.laprensa.hn.

Aurelio (Aurelio Martinez). 2023. "Biography." Aurelio (website), accessed June 16, 2023. http://www.aureliomusic.net/bio.

Avendaño, Alberto. 2016. "Marvin Figueroa, un garífuna dirige la campaña de Hillary Clinton en Virginia." *Washington Post*, July 8. https://www.washingtonpost.com/eltiempolatino/marvin-figueroa-un-garifuna-dirige-la-campana-de-hillary-clinton-en-virginia/2016/07/08/d65e907c-42c5-11e6-88d0-6adee48be8bc_story.html.

Averett, Nancy. 2021. "Social Capital in Black Communities Is Often Overlooked." *Scientific American*, October 1. https://www.scientificamerican.com/article/social-capital-in-black-communities-is-often-overlooked/.

Ávila, José F. 2004. "Hondurans Want to Be Stockholders Not Just Stakeholders and Share the Wealth—Shaping Hondurans' Future in the Bronx with a Wealth Sharing Vision." January 1. Email correspondence.

———. 2005. GarifunaNews.com, July 18. www.garifunanews.com.

———. 2006. "Honduran Garifuna Unification, Truth or Myth?" Garinet, February 14. https://www.garinet.com/cgi-bin/gksitecontent_ssi.cgi?ACTION=VIEW_ONE_CONTENT&ITEM=10&CATEGORY=57&CONTENT_ID=3998.

———. 2008. "The Garifunas and Happy Land Social Club Fire." Garifuna Coalition USA, Inc. newsletter, March 25. Retrieved from *GarifunaWorld Blog*. https://garifunaworld.blogspot.com/2008/04/garifunas-and-happy-land-social-club.html?m=0.

———. 2009. "Garifuna Coalition USA Inc. Garifuna Voter Registration Drive, Goal Is to Increase Registration by Garifuna and Others." Email correspondence.

———. 2010. "Legislative Resolution K1120—Garifuna Coalition USA Inc. 2011 Garifuna Heritage Month in New York Celebrating Garifuna Heritage and Culture in New York." November 1. Email correspondence.

———. 2011. "Carlos H Gotay Recibirá el Premio Coalición Garífuna." Garifuna link, September 26. Retrieved from Google Groups.

———. 2013. "Introducing GALENT to Serve a Diversified Entertainment Market Place." GALENT: Garifuna Afro-Latino Entertainment. Accessed October 25, 2017. Email correspondence.

———. 2014. "Garifuna Kids: The Garifuna Youth Music Sensation." Garifuna Coalition. News. May 6. www.garifunacoalition.org.

———. 2016a. "The Future of Garifuna Music." Garifuna Afro-Latino Entertainment, LLC. March 31. Email correspondence..

———. 2016b. "Rosemary Ordóñez-Jenkins Nominada Delegada Estatal." *La Voz de Honduras*, June 15. Accessed February 2, 2018. http://lavozdehondurasnews.com.

———. 2017a. "From Nurturing and Promoting the Garifuna Culture to Amending the State Education Law." In *2017 Garifuna Heritage Month: 220th Anniversary Garifuna American Heritage Month 1797–2017*. March 29. ISSUU. Providence, RI: Milenio.

———. 2017b. "The Garifuna Legacy in New York City." Garifuna Coalition USA. Accessed September 22, 2018. http://www.Garifunacoalition.org.

———. 2017c. "Insomie 'Mahogany Beatz' Leeper to Receive Lifetime Achievement Award." March 29. Email correspondence.

———. 2017d. "Seremein, Thank You Councilmember Rafael Salamanca Jr. for the $40,000 Discretionary Funding Allocation." Garifuna Coalition USA, May 20. Email correspondence.

———. 2018a. "'Intangible Cultural Heritage' Is 'Traditional, Contemporary and Living at the Same Time': Garifuna Music Records from 1952–1982." Garifuna Coalition USA, Inc., Facebook, October 17. Accessed March 5, 2021.

———. 2018b. "The Newly Created Garifuna Renaissance Arts and Culture Center." African Diaspora Tourism, December 18. http://africandiasporatourism.com.

———. 2019a. A Letter to Honduras's Minister of Human Rights by José Francisco Ávila López. Garifuna Coalition USA, Inc., August 27. Email correspondence.

———. 2019b. "Remembering New York City's Garifuna 2010–2019 Decade." GALENT, December 16. Email correspondence.

———. 2020. "Juan José Laboriel: The Legendary Honduran Garifuna Actor." GALENT Newsletter. Accessed February 10. Email correspondence.

———. 2021. *Pan-Garifuna Afro-Latino Power of Pride: My Quest for Racial, Ancestral, Ethnic and Cultural Identity*. Independently published.

Ávila, José Francisco, and Tomás Alberto Ávila. 2008. *Mundo Garifuna*. Providence, RI: Milenio.

———. 2017. "The Garifuna Reunion in St. Vincent (Yurumein): The Power of the Past and the Promise of the Future." In *2017 Garifuna Heritage Month: 220th Anniversary Garifuna American Heritage Month 1797–2017*. March 29. ISSUU. Providence, RI: Milenio.

Ávila, Tomás Alberto. 2014. *Dionisia "Mama Nicha" Amaya-Bonilla: La matriarca del Empoderamiento Garifuna / The Matriarch of Garifuna Empowerment*. Providence, RI: Milenio.

———. 2017. "First Garifuna Summit." In *2017 Garifuna Heritage Month: 220th Anniversary Garifuna American Heritage Month 1797–2017*. March 29. ISSUU. Providence, RI: Milenio.

Bardales Bueso, Rafael. 1985. *Imagen de un líder Manuel Bonilla*. Tegucigalpa, Honduras: Editorial Universitaria.

Barker, Cyril Josh. 2014. "Brooklyn BP Hosts Gariduna [sic] Heritage Celebration." *New York Amsterdam News*, April 17. https://amsterdamnews.com/news/2014/04/17/brooklyn-bp-hosts-gariduna-heritage-celebration/.

Barker, David, and Rose-Ann Smith. 2013. "Land and Livelihoods among the Black Caribs of North-East St Vincent: Case Studies of Farming and Cottage-Based Agro-Processing." *Caribbean Geography* 18:66–84.

Baver, Sherrie, Angelo Falcón, and Gabriel Haslip-Viera, eds. 2017. *Latinos in New York: Communities in Transition*. Notre Dame, IN: University of Notre Dame Press.

Beaucage, Pierre. 1970. "Economic Anthropology of the Black Carib of Honduras." PhD diss., University of London.

Beckles, Hilary. 1992. "Kalinago (Carib) Resistance to European Colonization of the Caribbean." *Caribbean Quarterly* 38 (2–3): Caribbean Quincentennial.

Bedolla, Lisa Garcia. 2005. "Resources and Civic Engagement: The Importance of Social Capital for Latino Political Participation." *Harvard Journal of Hispanic Policy* 17.

Belize Ex-Servicemen's League of New York. 2021. Global NPO. Accessed January 21, 2021. www.globalnpo.org.

"The Belize Ex-Servicemen's League of New York Inc. Message from the President." 2010. *Belize Music World*, accessed June 15, 2023. http://www.belizemusicworld.com/belize-ex-servicemens-league-of-new-york.html.

Bellamy, Lana. 2021. "Trail Blazer: Genesis Ramos Pulls Off Historic Win for Orange County Legislature." *Times Herald-Record*, November 4. https://www.recordonline.com/story/news/local/2021/11/04/newburgh-native-first-woman-color-elected-orange-county-legislature/6264452001/.

Biondi, Martha. 2003. "The Rise of the Reparations Movement." *Radical History Review*, no. 87:5–18.

Block, Dorian, and Corky Siemaszko. 2009. "Ex-NYPD Cop Rafael Lora Sentenced to 1-to-3 Years in Jail in Off-Duty Fatal Shooting of Fermin Arzu." *New York Daily News*, June 11. https://www.nydailynews.com/news/crime/ex-nypd-rafael-lora-sentenced-1-to-3-years-jail-off-duty-fatal-shooting-fermin-arzu-article-1.377026.

Blumenthal, Ralph. 1990. "Fire in the Bronx: Portrait Emerges of Suspect in Social Club Blaze." *New York Times*, March 27. https://www.nytimes.com/1990/03/27/nyregion/fire-in-the-bronx-portrait-emerges-of-suspect-in-social-club-blaze.html.

Booth, A. J., and T. W. Walker. 1999. *Understanding Central America*. 3rd ed. Boulder, CO: Westview.

Boyd, Herb. 2007. "Shooting 'Unjustified.'" *New York Amsterdam News*, May 24–30. www.amsterdamnews.com.

Brondo, Keri Vacanti. 2006. "Roots, Rights, and Belonging: Garifuna Indigeneity and Land Rights on Honduras' North Coast." PhD diss., Michigan State University. ProQuest (3216117).

———. 2017. *Land Grab: Green Neoliberalism, Gender, and Garifuna Resistance in Honduras*. Tucson: University of Arizona Press.

Bronx Chronicle. 2017. "Announcing New York City Council District 18 Nonpartisan Candidate Forum—September 7." August 16. http://thebronxchronicle.com.

Bronx [County] Historical Society (BHS). n.d. "The Bronx: A Historical Sketch." Accessed February 26, 2021. http://bronxhistoricalsociety.org/about/bronx-history/.

———. n.d. "Notable Bronxites." www.bronxhistoricalsociety.org. Accessed August 11, 2018. Web page no longer live.

Brooklyn Record. 1959. "Latin America Folk Dances in Manhattan." August 28, p. 6.

Burke, Kerry, Rocco Parascandola, and John Annese. 2019. "Man Stabbed Dead in Bronx Bodega; Suspect in Custody." *New York Daily News*, October 24. https://www.nydailynews.com/new-york/nyc-crime/ny-bronx-bodega-murder-stabbed-20191024-7exkppucanalbiuoqjffmliomu-story.html.

Burke, Kerry, Thomas Tracy, and Graham Rayman. 2019. "Mom of Two Young Children Stabbed to Death at Bronx Shelter." *New York Daily News*, October 2. https://www.nydailynews.com/new-york/nyc-crime/ny-woman-stabbed-death-shelter-20191002-s7f33s4n4zcb7j2f630ygx6m3e-story.html.

Bustamante, Luis Noe. 2020. "Amid COVID-19, Remittances to Some Latin American Nations Fell Sharply in April, Then Rebounded." Pew Research Center (website), August 31. https://www.pewresearch.org/short-reads/2020/08/31/.

Canelas Díaz, Antonio.1999. *La Ceiba, sus raíces y su historia, 1810–1940*. La Ceiba, Honduras: Renacimiento.

Caribbean Life. 2011a. "Coalition Welcomes Sulma Arzu Brown on Board." August 2. https://www.caribbeanlife.com.

———. 2011b. "Vincentians Get Taste of Garifuna Culture." October 4. https://www.caribbeanlife.com.

Carlislie, Nate. 2020. "What Utah's Coronavirus Task Force Wants Employers to Know." *Salt Lake Tribune*, March 10. https://www.sltrib.com/news/politics/2020/03/11/here-is-utahs-coronavirus/.

Caro, Robert. 1974. *The Power Broker*. New York: Alfred A. Knopf.

Caroom, Eliot. 2008. "Caribbean Ethnic Group Seeks New Street Name for Dawson St." *New York Daily News*. Accessed on March 10, 2022. https://www.nydailynews.com/new-york/bronx/caribbean-ethnic-group-seeks-new-street-dawson-st-article-1.288421.

Carrega, Christina. 2017. "Family of Bronx Man Shot to Death a Decade Ago by NYPD Cop Wins $2M." *NY Daily News*. August 24. https://www.nydailynews.com/new-york/bronx/family-bronx-man-fatally-shot-nypd-wins-2m-city-article-1.3439770.

Carrillo, Karen Juanita. 2004. "Honduran Sale of Black Community Lands Halted, with NYC Help." *New York Amsterdam News*, May 6–12.

Castillo, Kenny F. 2019a. "Apuntes sobre la migración garífuna en relación a la caravana migrante de hondureños 2018." *Diarios del terruño: Reflexiones sobre migración y movilidad*, no. 7, January–June. https://www.revistadiariosdelterruno.com/castillo-fernandez/.

———. 2019b. "El terrible año 2019 de violencia criminal contra los garífunas." Wa-dani, November 5. https://kennycastillo.com/garifunas-4/.

———. 2021. "Casa Yurumein concluye exitoso 'Mes de la herencia Garífuna' en Nueva York." Wa-dani, May 1. https://wa-dani.com/nueva-york-2/.

———. 2022a. "Congresistas de Estados Unidos introducen moción en favor del pueblo Garífuna." Wa-dani, December 17. https://wa-dani.com/congresistas-de-estados-unidos/.

———. 2022b. "Misión Evángelica Garífuna celebra asamblea en Houston, Texas y bajo el título 'Juntos.'" Wa-dani, March 12. https://wa-dani.com/mision-evangelica-garifuna/.

———. 2023. "Casa Yurumein reabre sus puertas en inolvidable noche garífuna en Nueva York." Wa-dani, February 27. https://wa-dani.com/casa-yurumein-abre-sus/.

Castillo Lewis, Stacey Caron. 2005. "Incidencia de la migración en la pérdida de la identidad cultural garífuna: (Caso específico, Livingston, Izabal)." Thesis, Universidad de San Carlos de Guatemala. Accessed March 3, 2019. http://www.repositorio.usac.edu.gt/4232/.

Castro, Jerry. 2005. "Garifuna in New York Rally for Hurricane Katrina Victims in the South." Garinet, September 6. https://www.garinet.com/main.php?module=gcms&node=gcms_front&action=get_content_detail&content_id=2931.

———. 2007. "Garifunas in the Bronx Seek Empowerment." Garifuna Coalition USA, May 8. (PDF). Accessed June 19, 2010. www.garifunacoalition.org.

Catholic New York. 2022. "Fe HondUreña." February 24. https://www.cny.org/stories/fe-hondurea,23495.

Cayetano, Marion, and Roy Cayetano. 2005. "Garifuna Language, Dance and Music: A Masterpiece of the Oral and Intangible Heritage of Humanity. How Did It Happen?" In *The Garifuna: A Nation across Borders*, edited by Joseph O. Palacio. Benque Viejo del Carmen, Belize: Cubola.

Cayetano, Roy E., ed. 1993. *The People's Garifuna Dictionary: Garifuna-Ingleisi, English-Garifuna*. National Garifuna Council of Belize.

Cayetano, Sebastian. 1993. *Garifuna History, Language and Culture of Belize, Central America and the Caribbean*. Belize: By the author.

Cayetano, Sebastian, and Emeri Cayetano. 2007. "The Garifuna Flag." In *Luba Garifuna: Footprints of the Garifuna Cultural Museum, Information Booklet*. 4th ed. Belize City: Sebastian and Isobel Cayetano.

Centeno García, Santos [José Hipólito Centeno]. 1997. *Historia del Movimiento Negro Hondureño*. Tegucigalpa, Honduras: Guaymuras.
———. 2001. *Historia del pueblo negro caribe y su llegada a las Hibueras el 12 de abril de 1797*. Tegucigalpa, Honduras: Universidad Nacional Autónoma de Honduras, Editorial Universitaria,
Chaney, James. 2012. "Malleable Identities: Placing the Garinagu in New Orleans." *Journal of Latin American Geography* 11 (2): 121–44.
Chiefs. 2017. "The Once-Released Rakeem Nunez-Roches Has Earned His Place." Kansas City Chiefs, December 17. https://www.chiefs.com/news/the-once-released-rakeem-nunez-roches-has-earned-his-place-19999213.
Chukwudi, Chudi. 2014. "Garifuna Coalition Honors a Leader." *Caribbean Life*, February 14. https://www.caribbeanlife.com.
Ciego, Arnold. 2021. "Conversando Con Arnold Ciego—Accion Civica Garifuna; entrevista con Consejal. #Fernando Cabrera." Facebook, June 14.
Clarke, Tangerine. 2013. "Rebirth of the Garifuna Culture in St. Vincent and the Grenadines." *Caribbean Life*, January 8. https://www.caribbeanlife.com.
Clawson, David. 2000. *Latin America and the Caribbean: Lands and Peoples*. 2nd ed. Dubuque, IA: Wm. C. Brown.
Cobb, R., and C. Elder. 1971. "The Politics of Agenda Building: An Alternative Perspective of Modern Democratic Theory." *Journal of Politics* 33 (4).
Coelho, Ruy Galvão de Andrade. 1981. *Los negros caribes de Honduras*. Tegucigalpa, Honduras: Guaymuras.
Coleman, James S. 1988. "Social Capital in the Creation of Human Capital." *American Journal of Sociology* 94, Supplement.
Collado, Maren Mohr de. 2007. "Los garínagu en Centroamérica y otros lugares: Identidades de una población afro-caribe entre la tradición y la modernidad." *Indiana: Estudios antropolológicos sobre América Latina y el Caribe* 24. https://doi.org/10.18441/ind.v24i0.67–86.
Colón, Mirtha. 2014. "Miss Garifuna Journal. Casa Yurumein Presenta 'Miss Garifuna 2014.'" https://casayurumein.org/.
———. 2015. "Hondurans Against AIDS Inc." *Premios Barauda Journal*, October.
Colon, Teofilo, Jr. 2010a. "Brooklyn Garifuna Settlement Day Celebration on Friday November 19th 2010." *Being Garifuna* (blog), November 19. https://beinggarifuna.wordpress.com.
———. 2010b. "First Annual Garifuna Heritage Awards and Cultural Night in New York City a Historic Success." *Being Garifuna* (blog), March 13. https://beinggarifuna.wordpress.com.
———. 2010c. "Garifuna American Student Nixon R. Arauz Is an Example of Perseverance Intelligence and Resilience Leading to Academic Success." *Being Garifuna* (blog), July 14. https://beinggarifuna.wordpress.com.
———. 2010d. "Garifuna Entrepreneur Lina Hortensia Martinez Loredo to Be Honored by the U.S. Department of State." *Being Garifuna* (blog), October 10. https://beinggarifuna.wordpress.com.
———. 2010e. "Garifuna Voter Education and Registration Drive to Take Place at Brooklyn's Linden Park on Saturday, August 28th, 2010." *Being Garifuna* (blog), August 27. https://beinggarifuna.wordpress.com/category/garifuna-power/.
———. 2010f. "Schedule for Soccer Games at Linden Park for Sunday, June 27th, 2010." *Being Garifuna* (blog), June 27. https://beinggarifuna.wordpress.com.
———. 2010g. "Third Garifuna Food Expo to Take Place on Saturday April 17th, 2010 in The Bronx." *Being Garifuna* (blog), April 17. https://beinggarifuna.wordpress.com

/2010/04/16/third-garifuna-food-expo-to-take-place-on-saturday-april-17th-2010-in-the-bronx/.

———. 2010h. "Third Garifuna Spirituality Assembly to Take Place In Bronx on Saturday June 19th, 2010." *Being Garifuna* (blog), June 19. https://beinggarifuna.wordpress.com/2010/06/17/third-garifuna-spirituality-assembly-to-take-place-in-bronx-on-saturday-june-19th-2010/.

———. 2010i. Video footage of the Garifuna Community Civic Meeting with New York City Mayor Michael R. Bloomberg. *Being Garifuna* (blog), October 6. www.beinggarifuna.com.

———. 2011. "Result of The Boxing Fight between Garifuna American Boxer EDDIE GOMEZ and Boxer MARCUS HALL." *Being Garifuna* (blog), August 29. https://beinggarifuna.wordpress.com/category/garifuna-video/.

———. 2012. "Garifuna Mass Honoring Virgin of Suyapa." *Being Garifuna* (blog), February 5. Accessed March 10 2013. https://beinggarifuna.com/.

———. 2014a. "18th Annual Central American Independence Parade and Festival in the Bronx on Sunday." *Being Garifuna* (blog), September 14. Accessed October 20, 2015. www.beinggarifuna.com.

———. 2014b. "Garifuna Soccer League President Barbie Lopez of Liga Honduras Unidos Presents Its 2014 Soccer League Awards on Saturday October 11, 2014 in the Bronx." *Being Garifuna* (blog), October 11. Accessed December 23, 2017. www.beinggarifuna.com.

———. 2014c. "Garifuna Veterans of America Organization Presents Its Second Annual Core Values Awards Ceremony on Sunday November 9th 2014 in the Bronx." *Being Garifuna* (blog), November 9. Accessed October 11, 2017. www.beinggarifuna.com.

———. 2014d. "Xiomara Esmeralda Arriola, Garifuna President of the NY Soccer League, Presents Its 2014 Soccer Awards on Friday October 10, 2014." *Being Garifuna* (blog). October 10. Accessed December 24, 2017. www.beinggarifuna.com.

———. 2018. "The Garifuna Americans in Law Enforcement Association Invite You to Network with Them. May 26, 2018." *Being Garifuna* (blog), May 26. Accessed October 11, 2017. www.beinggarifuna.com.

———. 2019. "Encuentro Garifuna y Centro Americano II 2019." NYC Mayor's Office of Immigrant Affairs. *Being Garifuna* (blog), September 28. Accessed February 5, 2020. www.beinggarifuna.com.

Cooper, Ayanna, and Awad Ibrahim, eds. 2020. *Black Immigrants in the United States: Essays on the Politics of Race, Language, and Voice.* New York: Peter Lang.

Corinealdi, Kaysha L. 2011. "Redefining Home: West Indian Panamanians and Transnational Politics of Race, Citizenship, and Diaspora, 1928–1970." PhD diss., Yale University.

Cortes de Solano, Zaira. 2015. "Madres garífunas viven 'nueva esclavitud' de ICE. El Diario Nueva York." *La opinión*, April 13. http://www.laopinion.com/garifunas-inmigrantes-condiciones-detencion-deportacion-ice.

Cosgrove, S., J. Idiáquez, A. J. Gorvetzian, and L. J. Bent. 2021. *Surviving the Americas: Garifuna Persistence from Nicaragua to New York City.* Cincinnati: University of Cincinnati Press.

Crawford, Amy. 2018. "Racism Kept Connecticut's Beaches White Up Through the 1970s." *Smithsonian Magazine*, July 2. https://www.smithsonianmag.com/history/connecticuts-beaches-were-largely-limits-african-americans-through-1970s-180969494/.

Crockett, Stephen A., Jr. "Danny Glover and Cedric the Entertainer Are Serving as Protection for an Exiled Revolutionary Returning to His Home Country." *The Root*, January 23.

https://www.theroot.com/danny-glover-and-cedric-the-entertainer-are-serving-as-1822350940.

Cruz, David. 2019. "Will the Bronx Elect a Cowboy-Hatted Congressman?" *City and State New York*, May 29. https://www.cityandstateny.com/politics/2019/05/will-the-bronx-elect-a-cowboy-hatted-congressman/177306/.

Cruz, José E. 2017. *Puerto Rican Identity, Political Development, and Democracy in New York*. New York: Lexington Books.

Culinary Backstreets. 2019. "Native Dish: Isha Sumner's Garifuna Tortillas." Culinary Backstreets, April 15. https://culinarybackstreets.com/cities-category/queens/2019/native-dish-4/.

Curran, Sara. 2002. "Migration, Social Capital, and the Environment: Considering Migrant Selectivity and Networks in Relation to Coastal Ecosystems." *Population and Development Review* 28, Supplement: Population and Environment: Methods of Analysis, 89–125.

Davis, RaVal. 2020. "Wilson Morales Launches New Venture BlackFilmAndTV.com with Focus on Highlighting Black Stories and Black Talent." *Forbes*, July 31. https://www.forbes.com/sites/raval/2020/07/31/wilson-morales-launches-new-venture-blackfilmandtvcom-with-focus-on-highlighting-black-stories--black-talent/?sh=329e7f234f75.

Dean, Kristina. 2019. "Speakers Discuss Human Trafficking in North Country." *North Country Catholic*, February 20. https://www.northcountrycatholic.org/Articles/2019/2_20talkinghumantrafficking.html.

Deen, Safid. 2019. "Five Things to Know about Brian Flores, Dolphins' Coaching Search." *South Florida Sun Sentinel*, January 12. https://www.sun-sentinel.com/sports/miami-dolphins/fl-sp-dolphins-brian-flores-20190112-story.html.

Defay, Jason B. 2004. "Identity Matters: Immigration and the Social Construction of Identity in Garifuna Los Angeles." PhD diss., University of California, San Diego.

Díaz, Rubén. 2015. "Diaz Team Announces the Fifth Abrazo Garifuna." New York State Senate website, April 7. https://www.nysenate.gov/newsroom/press-releases/ruben-diaz/diaz-team-announces-fifth-abrazo-garifuna.

Dooley, Tara. 1995. "Hondurans Find Few Breaks in Borough." *Bronx Beat*, September 22. Accessed December 2, 2014. http://www.columbia.edu/cu/bb/oldstuff/bb0220.17.html.

Dow, Jay. 2020. "Environmental Racism in the Bronx: Why the Asthma Rate Is So High in the Borough." *PIX 11*, October 19. https://pix11.com/news/created-equal/environmental-racism-in-the-bronx-why-the-asthma-rate-is-so-high-in-the-borough/.

Duhart, Bill. 2021. "N.J. Beach Was the Only One That Allowed Black Tourists, but They Made It a Hip Place to Be." *NJ.com*, updated February 15. https://www.nj.com/atlantic/2019/07/nj-beach-was-the-only-one-that-allowed-black-tourists-but-they-made-it-a-hip-place-to-be.html.

Duran, Gonzalo. 2019. "Garifuna Veterans Helping to Identify Garifunas in 2020 Census." Devil Dog USA Incorporated, May 23. https://devildogusainc.org/2019/05/23/garifuna-veterans-helping-to-identify-garifunas-in-2020-census/.

Election Results 2021. Spectrum News NY1. New York City. Accessed April 2, 2022. www.ny1.com.

Ellington Lambe, G. 1998. "Derecho Consuetudinario Garifuna sobre la Possession y uso de las Playas en el Perimetro Urbano del Municipio de Livingston, Departamento de Izabal." Thesis, Universidad de San Carlos Guatemala.

Endo, Isako, Sarah Hirsch, Jan Rogge, and Kamil Borowik. 2010. "The U.S.-Honduras Remittance Corridor: Acting on Opportunities to Increase Financial Inclusion and

Foster Development of a Transnational Economy." World Bank Working Paper no. 177. Washington, D.C.: World Bank, 2010.

England, Sarah. 1999. "Negotiating Race and Place in the Garifuna Diaspora: Identity Formation and Transnational Grassroots Politics in New York City and Honduras." *Identities: Global Studies in Culture and Power* 6 (1).

———. 2006. *Afro-Central Americans in New York City: Garifuna Tales of Transnational Movements in Racialized Space*. Gainesville: University Press of Florida.

Euraque, Dario A. 2003. "The Threat of Blackness to the Mestizo Nation: Race and Ethnicity in the Honduran Banana Economy, 1920s and 1930s." In *Banana Wars: Power, Production, and History in the Americas*, edited by Steve Striffler and Mark Moberg. Durham, NC: Duke University Press.

———. 2004. *Conversaciones historicas con el Mestizaje y su identidad nacional en Honduras*. San Pedro Sula, Honduras: Centro.

———. 2010. *El golpe de Estado del 28 de Junio de 2009, el patrimonio cultural y la identidad nacional de Honduras*. San Pedro Sula, Honduras: Centro.

Fadahunsi, Olayinka. 2003. "The Garifuna Exodus: Is Harlem God's Land?" *The African* 1 (15): 10.

Falcón, Angelo. 2005. "Latino New York City, the 2000 Elections, and the Limits of Party Loyalty." In *Muted Voices: Latinos and the 2000 Elections*, edited by Rodolfo O. de la Garza and Louis DeSipio. Lanham, MD: Rowman and Littlefield.

———. 2017. "The Racial-Ethnic Diversity of Latino Elected Officials in NYC." National Institute for Latino Policy (NiLP) Report on Latino Politics and Policy, April 16. https://myemail.constantcontact.com/NiLP-Report--Diversity-of-Latino-Elected-Officials-in-New-York-City.html?soid=1101040629095&aid=y7DhhcaE26U.

"Felipe N. Torres 1953–1963." Hunter College Felipe N. Torres Papers, Centro de Estudios Puertorriquenos, Guide to the Felipe N. Torres Papers. Accessed March 20, 2020. https://centropr.hunter.cuny.edu.

Fernandez, Manny. 2007. "Remembrance, and Protest, for a Man Slain by an Officer." *New York Times*, May 27. https://www.nytimes.com/2007/05/27/nyregion/27funeral.html.

Folkfest. 2013. "The 39th Annual New Jersey Folk Festival. Celebrating Garifuna Traditions Saturday." New Jersey Folk Festival (website), April 27. (PDF) https://www.njfolkfest.org/past-festival-themes/2013-garifuna-traditions/.

Fretz, Chris. 2015. "N.Y. Garifuna Mennonites Organize Assistance for Immigrants." *The Mennonite*, March 6. http://www.themennonite.org.

Garcia, Doris. 2013. "Transnational Ethnic Identities and Garinagu Political Organizations in the Diaspora." In *Crossing Boundaries: Ethnicity, Race, and National Belonging in a Transnational World*, edited by Brian D. Behnken and Simon Wendt. Lanham, MD: Lexington Books.

———. 2014. "Place, Race, and the Politics of Identity in the Geography of Garifuna Baündada." PhD diss., Louisiana State University and Agricultural and Mechanical College.

García, Jesús. 2022. "Representatives García, Bush, Omar, Schakowsky & Bowman Introduce Resolution to Affirm Rights of Honduras' Garífuna People." U.S. Congressman Jesus G. "Chuy" García (website), December 14. https://chuygarcia.house.gov/media/press-releases/representatives-garcia-bush-omar-schakowsky-bowman-introduce-resolution-to-affirm-rights-of-honduras-garifuna-people.

Gardiner, Sean. 2011. "Appeals Court Reverses Officer's Conviction." *Wall Street Journal*, June 16. https://www.wsj.com/articles/.

Gargallo, Francesca. 2005. "Garifuna: A Culture of Women and Men." In *The Garifuna: A Nation across Borders*, edited by Joseph O. Palacio. Benque Viejo del Carmen, Belize: CUBOLA.

Garifuna Nation. n.d. "Flag Story: History of the Garifuna Flag." Garifuna Nation (website), accessed June 15, 2023. https://www.garifunanation.org/history/.

Garinagu Quarterly Magazine. 1996. "Garinagu Enterprises Thanksgiving Dance a Success." January–March 1 (2).

Garinet. 2003. "Garifuna NBA Player, Milton Palacio, Needs Your Vote." Garinet, September 29. https://www.garinet.com.

Gartland, Michael, Tim Balk, and Chris Sommerfeldt. 2022. "Black Politicians, Long Shut Out, Ride Wave of Power in NYC and Beyond." *New York Daily News*, January 30. https://www.nydailynews.com.

Gil, Katy. 2019. BronxNet *Honduras Centro America Show*, hosted by Katy Gil, with guest Mirtha Colón.

Gil, Katy, and Murphy Valentine. 2018. BronxNet *Honduras Centro America Show*, hosted by Katy Gil; among the guests: Parade President, Evelyn Chamorro-Arauz, Communication Director, Arturito Martinez. August 27.

Glaberson, William. 2007. "Manhattan: Immigrant Advocate Pleads Guilty to Fraud." *New York Times*, March 17. https://www.nytimes.com/2007/03/17/nyregion/17mbrfs-maximo.html.

Goldberg, David E. 2016. *The Retreats of Reconstruction: Race, Leisure, and the Politics of Segregation at the New Jersey Shore, 1865–1920*. New York: Fordham University Press.

Gonzalez, Melecio. 1969. "El Soldado Garifuna en La Guerra con El Salvador Julio de 1969." Document provided by Melecio Gonzalez.

Gonzalez, Nancie L. Solien. 1969. *Black Carib Household Structure: A Study of Migration and Modernization*. Seattle: University of Washington Press.

———. 1979. "Garifuna Settlement in New York: A New Frontier." *International Migration Review* 13 (2): 255.

———. 1988. *Sojourners of the Caribbean: Ethnogenesis and Ethnohistory of the Garifuna*. Champaign: University of Illinois Press.

———. 1989. "Garifuna Settlement in New York: A New Frontier." In *Caribbean Life in New York City: Sociocultural Dimensions*, edited by Constance R. Sutton and Elsa M. Chaney. New York: Center for Migration Studies.

———. 2008. *Peregrinos del Caribe: Etnogenesis y etnohistoria de los garifunas*. Tegucigalpa, Honduras: Guaymuras.

Gonzalez-Ramirez, Patricia. 2017. "Garífuna Band Drums to Keep Culture Vibrant." *Hunts Point Express*, December 21. https://huntspointexpress.com/2017/12/21/garifuna-band-drums-to-keep-culture-vibrant/.

Gordon, Edmund T. 1998. *Disparate Diasporas: Identity and Politics in an African Nicaraguan Community*. Austin: University of Texas Press.

Gordon, Todd, and Jeffery R. Webber. 2016. *Blood of Extraction: Canadian Imperialism in Latin America*. Halifax, Canada: Fernwood.

Gorres, S. 2008. "Garifuna Place-Making: Hope for the Guatemalan Nation." MA thesis, University of Kansas

Grasmuck, S., and R. Grosfoguel. 1997. "Geopolitics, Economic Niches, and Gendered Social Capital among Recent Caribbean Immigrants in New York City." *Sociological Perspectives* 40 (3): 339–63.

Green, Oliver. 2005. "Music behind the Mask: Men, Social Commentary and Identity in Wanaragua (John Canoe)." Chapter 11 in *The Garifuna: A Nation across Borders*, edited by Joseph O. Palacio. Benque Viejo del Carmen, Belize: Cubola.

———, ed. 2018. *The Garifuna Music Reader*. San Diego, CA: Cognella.

Greene, David, Síle Moloney, and José A. Giralt. 2021. "Bronx NAACP President Sees Need for Voter Education in Future Elections." *Norwood News*, May 3. https://www.norwoodnews.org.

Greer, Christina M. 2013. *Black Ethnics, Race, Immigration, and the Pursuit of the American Dream*. Oxford: Oxford University Press.

Gullick, C. J. M. R. 1976. *Exiled from St. Vincent: The Development of Black Carib Culture in Central America up to 1945*. Malta: Progress.

Guzman, Omar. 2018. "The Garifuna Story, A Tale of Overcoming Obstacles." *In Shalom News* 38 (3).

Hamilton, Tod G. 2019. *Immigration and the Remaking of Black America*. Foreword by Douglas S. Massey. New York: Russell Sage Foundation.

Harmon, Dan'l, and Elaine Song. 2017. "Organizing Garifuna Communities in the Bronx and Honduras." *Collective Endeavor* 21 (1).

Henderson, Nia-Malika. 2004. "Garinagu Seek to Be Counted in Cultural Mix." *Bronx Beat*, April 19–24.

"Hen-Gee & Evil E: Biography." Last edited February 6, 2010. Last.fm (website). https://www.last.fm/music/Hen-Gee+&+Evil-E/+wiki.

Hernandez, Sadie. 2008a. "Garifunas en Nueva York rescatados para rescatar." *Subete al Arca*, no. 17 (November): 8–9.

———. 2008b. "Sonia Fernandez, Mujer Garifuna, Pastora, Periodista y lider comunitaria de character Cristiano." *Subete al Arca*, no. 17 (November): 8–9.

Hill, Robert A., et al., eds. 2014. "Honduras," "Belize," Nicaragua," "Guatemala," "Nicaragua." In *The Marcus Garvey and Universal Negro Improvement Association Papers*, vol. 12, *The Caribbean Diaspora, 1920–1921*. Durham, NC: Duke University Press.

Honduras Remittances. 2023. "Honduras: Remittances, percent of GDP." The Global Economy, Business and economic data for 200 countries. Accessed June 18, 2023. https://www.theglobaleconomy.com/Honduras/remittances_percent_GDP/.

Horne, Gerald. 2005. *Red Seas: Ferdinand Smith and Radical Black Sailors in the United States and Jamaica*. New York: NYU Press.

HRD Memorial. 2022. "Celebrating Those Who Were Killed Defending Human Rights. Silvinio Zapata Martinez." Accessed March 22, 2022. https://hrdmemorial.org/hrdrecord/silvinio-zapata-martinez/.

Hunter, Janae. 2015. "Nadia Lopez: Wonderful Educator." *New York Amsterdam News*, April 2. https://amsterdamnews.com/news/2015/04/02/nadia-lopez-wonderful-educator/.

Hutchinson, Janis Faye, Nestor Rodriguez, and Jacqueline Hagan. 1996. "Community Life: African Americans in Multiethnic Residential Areas." *Journal of Black Studies* 27 (2).

IACHR. 2019. "IACHR Condemns the Prevalence of Murders and Other Forms of Violence against Garifuna Women in Honduras." Report from Inter-American Commission on Human Rights, September 24. ReliefWeb. https://reliefweb.int/report/honduras/iachr-condemns-prevalence-murders-and-other-forms-violence-against-garifuna-women.

Iborra Mallent, Juan Vicente. 2019. "Eibuga Hama Wayunagu Garinagu (Caminando con los ancestros garífunas): Cosmopolíticas frente al despojo territorial en tiempos de la tercera expulsión." Master's thesis, UNAM.

———. 2021. "Migración garífuna, deportaciones y asilo político en un contexto de desplazamiento forzado." *Andamios* 18 (45). https://andamios.uacm.edu.mx/.

Investigation Report—SS *Smith Voyager*, Captain USCG A.W. Johnsen, Treasury Department, United States Coast Guard. September 22, 1966. Washington, D.C.

IWN. 2015. "Ramos Wants to Form 'Real' Garifuna Organization in St. Vincent." *iWitness News*, July 30. https://www.iwnsvg.com/2015/07/30/ramos-wants-to-form-real-garifuna-organisation-in-st-vincent/.

———. 2019. "Visiting Garifuna Want Balliceaux Declared Sacred Heritage Land." *iWitness News*, August 15. https://www.iwnsvg.com/2019/08/15/visiting-garifuna-want-balliceaux-declared-sacred-heritage-land/.

Izard, Gabriel. 2005. "Patrimonial Activation and Construction of Garifuna Identity in Contemporary Belize." In *The Garifuna: A Nation across Borders*, edited by Joseph O. Palacio. Benque Viejo del Carmen, Belize: Cubola.

Jamaica Observer. 2018. "OAS Marks Day of Remembrance for Victims of Slavery." March 25. http://www.jamaicaobserver.com.

James, Winston. 1999. *Holding Aloft the Banner of Ethiopia: Caribbean Radicalism in Early Twentieth-Century America*. New York: Verso.

John-Sandy, Rene. 1997. "The Garifuna Bicentennial Commemoration 1797–1997." *Black Diaspora: A Global Black Magazine* 18 (5): 26–28.

Johnson, Paul Christopher. 2007. *Diaspora Conversions: Black Carib Religion and the Recovery of Africa*. Berkeley: University of California Press.

Jones-Corrrea, Michael. 1998. *Between Two Nations: The Political Predicament of Latinos in New York City*. Ithaca, NY: Cornell University Press.

Jones-Correa, Michael A., and David L. Leal. 2001. "Political Participation: Does Religion Matter?" *Political Research Quarterly* 54 (4): 751–70.

Jonnes, Jill. 2002. *South Bronx Rising: The Rise, Fall and Resurrection of an American City*. 2nd ed. New York: Fordham University Press.

Kasinitz, Philip. 1992. *Caribbean New York: Black Immigrants and the Politics of Race*. Ithaca, NY: Cornell University Press.

Kerns, Virginia. 1997. *Women and the Ancestors: Black Carib Kinship and Ritual*. 2nd ed. Champaign: University of Illinois Press.

Kim, Julie Chun. 2013. "The Caribs of St. Vincent and Indigenous Resistance during the Age of Revolutions." In "Forming Nations, Reforming Empires: Atlantic Polities in the Long Eighteenth Century." Special issue, *Early American Studies* 11 (1): 117–32.

King, Nelson A. 2013. "Garifuna Coalition Supports Call for Reparations." *The Vincentian*, September 27. https://thevincentian.com/garifuna-coalition-supports-call-for-reparations-p3878-133.htm.

———. 2018a. "Garifuna Celebrates Heritage Month." *Caribbean Life*, March 13. https://www.caribbeanlife.com.

———. 2018b. "Vincentian Group Participates in Garifuna-American Event." *Caribbean Life*, May 23. https://www.caribbeanlife.com.

———. 2019a. "Garifuna Group Grateful for Discretionary Funds." *Caribbean Life*, April 5. https://www.caribbeanlife.com.

———. 2019b. "Garifuna Group Sponsors Free Heritage Camp in SVG." *Caribbean Life*, July 3. https://www.caribbeanlife.com/garifuna-group-sponsors-free-heritage-camp-in-svg/i90.

———. 2022a. "Garifuna Coalition 'Proud' to Celebrate Caribbean-American Heritage Month." *Caribbean Life*, July 7–13. https://www.caribbeanlife.com/garifuna-coalition-proud-to-celebrate-caribbean-american-heritage-month/.
———. 2022b. "Sen. Luis Sepúlveda Introduces Resolution to Celebrate Garifuna-American Heritage Month." *Caribbean Life*, March 10. https://www.caribbeanlife.com.
———. 2023a. "Adams Hosts Historic Garifuna Celebration at Gracie Mansion." *Caribbean Life*, April 20. https://www.caribbeanlife.com.
———. 2023b. "May Is Garifuna Arts & Culture Appreciation Month." *Caribbean Life*, May 3. https://www.caribbeanlife.com/may-is-garifuna-arts-culture-appreciation-month/.
Kirby, I. E., and C. I. Martin. 1997. *The Rise and Fall of the Black Caribs*. Kingstown: St. Vincent and the Grenadines National Trust.
Laguerre, M. 1984. *American Odyssey: Haitians in New York City*. Ithaca, NY: Cornell University Press.
Lakhani, Nina. 2020a. "Fears Growing for Five Indigenous Garifuna Men Abducted in Honduras." *The Guardian*, July 23. https://www.theguardian.com/global-development/2020/jul/23/garifuna-honduras-abducted-men-land-rights.
———. 2020b. *Who Killed Berta Cáceres? Dams, Death Squads, and an Indigenous Defender's Battle for the Planet*. New York: Verso.
Lambert, Aida. 2010. "We Are Black Too: Experiences of a Honduran Garifuna." In *The Afro Latin@ Reader: History and Culture in the United States*, edited by Miriam Jiménez Román and Juan Flores. Durham, NC: Duke University Press.
Lansing, David. 2009. "The Spaces of Social Capital: Livelihood Geographies and Marine Conservation in the Cayos Cochinos Marine Protected Area, Honduras." *Journal of Latin American Geography* 8 (1): 29–54.
Lentz, Philip. 1988. "Democrats Turn Bronx into Political Zoo." *Chicago Tribune*, June 26. https://www.chicagotribune.com.
Levitt, Peggy. 2001. "Transnational Migration: Taking Stock and Future Directions." *Global Networks: A Journal of Transnational Affairs* 1 (3): 195–216.
Lewis, Paul E. 2008. "Garifuna May Lose the Right to Visit the Island of Balliceaux." *Review of the Indigenous Caribbean* (blog), April 22. Accessed July 5, 2022. http://indigenousreview.blogspot.com.
Lewis, Rebecca C., and Zach Williams. 2022. "Black and Latino Faith Leaders Are Key to Any Cuomo Comeback." *City and State NY*, March 17. www.cityandstateny.com/politics.
Li, Victor. 2009. "New York Hondurans Brave the Cold for Soccer." *Columbia Journalism School*, November 13. Accessed January 10, 2019. http://www.victor-li-com.\
———. 2010. "The Happy Land Fire—20 Years Later." *Columbia Journalism School*, March 15. Accessed January 10, 2019. http://www.victor-li-com.
Longman, Jere. 2016. "Simone Biles Soars, Lifting Another Country with Her." *New York Times*, August 12. https://www.nytimes.com/2016/08/12/sports/olympics/simone-biles-gymnastics-belize-rio-games.html.
Loperena, Christopher. 2010. "Financiamiento del BID, enclave turístico y pérdida de la tierra Garífuna en la Bahía de Tela." *Americas*, May 10. https://www.americas.org/es/megaproyectos-del-bid-desplazamiento-y-migracion-forzada/.
———. 2016. "Radicalize Multiculturalism? Garifuna Activism and the Double-Bind of Participation in Postcoup Honduras." *Journal of Latin American and Caribbean Anthropology* 21 (3): 517–38.

———. 2017. "Settler Violence? Race and Emergent Frontiers of Progress in Honduras." *American Quarterly* 69 (4): 801–7.

———. 2021. "Frontiers of Dispossession, Territories of Freedom." *NACLA Report on the Americas* 53 (3): 211–14.

Lopez, Nadia. The Lopez Effect. Accessed March 29, 2021. www.thelopezeffect.com/aboutme.

López García, Víctor. 2006. *Tornabé ante el proyecto turístico*. Honduras: S N.

López Oro, Paul Joseph. 2016a. "Colón, Mirtha (1951–), Transnational Garifuna Activist and Political Organizer." In *Dictionary of Caribbean and Afro–Latin American Biography*, edited by Franklin W. Knight and Henry Louis Gates Jr. Oxford: Oxford University Press.

———. 2016b. "'Ni de aquí, ni de allá': Garifuna Subjectivities and the Politics of Diasporic Belonging." In *Afro-Latinos in Movement: Critical Approaches to Blackness and Transnationalism in the Americas*, edited by Petra R. Rivera-Rideau, Jennifer A. Jones, and Tianna Paschel. New York: Palgrave Macmillan.

———. 2021. "A Love Letter to Indigenous Blackness." *NACLA—Report on the Americas* 53 (3). 2021 North American Congress on Latin America (NACLA). August.

Lynn, Frank, and Michael Oreskes. 1987. "In Bronx Politics, Signs of City's Future." *New York Times*, June 15. https://www.nytimes.com/1987/06/15/nyregion/in-bronx-politics-signs-of-city-s-future.html.

MacCulloch, Christina. 2001. "IDB Approves $1,440,000 for microenterprise in Central America and Ecuador." IDB: Inter-American Development Bank, May 29. https://www.iadb.org/en/news/news-releases/2001-05-29/idb-approves-1440000-for-microenterprise-in-central-america-and-ecuador%2C1785.html.

Marable, Manning. 1996. *Beyond Black and White: Transforming African-American Politics*. New York: Verso.

Martínez, Edwin. 2018. "Violencia por armas de fuego en el tapete." *El Diario Nueva York*, April 17. www.eldiariony.com.

Martínez, Elena. 2016. "Echoes of Familiar Rhythms: Puerto Rican and Garifuna Drums." *Voices: The Journal of New York Folklore* 42 (3/4).

Matthei, Linda M., and David A. Smith. 1998. "Belizean 'Boyz 'n the 'Hood'? Garifuna Labor Migration and Transnational Identity." In *Transnationalism from Below*, edited by M. P. Smith and L. E. Guarnizo, 270–90. New Brunswick, NJ: Transaction.

Mays, Jeffery C. 2022. "New York City's Noncitizen Voting Law Is Struck Down." *New York Times*, June 27. https://www.nytimes.com/2022/06/27/nyregion/noncitizen-voting-ruling-nyc.html.

McLaughlin, Aidan, and Graham Rayman. 2016. "City Officials, Pastors Announce Upcoming Bronx Gun Buyback Event." *New York Daily News*, August 1. https://www.nydailynews.com/new-york/city-officials-pastors-announce-upcoming-bronx-gun-buyback-event-article-1.2734747.

Miller, Yawu. 2019. "Dorchester Resident Fighting to Protect Garifuna Community." *Bay State Banner*, September 5. https://www.baystatebanner.com/2019/09/05/dorchester-resident-fighting-to-protect-garifuna-community/.

Minsky, Tequila. 2015a. "Garifuna Celebrates Heritage at Boro Hall." *Caribbean Life*, April 12. https://www.caribbeanlife.com.

———. 2015b. "James Lovell." *Caribbean Life*, November 20. https://www.caribbeanlife.com/james-lovell/.

———. 2018. "Garifuna Celebrate Their Heritage at City Hall." *Caribbean Life*, April 20. https://www.caribbeanlife.com/garifuna-celebrates-heritage-at-boro-hall/.

Mitchell, Alex, and Jason Cohen. 2021. "Elections: Who's Running for City Council in the 16th District?" *Bronx Times*, April 6. https://www.bxtimes.com/2021-elections-whos-running-for-city-council-in-the-16th-district/.

Moberg, Mark. 1996. "Crown Colony as Banana Republic: The United Fruit Company in British Honduras, 1900–1920." *Journal of Latin American Studies* 28 (3): 357–81.

Molina, Alvaro Morales. 2007. "Extension for TPS Saves Hondurans in the USA." *Honduras This Week Online: Your Central American Weekly Review*, National News, May 7. Accessed at Issuu.com. https://issuu.com/94641567/docs/vol20n17.

Mollett, Sharlene. 2014. "A Modern Paradise: Garifuna Land, Labor, and Displacement-in-Place." *Latin American Perspectives* 41 (6). https://doi.org/10.1177/0094582X13518756.

Moore, Jim. 2021. "Jim Moore: Kache Palacio, Once a Terror on WSU D, Now in MMA Ring." *247 Sports*, January 30. www.247sports.com.

Moorer, D. Talise. 2007. "Cop Kills Bronx Man." *New York Amsterdam News*, May 24–30. www.amsterdamnews.com.

Moss, Jeremiah. 2017. *Vanishing New York: How a Great City Lost Its Soul*. New York: HarperCollins.

Moynihan, Ellen. 2019. "Man, 24, Stabbed to Death in Saturday Night Bronx Attack." *New York Daily News*, June 9. www.nydailynews.com.

Muraskin, William. 1972. "The Harlem Boycott of 1934: Black Nationalism and the Rise of Labor Union Consciousness." *Journal Labor History*, 13 (3): 361–73.

Museum of the City of New York. n.d. "Economic Rights: 'Don't Move, Improve': Reviving the South Bronx 1970–2012." *Activist New York*. Accessed February 26, 2021. https://activistnewyork.mcny.org/exhibition/economic-rights/Bronx.

Naison, Mark D., and Bob Gumbs. 2016. *Before the Fires: An Oral History of African America Life in the Bronx from the 1930s to the 1960s*. New York: Fordham University Press.

Newman, Jesse. 2011. "Garifuna Immigrants Bring Faith, Culture and Challenges to Brownsville." *Brooklyn Ink*, August 4. http://brooklynink.org.

News Americas (Staff writer). 2017. "Nationals from These Five Caribbean Countries Make Up New York City's Top Foreign Immigrant Groups." News Americas, Your Americas News and Lifestyle Portal, January 12. www.newsamericasnow.org.

Newsbreak. 2020. "Woman, 61, Shot in Leg When Caught in Crossfire of Bronx Gunfight: Police." *Newsbreak*, August 20. Accessed February 4, 2021. https://www.newsbreak.com.

News 12 The Bronx. 2018. "Central American Day Parade Held in West Farms." News 12 The Bronx, September 9. https://bronx.news12.com/central-american-day-parade-held-in-west-farms-39055751.

New York State. Track bill. Accessed March 22, 2022. https://trackbill.com/bill/new-york-assembly-legislative.

New York State Black, Puerto Rican, Hispanic and Asian Legislative Caucus. 2014. "1917–2014: A Look at the History of the Legislators of Color." New York State Assembly (website). Accessed March 20, 2020. https://nyassembly.gov/comm/BlackPR/20140213/index.pdf.

New York State Comptroller. 2021. "Recent Trends and Impact of COVID-19 in the Bronx." Office of the New York State Comptroller, NYS Comptroller Thomas P. DiNapoli. June. Accessed April 5, 2022. https://www.osc.state.ny.us/reports/osdc/recent-trends-and-impact-covid-19-bronx.

New York State Department of State, Division of Corporations. Corporation and Business Entity Database. https://apps.dos.ny.gov/publicInquiry/.

New York State Passenger and Crew Lists, 1917–1967 [database online]. https://www.ancestry.com/search/collections/1277/.

New York State 2020 Primary Election Summary. Accessed March 22, 2022. www.nysar.com.

NMU Pilot. 1976. "Shannon J. Wall. NMU's Friends, Allies Vow Continued Support, 'Convention Creates Impressive Road.'" *NMU Pilot* 41 (11): 2–3, 25, 29.

NYC Mayor's Office of Immigrant Affairs. "Temporary Protected Status: What Is Temporary Protected Status (TPS)?" Updated March 16, 2023. https://www.nyc.gov/site/immigrants/help/legal-services/temporary-protected-status.page.

NYC Planning. 2021. "Dynamics of Racial/Hispanic Composition in NYC Neighborhoods 2010 to 2020." New York City Department of City Planning, Population Division, November 10. https://storymaps.arcgis.com/stories/46a91a58447d4024afd00771eec1dd23.

NYC Votes. 2019. "2018–2019 Voter Analysis Report." New York City Campaign Finance Board, April 29. https://www.nyccfb.info/media/reports/2018-2019-voter-analysis-report/.

On a True Course: The Story of the National Maritime Union AFL-CIO. Washington, D.C.: Merkle.

Oneil, Vincent. 2004. "Dean Martinez is New Manager of Human Resources for Ogden City." CISION PR Web. November. Accessed January 21, 2021. www.prweb.com.

Opie, Frederick D. 2009. *Black Labor Migration in Caribbean Guatemala, 1882–1923*. Gainesville: University Press of Florida

———. 2014. *Upsetting the Apple Cart: Black-Latino Coalitions in New York City from Protest to Public Office*. New York: Columbia University Press.

Opoku Donyina, R. 2020. "Exploring How Social Networks Contribute to African Immigrants' Ability to Procure a Sustainable Livelihood in New York City." (Google—PDF file)

Orr, Matthew, and Vijai Singh. 2012. *Being Garifuna*. Video. January 13. Accessed March 25, 2022. https://www.nytimes.com/video/us/100000001285066/being-garifuna.html.

Palacio, Joseph O. 1992. "Garifuna Immigrants in Los Angeles: Attempts at Self-Improvement." *Belizean Studies* 20 (3): 17–26.

———, ed. 2005. *The Garifuna: A Nation across Borders; Essays in Social Anthropology*. Benque Viejo del Carmen, Belize: Cubola.

Palacio, Myrtle. 2001. "Dangriga BZ or USA? Out-migration Experiences of a Garifuna Community in Post-independent Belize." Belize Country Conference, Cavehill, Barbados: University of the West Indies, November. Retrieved from https://www.open.uwi.edu/sites/default/files/bnccde/belize/conference/papers/palaciom.html.

Pearson, Erica. 2011. "'Being Garifuna' Blogger Teofilo Colon Fans Flames of His People's Pride Online." *New York Daily News*, November 14. https://www.nydailynews.com/new-york/garifuna-blogger-teofilo-colon-fans-flames-people-pride-online-article-1.977231.

Perry, D. Mark. 1999. "Garifuna Youth in New York City: Race, Ethnicity, and the Performance of Diasporic Identities." MA thesis, University of Texas at Austin.

Pierre-Louis, Francois. 2006. *Haitians in New York City: Transnationalism and Hometown Associations*. Gainesville: University Press of Florida.

Portes, Alejandro, and Min Zhou. 2018. "The New Second Generation: Segmented Assimilation and Its Variants." In *Inequality in the 21st Century: A Reader*, edited by David B. Grusky and Jasmine Hill. New York: Routledge.

Proceso Digital. 2015."Inauguran aeródromo de Tela como una puerta al desarrollo del turismo." *Proceso Digital*, May 20. https://proceso.hn/inauguran-aerodromo-de-tela-como-una-puerta-al-desarrollo-del-turismo/.

Pro Football History. Clayton Lopez, coaching record, biography. Accessed June 15, 2023. https://pro-football-history.com/coach/1812/clayton-lopez-bio.

Putnam, Robert. 2000. *Bowling Alone: The Collapse and Revival of American Community*. New York: Simon and Schuster.

Queens Latino. 2016. "Hondureños de NY veneran a la Virgen de Suyapa en Catedral de San Patricio." *Queens Latino: Por Nuestra Communidad*, February 21. https://queenslatino.com.

Ramos, Adele. 2000. *Thomas Vincent Ramos: The Man and His Writings*. Belize: National Garifuna Council of Belize.

Ramos, T. V. 2000. "Stann Creek Faces a Period of Economic Crisis." In *Thomas Vincent Ramos: The Man and His Writings*, by Adele Ramos. Belize: National Garifuna Council of Belize.

Ramos, Wellington. 2008. "The Government of St. Vincent and the Grenadines Selling Balliceaux Is an Insult to the Garifuna People World-Wide." *Review of the Indigenous Caribbean* (blog), May 5. http://indigenousreview.blogspot.com.

———. 2014. "Commentary: A Mandate for a Garifuna Nation." *Caribbean News Now*, April 16. www.thecaribbeannewsnow.com.

———. 2017a. "Commentary: Election Petitions in St. Vincent and the Grenadines." *Caribbean News Now*, accessed September 28, 2018. https://thecaribbeannewsnow.com/.

———. 2017b. "Commentary: All Garifuna Must Oppose the Sale of Baliceaux." *Repeating Islands*, May 8. https://repeatingislands.com/2017/05/08/commentary-all-garifuna-must-oppose-the-sale-of-baliceaux/.

———. 2018. "Garifuna Response to the Guatemalan ICJ Referendum." *Caribbean Life*, April 24. https://www.caribbeanlife.com.

———. 2020. "Gonsalves Writes to UN, Honduras President Garifuna Abuse." *Garifuna Nation*, August 9. (Online source discontinued.)

Reklitis, George. 2003. "Remittances and Development in Central America." MA thesis, Dalhousie University (Canada).

Remeseira, C., ed. 2010. *Hispanic New York: A Sourcebook*. New York: Columbia University Press.

Rey, Nicolás. 2009. "La movilización de los garífunas para preserver sus tierras 'ancestrales' en Guatemala." *Revistas Pueblos y Fronteras digital* 4 (8). https://doi.org/10.22201/cimsur.18704115e.2009.8.171.

Reyes, Milton Leonel, and Mildred Gallo. 2021. "Garífunas: Las rutas del cuerpo entre el Aquí y Allá Imaginarios colectivos sobre el fenómeno migratorio en las comunidades de Sambo Creek y Corozal." *Migración y Desarollo* 14. Tegucigalpa: Universidad Nacional Autónoma de Honduras.

Reynoso, J. 2003. "Dominican Immigrants and Social Capital in New York City: A Case Study." *Latino Intersections* 1 (1): 1–28.

Ribando, Clare M. 2007. "CRS Report for Congress: Afro-Latinos in Latin America and Considerations for U.S. Policy." Congressional Research Service, Washington, D.C.

Rivas, Ramon D. 1993. *Pueblos indígenas y garífuna de Honduras (unacaracterización)*. Tegucigalpa, Honduras: Guaymuras.

Rivieccio, Anthony. 2015. "Who Will Be Next to Hold the Title: Chairman of The Bronx Democratic Party?" *Bronx Chronicle*, February 19. https://thebronxchronicle.com.

Roberts, Sam. 2006. "New York City Losing Blacks, Census Shows." *New York Times*, April 3. https://www.nytimes.com.

———. 2014. "Influx of African Immigrants Shifting National and New York Demographics." *New York Times*, September 2. https://www.nytimes.com.

Rodriguez, J., R. Hawkins, and A. Wilkes. 2019. "Social Capital: Social Capital, Gentrification, and Inequality in New York City." Chapter 15 in *Racial Inequality in New York City since 1965*, edited by B. P. Bowser and C. Devadutt. Albany, NY: SUNY Press.

Rodríguez, Néstor P. 1987. "Undocumented Central Americans in Houston: Diverse Populations." *International Migration Review* 21 (1): 4–26.

Sales, William W., Jr., and Rod Bush. 2000. "The Political Awakening of Blacks and Latinos in New York City: Competition or Cooperation?" In "Race, Class, and State Crime." Special issue, *Social Justice* 27 (1): 19–42.

Sander, Thomas, ed. 2012. "About Social Capital." The Saguaro Seminar: Civic Engagement in America. John F. Kennedy School of Government at Harvard University. http://www.hks.harvard.edu/programs/saguaro/about-social-capital.

———. 2015. "What Is Social Capital 2015—a Review." Updated version with a statement of Thomas Sander from Harvard Kennedy School from January 12. Project: World Social Capital Monitor.

Sandoval, Edgar. 2019. "Bronx Girl Seen Kidnapped in Video Admits It Was a Hoax, Official Says." *New York Times*, December 18. https://www.nytimes.com.

Schudel, Matt. 2012. "Thomas M. Zuniga, D.C. Housing Official and Consultant." Obituaries. *Washington Post*, October 12. https://www.washingtonpost.com.

Segura, Gary, Chris Garcia, Rodolfo de la Garza, and Harry Pachon. 1999. "Social Capital and the Latino Community." Research report. Claremont, CA: Tomás Rivera Policy Institute.

Segura, Gary M., Harry Potion, and Nathan D. Woods. 2003. "Hispanics, Social Capital and Civic Engagement." *National Civic Review* 90 (1): 85–97.

Selected Passenger and Crew Lists and Manifests. 2008. The National Archives at Washington, D.C. Available on Ancestry.com.

Sequeira, Robbie. 2021. "Bronx's Garifuna Community Is Finding Pathways to Vaccination." *Bronx Times Reporter*, September 17–23. www.bxtimes.com.

Servio, B. Harry. 1996. "Punta Rock, Garifuna Power." *Garifuna Quarterly Magazine* 1 (2): 22.

SHANY Corp. Humanitarian Organization. Accessed February 26, 2021. www.sociedadh.com.

Shaw-Taylor, Y., and S. A. Tuch, eds. 2007. *The Other African Americans: Contemporary African and Caribbean Immigrants in the United States*. New York: Rowman and Littlefield.

Sierra, Jorge. 2021. "Mirtha Colón, más de 50 años de lucha por los garífunas desde EEUU." *Proceso Digital*, April 11. https://proceso.hn/mirtha-colon-mas-de-50-anos-de-lucha-por-los-garifunas-desde-eeuu/.

Skelly, Richard J. 2013. "'Extinct' Culture Takes Center Stage at Folk Fest." *Princeton Info*, April 23. www.princetoninfo.com.

Skurnik, Jerry. 2017. "Who's Running in the 2017 New York City Primary Elections—Bronx Guide." *Bronx Chronicle*, July 18. https://thebronxchronicle.com.

Small, Eddie. 2014. "Bronx Garifuna Coalition Gets $20k in City Funds to Strengthen the Culture." South Bronx, Arts & Entertainment, DNAinfo, July 31. www.dnainfo.com.

———. 2016. "Turn in a Gun for $200 in The Bronx Next Weekend." *DNA Info*, July 27. www.dnainfo.com.

Smith, Rose-Ann. 2016. "Social Capital and Rural Resilience among the Garifuna Communities in Northeastern St. Vincent." In *Global Change and the Caribbean: Adaptation and Resilience*, edited by D. Barker, D. McGregor, K. Rhiney, and T. Edwards. Kingston, Jamaica: University of the West Indies Press.

Smithsonian Folkways Recordings. 2020. Garifuna Music. Smithsonian Institute, Washington, D.C. www.folkways.si.edu 2020.

SOA Watch. 2022a. "Congressional Delegation Visit to the Fraternal Black Organization of Honduras (OFRANEH)." School of the Americas Watch (website), December 4. www.soaw.org.

———. 2022b. "Members of Congress join Solidarity Organizations on a Fact-Finding Mission to Central America." School of the Americas Watch (website), April 4. www.soaw.org.

Soto, Juan Antonio. 2022. "How Houston's Afro-Latino Garifuna Community Is Keeping Its Culture Alive." Hispanic Heritage. *Houstonia*, September 28. https://www.houstoniamag.com/news-and-city-life/2022/09/houston-garifuna-population-and-culture.

SS *Texaco Oklahoma* Collection. 2005. MC 007 Records 1958–1971, Jack K. Williams Library, Texas A&M University at Galveston.

"The State of Black Immigrants." 2014. Part 1. Statistical Portrait of Black Immigrants in the United States. Part 2. Black Immigrants in the Mass Criminalization System. NYU Law Immigrant Rights Clinic, Black Alliance for Just Immigration. 2014 data.

Straughan, Jerome F. 2004. "Belizean Immigrants in Los Angeles." PhD diss., University of Southern California.

Stroud, Rick. 2020. "Bucs' Rakeem Nunez-Roches Is Talking Trash and Backing It Up." *Tampa Bay Times*, August 31. www.tampabay.com.

Suazo, Salvador. 2012. "Honduras Ha Sido Gobernada Por Mandatarios Garifunas." *El Libertador*, April. Tegucigalpa, Honduras p.63.

Sundstrom, Mark. 2020. "Woman, 61, Shot in Leg When Caught in Crossfire of Bronx Gunfight: Police." *PIX 11*, August 20. https://pix11.com.

Swain, Liz. 2000. "Garifuna Americans." *Gale Encyclopedia of Multicultural America*, edited by Jeffrey Lehman. 2nd ed. Vol. 1: 686–97. Detroit: Gale.

Swan, L. Alex. 1971. "The Harlem and Detroit Riots of 1943: A Comparative Analysis." *Berkeley Journal of Sociology* 16 (7): 75–93.

Taylor, Christopher. 2012. *The Black Carib Wars: Freedom, Survival, and the Making of the Garifuna*. Jackson: University of Mississippi Press.

Taylor, Douglas M. 1951. *The Black Carib of British Honduras*. New York: Wenner-Gren Foundation for Anthropological Research.

———. 1963. *The Black Carib of British Honduras*. Johnson Reprint.

Thevenot, C. G. 2012. "Las Vegas Council Renames Freedom, Doolittle Parks." *Las Vegas Review-Journal*, May 6. www.reviewjournal.com.

Thorne, Eva T. 2004a. "Ethnic and Race-Based Political Organization and Mobilization in Latin America: Lessons for Public Policy." Working Paper presented at the conference Inter-Agency Consultation on Race in Latin America, Washington, D.C. http://www.thedialogue.org/iac/eng/pubs/other_pubs.html.

———. 2004b. "Land Rights and Garífuna Identity." NACLA, Report on Race, Part I. (September–October).

Tuttle, Carlson John. 2012. *Bibliographical Collection on the Garifuna People*. Caye Caulker, Belize: Producciones de la Hamaca.

Twinn, Paul. 2006. "Land Ownership and the Construction of Carib Identity in St. Vincent." Chapter 5 in *Indigenous Resurgence in the Contemporary Caribbean: Amerindian Survival and Revival*, edited by Maximillian C. Forte. New York: Peter Lang.

UNIA Timeline. The Official Website of the Universal Negro Improvement Association and African Communities League. Accessed June 6, 2023. https://www.unia-aclgovernment.com/100-years-of-marcus-mosiah-garvey/.

United Negro Improvement Association (UNIA). 1945. The UNIA Rehabilitating Committee hosts a Mass Meeting at their Liberty Hall 2395 8th St , NY, NY. Cleophus Jacobs is Secretary. *New York Amsterdam News*, June 23, 1945.

United Negro Improvement Association and African Communities League (UNIA-ACL). 2019. "History of the Flag." Accessed March 22, 2019. www.theunia-acl.com.

United States Citizenship and Immigration Services (USCIS). 2007. "Temporary Protected Status." Washington, D.C.: U.S. Department of Homeland Security. Accessed February 22, 2008. www.uscis.gov.

U.S. Census Bureau. 2010. U.S. Census Bureau. Bureau of Census, Washington, D.C. Accessed September 30, 2018. www.census.gov.

———. 2013. U.S. Census Bureau. Bureau of Census, Washington, D.C. Accessed September 30, 2018. www.census.gov.

Vad, Jesse. 2020. "Garifuna Community Services, Virus Hampers Efforts at Full Census Count." *Hunts Point Express*, March 13. www.huntspointexpress.com.

Valdés, Javier H. 2015. "Gregoria Flores, United States." *Americas Quarterly*, July 28. https://www.americasquarterly.org/fulltextarticle/gregoria-flores-united-states/.

Valentine, Jerris J. 2002. *The Garifuna Understanding of Death*. Dangriga: National Garifuna Council of Belize.

Valentine, Murphy. 2003. "Centro America Show celebrando 10 años en el aire!" Garinet, September 4. https://www.garinet.com.

Van Sertima, Ivan. 1976. *They Came before Columbus: The African Presence in Ancient America*. New York: Random House.

Vargas-Ramos, C. 2003. "The Political Participation of Puerto Ricans in New York City." *Centro Journal* 15 (1).

VCU News. 2021. "School of Medicine Ph.D. Candidate Uses National Fellowship to Advance Goal of Reducing Health Disparities." Virginia Commonwealth University (VCU) News, December 16. https://news.vcu.edu/article/2021/12/phd-candidate-uses-national-fellowship-to-advance-goal-of-reducing-health-disparities.

Waldman, Amy. 2000. "Housing Radical Meets Bottom Line; In the Rebuilt South Bronx, A Pioneer of Sweat Equity Fights to Keep His Ideals." *New York Times*, January 18, B1.

Walker, Simon, and Rosalia Reyes. 2017. "Chapter Eight Central Americans in New York." In *Latinos in New York: Communities in Transition*, edited by Sherrie Baver, Angelo Falcón, and Gabriel Haslip-Viera. 2nd ed. Notre Dame, IN: University of Notre Dame Press.

Wall, Patrick. 2012a. "Honduran Soccer League Can't Use New Crotona Park Field They Fought For." *DNA info*, May 31. https://www.dnainfo.com.

———. 2012b. "No Bathrooms, No Water for Ferry Point Park-Goers." *DNA info*, July 5. https://www.dnainfo.com.

———. 2013a. "Four Members of Bronx African Community Vie for a Single City Council Seat." *DNA info*, January 22. https://www.dnainfo.com.

———. 2013b. "Friends Form Company to Bring Garifuna Music to the World." *DNA info*, August 9. Accessed January 9, 2021. https://www.dnainfo.com.
Washburn, Gary. 2020. "Former Celtic Milt Palacio Still Mystified by News Story Reporting His Death." *Boston Globe*, January 11. www.bostonglobe.com.
Waters, M. C. 2001. *Black Identities: West Indian Immigrant Dreams and American Realities*. Boston: Harvard University Press.
Webster, Nancy, and David Shirley. 2016. *A History of Brooklyn Bridge Park: How a Community Reclaimed and Transformed New York City's Waterfront*. New York: Columbia University Press.
WHRDAlert Honduras. 2019. "Assailants Kill Mirna Teresa Suazo, Community Leader and Garifuna Territorial Defender." Iniciativa Mesoamericana de Mujeres Defensoras de Derechos Humanos/Mesoamerican Initiative of Women Human Rights Defenders, September 10. (Accessed March 22, 2022). https://www.im-defensoras.org.
Wilkinson, Tracy. 2013. "Johnny Laboriel Dies at 71: Mexican Rock 'N' Roll Star." *Los Angeles Times*, September 19. https://www.latimes.com.
Wilson, Samuel M. 1993. "The Cultural Mosaic of the Indigenous Caribbean." *Proceedings of the British Academy* 81:37–66.
Wirsing, Robert. 2017. "Electeds Celebrate Abrazo Garifuna in New York." *Bronx Times*, April 4. https://www.bxtimes.com.
Wong, J. 2001. "The New Dynamics of Immigrants' Political Incorporation: A Multi-Method Study of Political Participation and Mobilization among Asian and Latino Immigrants in the United States." PhD diss., Yale University.
Wrathall, David J. 2012. "Migration amidst Social-Ecological Regime Shift: The Search for Stability in Garífuna Villages of Northern Honduras." *Human Ecology* 40 (4): 583–96.
Wright Austin, Sharon D. 2018. *The Caribbeanization of Black Politics: Race, Group Consciousness, and Political Participation in America*. Albany, NY: SUNY Press.
Yonow, T., et al. 2019. "Black Sigatoka in Bananas: Ecoclimatic Suitability and Disease Pressure Assessments." *PLoS ONE* 14 (8): e0220601. https://doi.org/10.1371/journal.pone.0220601.
Zambito, Thomas. 2006. "An American Nightmare." *New York Daily News*, April 5. https://www.nydailynews.com.
Zéphir, Flore. 1996. *Haitian Immigrants in Black America: A Sociological and Sociolinguistic Portrait*. Westport, CT: Bergin and Garvey.
———. 2004. *The Haitian Americans*. Westport, CT: Greenwood.

INDEX

Abrazo Garifuna, 137–38, 182, 258
Abrazos Garifuna event, 145
activists, 24, 86, 168, 170–72, 233n43, 234n4
African American and Latino candidates, 25, 119
African Americans, viii–ix, 1, 3, 5–6, 13, 16–20, 23, 25, 51, 53, 57–58, 62–63, 94, 131–33, 152–53, 180–82, 185
African Communities League (ACL), 58, 257
Africans, 2, 17, 19, 26, 28–29, 38, 91, 111, 115, 221n2, 246
Afro-Central Americans in New York City, 246
Afro-Hondurans, 37, 116
Afro-Latinos, 114–16, 251, 255
AIDS, 121, 125, 127, 129, 139, 144, 157, 217, 231n6, 231n20
AIDS organization, 106, 122–23, 162, 166
Albany, 134–35, 144–45, 174, 232n23, 233n40, 255, 258
albums, 65, 81, 87–88, 225n22, 226n15, 228n40, 236n3
Americas, 28–29, 45, 52, 114–15, 199, 201, 232n24, 236n13, 238, 245–46, 251, 255, 258

ancestors, 3, 27–28, 45, 55, 89–90, 95, 102–4, 135, 177–78, 185, 249
annual New York City Hispanic parade, 14
Aranda, Theodore, 114–15, 157–58, 238
arrival, 2, 15, 61–62, 65, 134, 160, 190–209
Arrivillaga Cortés, Alfonso, 34, 36, 47, 238
associations, 5, 18, 53, 55, 60–61, 63, 67, 86, 88, 90, 224n4
asylum, political, 10, 165–66
Ávila, José, 77–78, 96–97, 103, 115–16, 127–29, 134, 136–37, 139–40, 142–43, 145–46, 149, 157, 160–64, 176–77, 216, 239–40
Avila, Victor R., 52, 55, 57, 224n1, 224n3, 224n10, 226n6

Balliceaux, 32, 177, 250
bands, 38, 66–67, 78, 95, 228n48, 226n12
basements, 83–84, 95, 102
beaches, 22, 47, 65, 245
Being Garifuna, 106, 155
Believers Mennonite Garifuna Ministries, 104, 172
Belize, 1–3, 8, 21, 23, 33–35, 37, 45–47, 57–58, 82, 88–89, 99, 108–11, 157–60, 172–73, 180–81, 230n15, 234n3, 242–43, 247–49, 254, 257

259

Belizean Garifuna, 7–8, 11, 15, 24, 63, 66–67, 77, 81–82, 87, 94, 99, 103, 105, 107, 114–15, 125, 128, 137, 139, 181, 228n40, 229n52
Belizean Garifuna Mennonite, 99
Belizean organization National Garifuna Council, 160
Belize City, 9, 173, 243
Belize Honduran Association, 63
Black, 16–19, 29–30, 33, 35, 43–45, 51–54, 61–62, 65, 72, 75, 77, 131, 146–47, 180, 239, 250–51
Black Americans, viii, 5, 12–13, 19–20, 26, 79, 146, 151, 185, 189
Black Caribs, 2, 22, 28–32, 56, 63, 65, 157, 240, 250, 225n22, 240, 256–57
Black ethnic groups, 3–6, 26, 152, 185, 189, 248
Black Fraternal Organization of Honduras (OFRANEH), 9, 86, 122, 148, 159, 163–64, 166, 168–69, 171–72, 231n5, 256
Black Hondurans, 79, 86, 116
Black immigrants, 1, 3–4, 6, 16–17, 19–20, 23, 25, 51, 53, 132, 155, 244, 249, 256
Black organizations, 94, 158
Blacks and Latinos, 12, 51, 94, 123, 132–33, 253, 255
Bloomberg, Michael R., 244
Bodoma and Budari Garifuna Cultural Group, 109, 230n15
British, 2, 28–29, 31–35, 107, 177
British Honduras, 1, 23, 34–35, 41, 43–47, 49–52, 56–58, 60, 63, 66–67, 81, 252, 256–57
Bronx, 62–63, 65–66, 69–70, 72–75, 88–89, 97–99, 101–8, 110–14, 127–30, 132–38, 141–44, 149–51, 153, 156, 166–67, 183, 229n1, 229n9, 236n10, 244–45, 252–53
Bronx borough president, 141, 145, 149, 151, 216, 234n7
Bronx Community Board, 97, 136, 143, 215–16, 233n41
Bronx Democratic Party, 215, 255
Bronx Garifuna Church Community Center, 140–41

Brooklyn, 4–5, 62–63, 81–84, 88–89, 98–99, 103–4, 107–8, 110–12, 132, 137, 180–81, 187, 222n11, 229n54, 229n7
Brooklyn Record, 63–64, 241
Bulnes, Cresencio, 123, 124, 166–67
Burke, Biarni, 152–53, 186–87, 241, 248
businesses, 27, 55–56, 93, 139–40, 143, 158, 161, 163, 182–83, 231n13

candidates, 5, 46, 115, 133, 137, 142, 145–47, 149–51, 153, 233n35, 257
Carib American Association, 52, 55–61, 63, 65–70, 76, 81, 84, 223n14, 224n1, 224n2, 224n6, 227n31
Caribbean, vii–viii, 1–2, 17–18, 22, 28–29, 32, 111–12, 115–6, 131, 222n11, 240, 243, 247, 251
Caribbean Coast, 2, 23, 41–50, 54, 170, 223n1
Caribbean Community (CARICOM), 168, 173, 177, 235n18
Carib Community Association, 81–82
Carib Development Society (CDS), 46, 57
Carib Disembarkation Day, 45, 57
Carib International Society (CIS), 46, 57
Caribes, 35, 226n9, 226n15, 228n40, 247
Caribs, 29–34, 36, 40, 46, 56, 77, 83, 175, 240
Casa Yurumein, 106, 107, 109, 122–23, 137, 139, 144, 146, 149, 230n15, 231n6, 231n16, 235n15, 237, 242
Castro, Celso, 86–87, 218, 227n23, 227n25, 227n30, 228n37, 228n38
Castro, Efraim, 83, 85–86, 227n23, 227n24, 227n25, 227n31
census, 21, 116, 135–36, 143, 179, 233n39, 246, 255, 257
Central America, 2, 9, 21–23, 25, 33, 35–44, 47, 49–51, 56, 58–60, 88–91, 93–96, 98–99, 103–4, 111–12, 114–15, 147–49, 155–79, 182–85, 237–38, 234n48
Central American, 7–8, 11, 13, 22–24, 34–35, 40–41, 44–46, 77–78, 111–14, 121–22, 140, 156, 183–84, 186, 189–90
Central American Black Organization (CABO), 116, 122, 158, 167, 234n3

Central American Day Parade, 134, 230n19, 253
Central American Federation, 36
Central American Independence Parade, 113–14
Centro America, 102–3, 108, 120, 179, 257
Chief Joseph Chatoyer Garifuna Folkloric Ballet, 105, 109, 231n20
children, 7–8, 44, 47, 67, 91, 120, 127, 176, 186, 233n32
city, 1–5, 11–14, 17–18, 21, 24–26, 41–43, 51–54, 60–63, 72–75, 97–101, 107–10, 118–21, 125–29, 131–35, 147–49, 156–59, 174–76, 182–84, 186–89, 232n25
City College, 66, 103, 108, 227n28
city council, 124, 133, 142, 145, 150–52, 252
City Hall, 149, 252
city of Trujillo, 222n12
City University, 107, 120, 157
City University of New York (CUNY), 107, 120, 157
civil rights period, 73, 75, 132
classification, ethnic, 24, 114–17
Clotter, Hermenegildo, 48–49
Club Cangrejeros, 67–68, 80, 227n19
Colon, Sandra, 84, 86
Colon, Teofilo, 89, 97, 104, 106, 111–12, 114, 136, 138, 144, 187
Colón, Mirtha, 48, 88, 96, 107, 110, 121–23, 137, 167, 179, 243, 251
communities, 2–5, 10–13, 15–17, 19–26, 40–43, 72–76, 78–82, 90, 99–100, 102–4, 114–20, 122–30, 136–37, 141, 143–44, 149–55, 158, 161–64, 170–73, 179–80, 182–84, 188–90
Congress, 146–48, 150, 168, 173, 224n16, 255
Congressional Black Caucus, 147–48, 235n12
coup, 9–10, 168–69, 233n43, 238
Creole Blacks, 44–45
Crew Lists, 49–50, 52, 56, 59, 61–62, 209, 224n2, 226n7, 226n8, 253, 255
crime, 93, 125, 127, 151, 153, 165
Crotona Park, 101, 110, 112–13, 136–37, 229n1

culture, 2–4, 9–13, 15, 19–20, 22–25, 27–38, 63, 73, 83–84, 87–88, 94, 97–98, 100–102, 104–5, 107–10, 115–17, 133–34, 137, 155, 174–76, 246–47, 256

dance groups, 24, 96, 99, 101, 103–4, 107–110, 113, 117, 143, 166
Dangriga Development Association, 81–82, 88, 98
deaths, 10, 21, 54–55, 95, 131, 171, 241–42, 252, 257–58
Deferred Action for Childhood Arrivals (DACA), 123
Democratic Party, 18, 72, 75, 131–33, 146, 233n35
diaspora, 105, 177, 244, 246
Díaz Jr., Rubén, 112, 134
Díaz Sr., Rubén, 124, 137–39, 142, 145–46, 245
discrimination, viii, 3, 8, 16–18, 20, 26, 41, 44, 52–54, 72–73, 151, 153
districts, 72, 120, 124, 134, 140, 145–48, 150–51, 153, 231n21, 252
dugu, 38, 89, 174

education, 4, 9–10, 16–18, 96, 119–20, 126, 133, 136, 138, 140, 168, 173, 187–89
voter, 137, 152, 248
elected officials, 113, 131–32, 154, 190
elections, 11, 83, 133, 142, 144–46, 149, 152, 216, 246, 248, 252
ethnic group, 1–5, 9–10, 13, 24, 34–35, 60, 77–78, 91, 95–96, 98–102, 105, 107, 115–16, 129–30, 141, 145–46, 148–49, 152–53, 171–72, 182–83, 185–86
ethnicity, 13, 18, 45, 63, 70, 146, 152, 179–80, 206, 246, 254
Evangelical Garifuna Church, 98–99, 141, 183, 229n53
Evangelical Garifuna Council of Churches (EGCC), 125–26, 138, 141, 159, 174–75, 231n10, 235n21

Federation of Honduran Organizations of New York, (FEDHONY), 13–14, 97, 119–21, 125, 127–28, 217, 230n3, 230n4
Fenix Social Club, 69–71, 84

Flores, Gregoria, 140–41, 164–67, 181, 258
folkloric, 21, 24, 96, 101, 107, 109–10, 113, 117, 166
forums, 69–70, 90, 104, 142, 156–57, 160, 169–70, 233n32, 235n15
Francisco, José, 212, 216, 218, 240
Frente Unido Hondureño (FUH), 82–84, 86–87, 157, 227n29

García, Centeno, 33, 35–36, 42–43, 223n4, 223n6, 223n10, 243
Garcia, Victor Virgilio Lopez, 3, 12–13, 84, 99, 102, 106, 110–11, 115, 120, 157–59, 163
Garifuna Afro-Latino Entertainment (GALENT), 106, 139, 143, 216, 218, 230n12, 233n33, 239–40
Garifuna American Heritage Foundation United (GAHFU), 104, 230n10
Garifuna American Heritage Month, 103, 134, 140, 150–51, 142, 150, 232n22, 232n25
Garifuna American Law Enforcement Association, 115, 138, 149
Garifuna American Legislative Day, 134–35, 182
Garifuna American Veterans Association, 115, 138
Garifuna Amerindian, 114, 116
Garifuna anthem, 27, 95
Garifuna choreographer Crisanto Armando Melendez, 94, 109
Garifuna churches, 126, 141
Garifuna Coalition, 97, 105–6, 115, 126–31, 133–40, 142–47, 149–50, 160–62, 175, 231n11, 231n17, 233n31, 233n40, 239–40, 250
Garifuna communities, 13–15, 21–23, 46, 51–69, 72–73, 97–99, 106–7, 120–22, 124–26, 139, 141–43, 146–49, 151–52, 160–63, 166–71, 174–77, 179–80, 182–83, 185–86, 222n12
Garifuna Community Services, 140–41, 143, 147, 166, 257
Garifuna Council, 127, 157–58, 217
Garifuna Cultural Museum, 243
Garifuna Cultural Performance Arts, 108
Garifuna culture, 24, 75, 77, 80, 84, 87, 90–91, 97–98, 102–3, 106, 108–10, 113, 125, 127, 158, 160, 237, 239
Garifunadao, 23, 74–84, 86–100, 225n34
Garifuna Day, 120, 125, 156
Garifuna Diaspora, 83, 188, 246
Garifuna families, 7, 62, 91, 112, 118
Garifuna flags, 47, 183, 186, 247
Garifuna folkloric and music groups, 103, 107, 108 110, 143
Garifuna food, 106, 114, 182
Garifuna for Christ Ministries committee group, 175
Garifuna groups, 24–25, 75, 83, 88, 108, 116, 138, 143, 145–46, 155, 157, 159, 163, 175, 177
Garifuna Heritage, 120, 233n37
Garifuna Heritage Day in New York City, 233n36
Garifuna Heritage Month, 107, 140, 147, 232n25, 239–40
Garifuna History, 2, 28, 142, 243
Garifuna House, 127, 217
Garifuna identity, 12, 37–38, 40, 107, 114–15, 179, 185, 249
Garifuna immigrants, 4–5, 8, 10–11, 15, 53, 70, 94, 125–26, 140, 164–65, 183, 185 253
Garifuna International Promotions (GIP), 102
Garifuna Kids, 96, 102, 239
Garifuna lands, 123, 165–66, 169, 171–72, 252
Garifuna language, vii–viii, 20–21, 24, 27, 40, 77–79, 82, 89, 91, 94–96, 98–99, 121, 125, 176, 179
Garifuna leaders, 21–22, 115–16, 127, 137, 149, 153–54, 162, 166–67, 169–70, 230n4, 234n47
Garifuna leagues, 101, 110, 229n1
Garifuna Mennonite Mission (GMM), 126
Garifuna migration, 2, 7, 22, 40, 88, 90, 164–66
Garifuna music, 37–38, 65, 79, 81, 83, 102, 105–6, 108, 124, 155, 231n9, 235n10, 239, 256

INDEX · 263

Garifuna Nation, 162, 167–68, 171, 173, 176, 235n11, 235n12, 235n18, 235n19, 247, 254
Garifuna organizations, 1, 9–10, 12–13, 15, 20–21, 23–26, 45, 52, 69, 77, 97–100, 104–5, 113, 117, 119–21, 126–30, 137–38, 140, 143–47, 149–52, 154, 158–60, 167–69, 172, 177–79, 184, 223n10
Garifuna origins, 22, 96, 114, 116–17
Garifuna Political Action Committee (GAPAC), 129, 145–46
Garifuna population, 7, 9–10, 12, 75, 94, 120, 122, 126–27, 134–35, 137–39, 150, 182, 184–85, 221n2, 222n6
Garifuna seamen, 6, 23, 47–50, 52–53, 57, 59–62, 76–77, 99, 191
Garifuna Settlement, 2, 23, 77, 94, 232n24, 232n25, 238, 247
Garifuna Settlement Day, 45, 57, 77, 104, 120, 226n10, 229n8–9
Garifuna soccer clubs, 91, 101, 110–11, 117, 137
Garifuna Veterans of America Organization, 244
Garifuna woman, 3, 57, 74, 96–97, 99, 159, 165, 187
Garifuna Women for Progress in Education, 96
Garifuna World, 127, 155, 217
Garinagu Ethnic Group Action Committee (GEGAC), 152
Gibson, Vanessa, 139, 142–43, 149, 151, 164
Gomez, Pablo, 113
Gonsalves, Ralph Everard, 173, 235n18, 235n19, 254
Gonzalez, Nancie L. Solien, 11, 33–36, 42, 48–49, 67, 77, 88, 98–99, 229n52, 234n4, 247
Gotay, Carlos, 98, 102
government, 9, 158–59, 161, 165, 168, 171, 175–77, 221n4, 223n10, 255, 259
Grenadines, 14, 28, 106, 157, 167, 173–78, 228n42, 243, 254
Grenadines, Inc. (GIPSVG), 174–75, 235n21

groups, 4, 12–15, 17–26, 28–29, 52–54, 56–58, 81–84, 86–88, 95–97, 99, 101–2, 104, 108–10, 120–27, 137, 145–47, 151, 157–60, 166–67, 173–74, 183–85, 215, 221n2
Guatemala, 1–2, 6–8, 14–15, 34–37, 40–42, 44–46, 48–51, 53, 89, 110–11, 157–60, 172, 193, 237–38
Guatemalan Garifuna, 7–8, 60, 66, 88, 96, 184, 189, 217, 222n6, 227n20, 228n41
Guatemalan Garifuna Organization, 127

Haitians, 5, 16, 18–19, 147, 152, 221n2, 250, 254, 258
Hamalali Wayunagu Garifuna Dance Company, 105–6
HAMPAC (Honduran Political Action Committee), 128–29, 234n7
Happy Land, 102, 120, 123, 156, 185, 251
Harlem, 17, 23, 47, 50–54, 56–58, 62, 65, 69–70, 73, 78, 83
hometown associations, 2, 4, 18, 42, 86–87, 99, 184, 228n33, 254
Honduran Active Society of New York, 123
Honduran American Association, 54–55, 79
Honduran American Cultural Association, 97, 128
Honduran and Central American Bronx Day Parade, 114
Honduran army, 67, 227n26
Honduran Congress, 169–70, 234n5
Honduran Football and Social Club, 70, 72, 79–80, 84, 91–92
Honduran government, 9, 43, 94, 116, 128, 148, 156, 161–65, 168, 170–71, 234n5
Honduran Parade Committee, 113–14, 125, 218
Honduran politics, 124, 166
Honduran president, 162, 211, 223n4, 235n18
Hondurans, non-Garifuna, 83, 112, 120
Honduran Social Circle club, 67, 69, 78–79
Honduras, 1–2, 6–7, 9–10, 12–15, 33–34, 40–43, 45–49, 51–53, 55–62, 82–84, 86–87, 109–11, 121–23, 147–49, 157–70, 211–13, 238–41, 243, 246–52, 255–56
Honduras Centro America, 235n1, 247

Honduras Imperial Social Club, 79–80
Honduras Remittances, 161, 248
Honduras Soccer Club, 79–80
human rights, 25, 148, 156, 164–65, 168–69, 171, 173, 178, 235n16, 240, 249

identity, viii–ix, 2, 4, 6, 12, 15, 24, 38, 40, 53, 55, 75–102, 107, 109, 116–17, 125, 185, 216, 218, 240, 245, 247–48
Illagulei, 103, 108
immigrant groups, 2, 4, 6, 16–17, 19–20, 23, 90, 183
immigration, 11, 93, 129, 140–41, 143, 149, 190, 245, 248, 256
Indigenous Organizations of Honduras, 9
indigenous populations, 44–45, 165
institutions, international, 148, 161–63
International Garifuna Council, (IGC), 152–53, 234n45
International Honduran and Central American Day Parade, 230n19
Iseri Imenigi Garifuna Cultural Dance Group, 113
island, 2, 22, 27–28, 30–32, 44, 167, 174–77

Jaime, Celso 99

La Ceiba, 41–42, 45, 160, 163, 167, 170, 205–7, 209, 211–12, 222n12, 223n4, 223n5, 241
Lambert, Aida, 12, 71, 80, 225n28, 227n19, 227n20, 227n23, 227n28
Lambert, Alejandro, 60, 62–63, 65, 223n8, 224n10, 224n15, 224n17, 225n21, 225n23, 225n24, 225n31, 225n32, 228n34
Lambert, Amado, 83–84, 227n23, 227n31
land, 28, 31–32, 42, 50–51, 53, 60, 74, 76, 98–99, 148, 159–60, 162, 164, 168, 171–72, 174, 178
land abuses, 148, 168
Latin America, 63, 70, 116, 148, 169, 235n13, 237–38, 243, 248, 255, 257
Latino communities, 16, 99, 129, 131, 180
Latinos, viii–ix, 1, 3–4, 11–12, 23, 51, 72, 94, 100–101, 103, 107–8, 113, 115, 132–33, 231n15

Latinos in New York, 13, 14, 240, 249, 258
Long Island, 53, 65, 83, 223n9, 224n3, 224n8, 225n32
Los Angeles, 3, 7, 11, 66, 75, 77–78, 99, 105, 156–57, 181, 232n25, 253, 256
Louisiana, 50, 52, 61–62, 126, 224n10

Malcolm X, 66, 83
Manhattan, 63, 65, 67, 70, 79–80, 111–12, 118, 222n11, 228n35, 229n1, 241, 247
Marin, Juan, 70
Martinez, Juan, 49–50, 53, 58, 61, 66, 224n3, 224n10, 226n4, 226n5, 226n6, 227n26
Martinez, Timothy, 55, 57–58, 60–62, 67, 80, 84, 192, 223n14, 224n1, 224n10, 225n2
meetings, 58, 83–84, 86, 128–30, 136, 138, 153, 157–60, 162, 164, 168, 170, 172–73, 225n28, 231n6
Mena, René, 70, 80, 91–92, 225n28, 225n29, 225n30, 225n33, 226n17, 228n47
merchant marines, 59–60
mestizos, 37, 43–45, 113, 122, 172
Miami, 3, 17, 126, 162, 181
migration, 2, 6–8, 10–11, 15, 17, 40, 148, 156, 164–65, 245, 247
Migration waves, 7, 10, 17, 101, 167
minority groups, 1, 4, 26, 131, 189
Miranda, Felix, 98, 120–21, 157, 217, 234n3
Miranda, Miriam, 169–70, 235n14
Miskitos, 33–35
MUGAMA, 96, 120, 127, 211, 217, 228n50
music, 3, 6, 37–38, 75, 78, 81, 84, 88–89, 95, 101–17, 226n15, 229n2, 229n55, 230n12, 234n2, 236n4, 242

National African American Reparations Commission (NAARC), 177
National Garifuna Council (NGC), 46, 158, 160, 173, 223n12, 242, 254, 257
National Maritime Union (NMU), 52–53, 59, 76, 225n3

networks, 14, 16–17, 20–21, 24, 75, 143, 244–45
New Orleans, 11–12, 50, 52, 56, 61–62, 126–27, 129, 135, 224n10, 231n15, 232n26
New York, 2–5, 10–11, 13–14, 16–17, 50–55, 57–58, 60–61, 76–82, 86–99, 103–5, 121–23, 132–35, 137, 140–41, 150–51, 156–59, 166–68, 173–76, 192–209, 226n18, 227n22, 229n53, 230n19, 232n22, 235n20, 236n10, 237–42, 247–58, 253
New York City, vii–ix, 1–5, 10–14, 16–20, 23–25, 49–53, 60, 62, 65–67, 74–76, 86–87, 90–91, 94–97, 107–10, 115–54, 156–60, 164–67, 175–80, 245–50, 253–55
New York City Department of Education, 120, 136
New York City Garifuna, 14, 87, 114, 128, 139, 155–56, 160, 162, 175–76, 184
New York City Hispanic Chamber of Commerce, 139
New York City Mennonite Central Committee, 140
New York Daily News, 237, 241–42, 247, 252, 254, 258
New York Garifuna, 11–12, 123, 129
New York Hispanic Clergy Association, 138, 154
New York State Assembly, 4–5, 122, 134, 137, 142, 150, 153, 231n19, 253
New York State Department of State, 63, 69, 81–84, 224n6, 225n29, 228n50, 229n53, 231n7, 236n10, 236n11, 253
New York State Passenger and Crew Lists, 209, 253
New York State Senate, 124, 138, 144–45, 150, 232n22, 245
New York Times, 131, 136, 239, 241, 246–47, 251, 255, 257
New York University (NYU), 170
Nicaragua, 1–3, 7, 13, 36–37, 40, 42, 44–45, 158, 160, 221n4, 245, 248
Nicaraguan Garifuna, 14, 44
Nunez, Andrew, 99

Organization for Ethnic Community Development (ODECO), 116, 121–22, 127, 163, 167–69, 217, 231n5
Organization of African Unity (OAU), 173
organizations, 5, 13–15, 21–27, 56–58, 69, 77–79, 81–84, 86–87, 96–99, 106–8, 113–23, 125–29, 138–39, 146–47, 152–54, 156–59, 163–64, 166–68, 173–74, 184–85, 188–89

Palacio, Joseph O., 2–3, 6, 9, 29, 34, 40, 77, 89, 152, 181, 232n26, 253
Pan-Garifuna Afro-Latino Power, 115, 218, 240
parade, 113–14, 137
performances, 32, 103–5, 107, 110, 142, 254
Political Action Committee (PAC), 128–29, 145–46, 215
political participation, 13, 20, 130, 137–38, 141, 189–90, 249, 257–58
politics, 18, 119, 132, 146, 153, 190, 243, 247–48, 251
population, 1–2, 4, 8–11, 14, 23, 28, 37, 44, 72–73, 75, 78, 122, 183, 189–90, 245
proclamation, 32, 120, 134, 232n25, 232n26
program, 120, 122–23, 130, 138–39, 141, 143, 157, 159, 229n5, 229n6, 229n7, 229n9, 230n10, 230n11, 230n13, 231n10
Prometra Garifuna Society, 97, 158, 160
Puerto Barrios, 41–42, 44–45, 53, 191, 193–94, 200–201, 222n6
Puerto Castilla, 49, 51, 56, 192
Puerto Cortés, 42–43, 47–49, 61, 162, 192–96, 200, 203–6, 208, 211, 223n8, 223n13, 223n14, 224n5, 224n8, 224n9, 224n13, 224n14, 224n15, 224n17, 225n21, 228n34
Puerto Ricans, 62–63, 67, 72, 75, 110, 113, 118–19, 132–33, 137–38, 147, 149, 151, 224n10, 226n16
punta, 38, 95, 101, 103–4, 124
Punta Gorda, 41, 223n1, 223n10

race, 13, 45, 47, 146, 149, 165, 191, 194, 196, 244, 246–49, 254–55, 257–58

racism, 16, 19–20, 43, 50–53, 65, 70, 116, 188–89, 245
Ramos, Thomas Vincent, 45–47, 57, 103–4, 224n7, 229n9, 254
Ramos, Wellington, 81, 91, 167–68, 173, 176–77, 223n7, 228n43, 228n46, 235n11, 235n12, 235n19
Reflejos, 83, 227n23, 227n24
remittances, 161, 163, 189, 241, 248, 254
reparations, 156–58, 173, 177, 235n23, 238, 250
representatives, 75, 114, 122, 134, 137–38, 140–41, 143, 148, 160, 164, 173–74
resolution, 134, 148, 168, 171, 232n22, 232n25, 233n36
Roatan, 32, 34, 134
Ruiz, Francisco Yoba, 113

Saints Lutheran Parish, 234n1, 238
San Pedro Sula, 87, 170–72, 246
Santa Fe, 67, 87
seamen, 23, 48–50, 52–53, 58–61, 225n25
Selected Passenger and Crew Lists, 49–50, 52, 56, 59, 61–62
Sepulveda, Luis R., 142, 150
settlements, 2, 6–7, 33, 41, 131, 174
settlers, 31, 94
ships, 48–49, 51–53, 59, 76, 101, 123, 193
shipwreck, 28–29, 77
soccer leagues, 110–12, 229n1, 244
social capital, 15–17, 20, 222n7, 243, 245, 250, 255
Social Club, 63, 69–70, 72, 79–80, 84, 91–92, 226n18
social functions, 58, 60–61, 65, 96
social networks, 15–16, 20, 109
social organizations, 20, 24, 72–73, 101
social, services 4, 12, 119, 126, 130, 231n15, 231n17
Sociedad Honduras New York, 80, 227n20
Sociedad Hondureña Activa de New York (SHANY), 123–25, 138, 166, 231n7
Solis, Luz, 108, 126, 230n13
Solis, Rejil, 128
South Bronx, viii, 72, 93, 118, 130, 140, 150, 153, 237, 252, 256
Spaniards, 33–35

sports, 4, 24, 37, 75, 82, 91–92, 101–17, 176, 180–82, 229n55, 252
St. Vincent, 2, 14–15, 22, 25, 27–33, 40, 96, 106–7, 130, 155–57, 167, 173–78, 184–85, 248–50, 254
Suazo, Omar, 168
support, 5, 25, 81–82, 98, 112–14, 121, 123–24, 128–29, 134, 136–38, 140, 142–43, 146, 153–54, 159, 163, 166–67, 173–74

teams, 91, 110–12, 229n1
Tela, 41–42, 45, 49–50, 169, 192–93, 195–98, 202–3, 207, 222n12, 251, 254
Tela Bay, 162, 166–69
Tela Railroad Company, 42–43, 48–49
temple, 89–90
Temporary Protection Status, (TPS), 123, 126, 140–41, 147, 190, 221n4, 252–53
Tornabé, 162, 168, 223n2
Torres, Ritchie, 147–48
trade, 29–30, 33, 124
traditions, spiritual, 38, 77, 88, 90–91, 174
treaty, 29, 31–32
trip, 61, 65, 89, 148, 159, 175, 234n43, 234n4
Trujillo, 33–34, 41, 45, 49, 67, 70, 172, 222n12, 223n11

Unificación Cultural Garifuna, 127, 158, 217
United Fruit Company (UFCO), 42, 44, 49
United Garifuna Association (UGA), 81, 98, 114, 158, 172, 176, 235n17
United Negro Improvement Association (UNIA), 23, 45–47, 57–58, 257
United States, vii–viii, 1–8, 10–11, 18–22, 40–41, 52–53, 59–61, 63, 82, 91, 93–95, 125–27, 147, 152–53, 158–60, 164–66, 168, 181, 255–59

Valentine, Murphy Zenon, 102–103, 149, 257
villages, 13, 22, 42, 59, 72, 86, 89, 173, 175

war, 6, 7, 29, 31–32, 35–36, 51–52, 59–60, 67, 93, 105, 189

Washington, D.C., 128, 141, 146, 188, 209, 214, 246, 249, 253, 255–57
West Africans, vii, 38, 112, 151, 183

West Indians, 4, 17–19, 23, 26, 37, 51, 79, 91, 131–33, 221n2, 222n11
work, 43–44, 49, 59–60, 84, 97, 134, 136, 148, 152, 163–64, 232n26, 232n27
World War II, 6, 23, 48–49, 59–60, 65, 158

Yellow Caribs, 28–30, 32
Young Garifuna, 107, 110, 125, 230n15
youths, viii, 52, 97–98, 108–9, 111–12, 119, 123, 125, 154, 184, 186
Yurumei Garifuna Cultural Retrieval (YuGaCuRe), 176
Yurumein, 27, 96, 240

Zuniga, Belizean Garifuna Thomas M., 188

Maximo G. Martinez is Professor of Government at Blinn College in Bryan, Texas. His research focuses on Latin American politics and Afro-Caribbean immigrants in the United States. He is the author of *"Other Hispanics": An Analysis of New York City Honduran Political Participation* (2009).

www.ingramcontent.com/pod-product-compliance
Lightning Source LLC
Chambersburg PA
CBHW020359080526
44584CB00014B/1098